The
End of the
European Empire

PROBLEMS IN
EUROPEAN CIVILIZATION

Under the editorial direction of
John Ratté
Amherst College

The End of the European Empire

Decolonization after World War II

Edited and with an introduction by

Tony Smith
Tufts University

D. C. HEATH AND COMPANY
Lexington, Massachusetts   Toronto   London

D
843
.E48

68793

CONTENTS

INTRODUCTION   vii
CHRONOLOGY   xxv
MAPS
1 The British Empire Before World War II   xxviii
2 The French Empire Before World War II   xxix
3 Asia in 1975   xxx
4 Africa in 1975   xxxi

I ROOTS OF DECOLONIZATION DURING THE INTERWAR YEARS

Rudolf von Albertini
THE IMPACT OF THE TWO WORLD WARS
ON THE DECLINE OF COLONIALISM   3

II THE END OF THE BRITISH EMPIRE

Nicholas Mansergh
BRITAIN LEAVES INDIA   23

Francis Hutchins
INDIA LEAVES BRITAIN   31

Debates of the House of Commons
PRIME MINISTER ATTLEE ON INDIA, MARCH 15, 1946   41

CHURCHILL VERSUS ATTLEE OVER BURMA,
DECEMBER 20, 1946   46

CHURCHILL VERSUS ATTLEE OVER INDIA,
FEBRUARY–MARCH, 1947   52

A. P. Thornton
THE DECLINE OF BRITISH POWER IN THE MIDDLE EAST   60

John Hatch
THE DECLINE OF BRITISH POWER IN AFRICA   72

Harold Macmillan
THE WINDS OF CHANGE   96

III THE END OF THE FRENCH EMPIRE

Tony Smith
THE FRENCH COLONIAL CONSENSUS AND
PEOPLE'S WAR, 1946–1958   103

Prime Minister Ramadier
THE FRENCH STAND IN INDOCHINA, MARCH 18, 1947   123

Prime Minister Mollet
THE FRENCH STAND IN ALGERIA, MARCH 27, 1957   128

Alfred Grosser
DE GAULLE AND DECOLONIZATION   131

Charles de Gaulle
MEMOIRS OF HOPE   148

IV THE END OF THE DUTCH AND BELGIAN EMPIRES

Rudolf von Albertini
THE DECOLONIZATION OF THE DUTCH EAST INDIES   171

Arend Lijphart
THE DUTCH AND WEST NEW GUINEA   177

Crawford Young
THE END OF THE BELGIAN CONGO   183

V THE QUESTION OF NEO-COLONIALISM

Kwame Nkrumah
NEO-COLONIALISM: THE LAST STAGE OF IMPERIALISM   199

Frantz Fanon
THE COLLABORATING CLASS IN NEO-COLONIALISM   209

P. T. Bauer
THE ECONOMICS OF RESENTMENT   214

Peter Evans
NEO-COLONIALISM AND THE MULTINATIONALS   229

Tom Soper
THE EUROPEAN ECONOMIC COMMUNITY AND AFRICA   245

SUGGESTIONS FOR ADDITIONAL READING   257

INTRODUCTION

During the two decades following World War II, the maps of overseas empire which had established their place in so many classrooms of Europe were drained of their traditional colors of rose and blue: one-third of the people of the earth were freed from colonial rule. At the same time millions of others who had been subject to European power without falling under formal colonial jurisdiction reestablished their national identities. With the entry of the Communist Chinese into Peking in January 1949, the outlines of a new period of world history, one that signaled the end of a long era of unquestioned European hegemony over the technologically backward areas of the globe, seemed to be emerging from the ruins of World War II. Through Asia, the Middle East, North Africa and Africa south of the Sahara, a tidal wave of local nationalism was gathering to cast out the European rulers.

Many commentators on this period characterize the process of decolonization most highly by its speed. Yet this is to neglect the history of nationalist agitation and organization that began in modern form with the success of the Young Turks in overthrowing the Sultan in 1908, and with the hesitant emergence of republican government in China under Sun Yat-sen following the collapse of the Manchu dynasty in 1911. The contact of these two bureaucratic empires with European power in the nineteenth century had contributed to setting into motion forces that spelled the eventual disintegration of their traditional orders. But in the very process, groups that were dedicated to reworking the character of their countries had begun to mobilize so that they might meet the threats of the international system. Only in Japan had a modernizing elite emerged to save the country from European sway, but the significance of this example was also appreciated by other nationalists, from China to the Middle East, who were opposed to Western rule. European rivalries also undermined colonial regimes. The impact of World War I prompted a liberalization of imperial rule in an effort to secure more wholehearted colonial support in the provision of men and materiel. So in 1916 France moved fully to assimilate the Four Communes of Senegal into the French Republic, and offered a series of overdue reforms to the Muslim elite in Algeria, including an end to special native taxes, a relaxation of the provisions of the native penal code, and a token increase in the political voice of the Muslim community at the local level. Similarly Great Britain found herself obliged to declare that the eventual goal in India was self-government (the Montagu-Chelmsford Commission leading to the reforms of 1919), and entered into negotiations with the local political leadership in Egypt, which led to a form of semi-independent status for this country in 1922. (But it was not until the Anglo-Egyptian Treaty of 1936 that the Egyptians themselves recognized a relaxation of London's grip.) Such examples could easily be multiplied.

In the years following World War II, the pace of colonial nationalism quickened. The slow spread of Western education, the increasing economic development of areas related to European capitalism, and the accumulating wisdom acquired from political discussion and agitation by colonized subjects of many different social and economic categories were serving to create the necessary basis for strong nationalist movements after 1945. During this period a hallmark of modernity—political parties—began to form for the first time in many of these areas. The National Congress Party of India had been founded in 1885, substantially earlier than an organized Western local elite arose in most of the imperial domains, but its functional equivalent could clearly be discerned throughout the lands of European rule by the early thirties (with the exception of certain parts of black Africa), while the Congress Party's own stance became substantially more antagonistic to continued British rule.

Outside the colonial order, other challenges to the international supremacy of Western Europe were beginning to be sounded in the interwar years. The most striking initial defiance was that of the Turkish nationalist Mustafa Kemal, or Ataturk. Reacting to the wartime designs of France, Britain, Greece, Italy and Russia to reduce

his nation to an area of some 20,000 square miles, Ataturk in 1919
stirred his countrymen to a resistance effort that by 1923 had established the boundaries of a modern state of 300,000 square miles.
So, too, in China, first the Kuomintang and—by 1921—an indigenous
Communist Party, were beginning their organizational efforts to reestablish the sovereignty and international autonomy of the Chinese state.

It was the Russian Revolution of 1917, however, that presented
the most fundamental challenge to the imperial order. Not only was
Lenin capable of formulating a theoretical attack on Western colonialism that was ideological dynamite, but he was able to back it up
with an organizational method and the resources of the Soviet state.
His new socialist government immediately renounced Czarist designs on Constantinople, the northern part of Persia and Manchuria.
Instead Lenin offered material aid to Ataturk, Reza Khan Pahlevi in
Teheran, the emir of Afghanistan, the Wafd Party in Egypt, and the
Kuomintang in China in their respective efforts to diminish Western
influence in their national affairs. The subsequent growth of local
Communist parties, the action of Comintern, and the conduct of other
national Communist parties—most notably the French—played an
undeniably important role in the ground-swell of opposition to Western rule (although Communist influence fell far short of being the
"international menace" that Western statesmen immediately after
1921 began to use as a scapegoat in their explanations of colonial
discontent).

The challenge of the Russian Revolution and the growth of anti-
Western nationalist sentiment in Asia, the Middle East and Africa
did not go unnoticed in Paris and London. Nor did these capitals
fail to recognize how gravely the terrible toll of World War I—the
millions dead, the material destruction, the pretentions of cultural
superiority debunked—crippled their own ability to maintain their
international rank. They could, however, look to the map, where
substantial gains had been registered. Not only had these countries
claimed Germany's African colonies (leaving to Japan Berlin's Pacific holdings north of the Equator, while Australia and New Zealand
took those to the south), but they had proceeded to the final dismem-
berment of the Ottoman Empire (after the occupation of Algiers in
1830, Egypt in 1882, and machinations in the Balkans over the preceding several decades). The League of Nations duly sanctioned

these arrangements, and the evident powerlessness of the Arabs—
the most politically advanced group of people under colonial rule—
suggested that European might had no serious challengers.
More, World War I had amply demonstrated to public opinion and
to the leadership of both France and Great Britain the practical advantages of empire, for there was general agreement that the hundreds of thousands of workers, the vast stores of supplies, and the
million and a half fighting men furnished by the two empires had
given these countries a decisive edge in the struggle against Germany. At the same time, the increasing participation of socialist
parties in their respective national governments meant that except
for the nascent Communist parties and a scattering of intellectuals,
fundamental opposition to imperial possessions ceased in the Western democracies. Leftist critics no longer directed their attacks
against colonialism as a system, but instead called for remedies to
specific abuses, and this in the interests of the mother country as
well as the foreign subjects. In short, just at the moment when powerful forces were beginning to assemble to put an end to European
rule overseas, many Europeans were for the first time coming to the
conclusion that their national survival might depend on the preservation of empire. Faced with the growing power of the United
States, Japan and the Soviet Union, the proposition that local nationalisms would be the wave of the future appeared a bit absurd.
It was easy, then, to predict the international role of a European nation bereft of empire. The example of Spain was there for all to
ponder.

Whatever the European will, the increasing strength of nationalist
organization in most areas of European domination proceeded
apace in the 1930s. Here the impact of World War II proved decisive. The fall of Singapore in February 1942, and the surrender of
Rangoon a month later, climaxed the expansion of Japan's Greater
Asian Co-Prosperity Sphere and encouraged (as in the case of the
Dutch East Indies), or permitted by default (as in the case of French
Indochina), the mobilization of such strong nationalist forces that it
seemed highly improbable that the old colonial regimes could rein-
state themselves without being severely contested. Similarly, World
War II exacerbated tensions in the most important of imperial pos-
sessions—India—sharply intensifying the demands for independence at the same time that it placed the British in a more unfav-

orable position either to refuse or to stall. In Africa, although its influence was less direct, the war strained colonial relations as well, since the northern part of the continent was an important theater of military action (with the conspicuous absence of the dominant colonial authority, France, noted by all), while southern Africa suffered harsh requisitions in order to further the Allied war effort.

Despite the established pedigree of local nationalism in most imperial domains by 1945, and despite the apparent decline of European power internationally, virtually no one foresaw the scope of the decolonization process—much less its speed—in the immediate aftermath of the war. Part of the reason is undoubtedly that changes of such magnitude are very seldom predicted. More specifically, however, the Europeans professed pride in the solidarity of their empires during the conflict, while interpreting the character of the emerging postwar international order as one to be marked by the increasing interdependence of nations—not by their fragmentation at the hands of local nationalists. National independence seemed a vain, anachronistic goal. Better, then, to refurbish the imperial system, the British by the addition to the Commonwealth of non-European members (first of all India), while the French energetically began debating the structure of the projected French Union.

The forecast of the character of the new international order was to turn out to be correct; the forecast of which units would join in association proved mistaken. For in the decade and a half after the end of World War II, London and Paris came to realize that their best safeguards lay not in revitalized empire but in a united Europe. In the meantime, especially on the Continent, the imperial reflex held sway, motivated by established myths about colonial rule. Except now the first victims of the web of postponed good intentions, half-truths, and paternalistic stances were not the colonized but the colonizers. How else can we understand declarations such as that by Vincent Auriol, a Socialist and the first President of the French Fourth Republic, who found on his visit to Algeria in the summer of 1949 "unforgettable signs of affection, loyalty and confidence"? More than a year after a series of rigged elections had begun to ensure that nationalist agitators did not obtain a public forum, Auriol could report that everywhere "the people cried their love for France."

A further reason for discounting the significance of colonial unrest after 1945 was that the major menace to the West seemed to come from Soviet Russia. Outright opposition over the fate of Poland began in 1945, and the Cold War was officially inaugurated in the West with the announcement of "containment" in the Truman Doctrine of March 1947. Western strategic thinking at this time was preoccupied with such problems as calculating the damage a nuclear attack would inflict on the Soviets as against the number of hours it would take Russian divisions to occupy Western Europe. It remained unanticipated that the major theater of conflict in the postwar period would be the so-called Third World.

Yet in short order the first violence to wrack these politically unstable areas of the world made its appearance. On May 8, 1945, the very day Paris was celebrating the defeat of Germany, Muslim riots around the town of Sétif in Western Algeria claimed over a hundred European lives. Reaction was swift. French planes strafed forty-four Muslim hamlets, a cruiser offshore bombarded more, and groups of settler vigilantes summarily executed hundreds of natives. As testimony to the ferocity of the repression, how many Muslims died in these events has never been determined, though estimates range from 6,000 to 45,000. The following year war broke out in Indochina, in a struggle that would eventually kill 100,000 French (including mercenary auxiliaries) and cost the lives of untold thousands of Vietnamese. Again, in 1947, an uprising in Madagascar killed some 100 Europeans, provoking a French repression that by official estimates took 80,000 native lives. By the time the Algerian conflict ended in 1962, another 750,000 deaths had been added to the rolls of decolonization.

"Police action" that mushroomed into armed repression occurred in the British Empire as well, most notably in Malaya (1948–1954) and in Kenya (1952–1955). But the British possessions came more to be noted—as the Conservatives especially had warned—for the violence the subject masses inflicted on each other rather than for nationalist confrontations between London and the various local leaders. Thus it was Greek against Turk on the island of Cyprus, Jew against Arab in Palestine, and most tragic of all, Hindu against Muslim on the Indian subcontinent. Struggles between blacks and Asians in East Africa, between Africans and Arabs in the Sudan and Zanzibar, between Nigeria and Biafra and within

Northern Ireland have been later indirect consequences of this same decolonization process.

After the books on imperialism come the studies on decolonization. Yet in addition to emphasizing that decolonization was not so speedy a movement as it is sometimes described, it is also important to point out that the imperialist phase of the relations between industrial and technologically backward countries is far from concluded. Surely some skepticism is warranted toward the statement of the noted historian of imperialism, William F. Langer, when he writes in "Farewell to Empire" (*Foreign Affairs,* October 1962) that "thoughtful people, particularly in the Western world, are bound to reflect on this epochal upheaval and to realize that one of the very great revolutions in human affairs has taken place." One may similarly doubt that Rupert Emerson, another dean of colonial studies, is justified in writing in *The Journal of Contemporary History* (January 1969) of the "spectacular demise" of the old imperial order, while asking, "Is there any other occasion on which so global and commanding a scheme of things was swept away in so brief a time?" For although Portugal has at long last agreed to independence for Angola and Mozambique, white-settler regimes remain strongly ensconced in Rhodesia and the Union of South Africa, and a multitude of cultural, economic and political ties still bind many of the former imperial possessions to the capitals of Europe. France, for example, continues to control the education, currency and armies of a number of her former African colonies. Indeed, it is common to hear it observed that through her teachers, fiscal controls and army personnel, France is more influential today at all levels of African society than in the heyday of direct political control from Paris.

Today the argument that imperialism has not ended goes under the heading of "dependency theory" or "neo-colonialism." While it is obviously oversimplifying to reduce a complex and variously interpreted position to a few propositions, a summary presentation of the argument is basic to efforts to conceptualize accurately the character of present-day decolonialization. According to the theory of neo-colonialism, most Third World nations have become dependent on the international economic system dominated by the Western capitalist powers and Japan for markets, technology, financing and even basic foodstuffs to such a point that these less-developed countries may be called "hooked": they cannot do with their dependence, but, just as well, they cannot do without it.

They cannot do with dependence because their form of incorporation into the international system has tended to preclude their industrialization, relegating them instead to the less dynamic forms of growth associated with agriculture or the extractive industries. Where manufacturing occurs it is generally under the auspices of multinational corporations with their headquarters in the West which, for whatever benefits they may bring in the form of managerial know-how, marketing and the like, take far more than they bring and—what is more important—make it virtually impossible for local, self-sustaining industrialization to develop. At the same time, however, so this theory runs, the necessary remedy to the problem —a break with the international system—is not available to most of these countries. In some cases the economies of the less-developed countries have become so dependent on exports to the international system that the requirements of their single-crop economies dictate continued participation in the very process that is victimizing them.

In other instances adjustments might be made, but not without cutting the base from under the present dominant classes that rely on the international system for the trade, investment and military aid, which secure the power and privileges of these elites. In short, dependence grows from and serves to perpetuate an asymmetrical power relation internationally, from which the less-developed countries can only escape with great difficulty. A few, like Algeria, may have the sort of natural resources, population base and national leadership that make this break possible. For the rest, only war or a serious depression afflicting the industrial West will weaken the international system sufficiently to allow local autonomous development. Thus the direct political control through colonization is replaced by the indirect economic control of decolonization. The result is the same: imperial domination. From this point of view, the national anthems and flag ceremonies of decolonization were nothing more than ideological smokescreens covering a more rationalized economic exploitation of the world.

In order to determine the validity of this thesis, the student must look to the series of accords signed since 1958 between the European Economic Community (EEC) and those areas of the world over which these countries once exercised direct or informal control. In such an analysis the year 1975 serves as an appropriate watermark date. For in the winter of 1975, the EEC, enlarged by the entry of Great Britain, concluded a convention at Lomé, Togo, associating forty-six less-developed states with the EEC in a form of international economic bloc. The convention thereby marks clearly the emergence of a new order restructuring relations between Europe and many of the less-developed countries that had previously gravitated toward Western capitals, but which in the aftermath of World War II had moved to establish their own political identities.

Thus the rapid disintegration of the imperial order politically in the first two decades following the war has seemingly given way to a decade of economic reintegration. The easy dislocation of the new system is difficult to imagine. To be sure, the outlines of such an order are still sketchy and remain fragile; the reintegration of Europe with these areas of its former dominance is by no means devoid of problems. Preeminent among these are: (1) the rivalries among the European capitals—and particularly Paris and London—however much they may recognize overriding common interests in their association; (2) the rivalries among states of the less-developed countries as they seek a common front in their negotiations with the EEC; and (3) the rivalries between the Europeans to one side and the members of the Associated States to the other—or the question of neo-colonialism.

It is, of course, by no means self-evident that such an arrangement will fail to serve the interests of all parties involved in it (albeit some more than others). Certainly relations may be "imperial" without being "exploitive." So long as an imperial center is not threatened by the growth in power of a dependent to it, it may actually see its own interests served. (One thinks, for example, of the relation between Britain and Portugal in the nineteenth century, or that between the United States and Iran today.) To be able to establish theoretically that an imperial relation is exploitive —as the present-day interpreters of neo-colonialism and dependency would have it—is by no means to establish that such a relation actually exists. The distinction between the logic of a theory and the logic of history appears too often to be forgotten.

Whatever the merits of the debate, the term neo-colonialism seems a misnomer for this phenomenon, however, since Britain established a somewhat similar arrangement in the nineteenth century with Latin America after Spain's prostration during the Napoleonic Wars. From the perspective of the past, then, the satellite states of "informal empire" are certainly not unique to the contemporary period. Nor are economic motives the only impetus to domination. Imperialism of the strong against the weak is as old as human history, and there is little reason to be confident that the period described as one of decolonization will guarantee the undisturbed sovereignty of the new nations of the world. Like a chameleon changing colors, imperialism may be expected to appear in different form but with similar consequences. We would be naive indeed not to anticipate that among its chief practitioners may well be some of its former victims and most outspoken critics.

The debate over the causes of the "new imperialism," which began in the final quarter of the nineteenth century, exhibits far more unity and erudition than does contemporary discussion of the decolonization process. There simply are no works today that attempt to be as comprehensive in accounting for the loss of empire as Hobson, for one, was comprehensive in his explanation of its acquisition. This is the case because, in part, economic interpretations of the root motivations of imperial policy (still the pacesetters in discussions of four centuries of European overseas expansion) fail to elucidate at all well the vicissitudes of decolonization. So Great Britain, whose security for three centuries had depended closely on foreign trade, investment and domination, decolonized with relative ease, while France, with far less material interest in her possessions, dug in to stay. More fundamentally, perhaps, the exponents of an economic interpretation of history have tended to doubt how genuinely revolutionary a development decolonization actually has been, and have stressed instead the continued cultural, social and political weight of neo-colonialism based on the character of the contemporary economic international order. Whatever the reasons, the present debate lacks the hard analytical edge of the earlier (and still continuing) controversy over the origins of European expansion.

The problem, then, is to attempt to establish, by a more systematic approach than case studies alone permit, the primary factors at work in creating the various patterns of decolonization. Here, as I have suggested, economic considerations do not now appear to be of much significance, although one line to take might be that the more advanced economy of the British was able to adjust more easily to control without political domination than was the case for the French. Instead, commentators make reference to a host of causative forces behind political policies—such as the influence of past imperial ideology, of past experience in colonial matters, of national psychology, or contemporary domestic politics, and of international strategic calculations—without, however, expending much effort on refining the guiding concepts invoked, assigning them relative weights as motivating factors behind the various imperial policies, framing them as disprovable interpretations of political behavior, or putting them within a broadly historical and comparative framework.

Suppose, then, that we attempt briefly to account for the more signal differences in the British and French responses to the challenge of decolonization. Surely an important part of the answer must be the historical experiences that had come to establish a characteristically national attitude and method for handling colonial affairs. Thus, unlike the French, who had aspirations for making fellow citizens out of their colonial subjects and so creating "the Greater France of 100 million Frenchmen," the British had typically spoken of eventual self-government. It could be that this goes back to a fundamental difference in philosophic temperament: when the French were declaring the universal Rights of Man, Burke was moved to say that he knew only of the Rights of Englishmen. In other words, leaving aside such important exceptions as Lyautey and Jules Harmand, who championed "association" rather than "assimilation" as goals for national policy, the French claimed a general relevance for their national values that the British never assumed, believing instead in the basic distinctness of different social patterns.

In each case, of course, the dominant culture was asserting its superiority over the natives, but the British version of this common claim proved more amenable to fulfillment in the light of the course of history (however much it, like the French policy of assimilation, had attached its promise in practice to an infinitely receding historical horizon).

Nor should we forget that the nineteenth century had given the British long acquaintance with the practice of what today would be called neo-colonialism. That is, the British came early to appreciate the advantages of "informal empire," of supporting a dependable local elite in order to assure a stable environment for trade and investment. Such an arrangement worked well with Latin America after the Napoleonic Wars and was contemplated for China, Persia, the Ottoman Empire and Africa thereafter. Only the inability of native regimes to maintain themselves in the face of mounting domestic and foreign pressures prompted Britain's direct (and generally begrudging) intervention. Although London finally had undertaken to experiment with a protectionist empire during the interwar period, this style had never suited the Free Trade Imperialists anything like it had the French.

Still more importantly, the British, unlike the French, had developed a successful method for dealing with colonial discontent long before 1945. In a sense, one may mark the first phase of British decolonization as stretching from the Durham Report of 1839 relative to Canada, to the Statute of Westminster of 1931. By this series of measures, Britain created the Dominion system and institutionalized a procedure for gradually loosening control over her possessions. For a time, to be sure, the final character of the Commonwealth, as it came to be called, was in doubt. During the interwar years (if not earlier), however, it became clear that the sometime dream of Imperial Federation, whereby London would control the economic, defense and foreign policies of the several allied Anglo-Saxon peoples, would never come to fruition. Instead the measured progress within the colonies from representative to responsible government and from there to Commonwealth status would culminate in the establishment of fully sovereign states.

Of course there is the mistake, encountered frequently in the works of Britishers especially, of seeing in retrospect a grand design for decolonization that in fact did not exist. Closer inspection commonly reveals the British to have been following Burke's sage counsel to "reform in order to preserve": London made concessions more usually to subvert opposition to British rule than to prepare for its demise. So, for example, to see Indian independence in 1947 as necessarily following from the Government of India Act of 1935, which in turn unerringly confirmed the intentions of the Government of India Act of 1919 (itself the natural product of the Morley–Minto reforms of 1909), assumes a British gift for prophecy that a closer examination of the historical record fails to sustain. What is lacking in these accounts is a sense of the conflicts, hesitations and uncertainties of the past and of the attempts to reinterpret or renege on the promise of eventual independence for India. Nonetheless, the British *did* establish a tradition of meeting colonial discontent by reforms that associated the subject peoples more closely with their own governing. The prior evolution of the Dominion system *did* exert an important influence on the style of British policy toward India. And the ultimate decision to grant India independence and to permit her to withdraw if she wished from the Commonwealth *did* constitute a momentous precedent for British policy toward the rest of her empire. Seen from this perspective, there is something a bit pathetic about the French, whose naiveté and relative paucity of experience found expression in resolutions voted from the Brazzaville Conference of January 1944 through the debates establishing the ill-fated French Union in 1946.

Prewar theory and practice did not alone decide postwar imperial policy, however. The international situation after 1945, as well as past precedent, was crucial in determining British and French responses to the pressures of decolonization. Here the character of relations with the United States was central. Thus, although Great Britain had been a greater international power than France before 1939, she adjusted more easily to her postwar decline in part, certainly, because of her greater confidence in the United States. Wartime experience had been important in laying the ground for this trust, as one can see in comparing the quite different relationships Roosevelt had with Winston Churchill and Charles de Gaulle. For de Gaulle, Roosevelt had little but distrust; for Churchill, the American leader had unstinted admiration. In turn, the French sought an international role after the war as little dependent as possible on the United States (although to their continual annoyment this proved to be no easy task), while Britain looked forward eagerly to what Churchill in his Fulton, Missouri speech of March 1946 called "the fraternal association of the English-speaking peoples . . . a special relationship between the British Commonwealth and Empire and the United States."

When should the beginning of this alliance between the English-speaking peoples be dated? Is 1823 too early, when the British celebrated the Monroe Doctrine as a policy well suited to support

Pax Britannica? Or the Open Door Notes of the late nineteenth century when the United States lent its support to the British scheme of things in China? Perhaps the decisive moments would be better put after World War I, when the British had to reckon with America's coming international paramountcy. So at the Washington Naval Conference in 1921, Britain finally accepted parity with the United States in sea power and moved away from her alliance with Japan—clear indications that her most important international alliance would henceforth be with her former North American colony. The Anglo-American Trade Agreement of 1938 only confirmed this orientation, when the British agreed partly to dismantle their imperial preference system, both in response to American pressures and in the hope of securing greater assistance from Washington to counter the growing menace of Hitler. Subsequently the Americans exacted imperial concessions in return for Lend Lease and in the name of the Atlantic Alliance. Not that London gave in willingly during these negotiations. To the contrary, British leaders sought to preserve as many advantages for their country as possible and greatly resented many of the demands made by the Americans. But there was nothing like the French feeling—born of decades of lack of national confidence—that others were waiting like vultures for her to show weakness in order to redivide her empire. One need only consider the ease with which the United States replaced Britain in Greece and Turkey in 1947 to appreciate the gap between French and British attitudes in regard to the expansion of American power. In an important sense, then, one can mark the beginning of British decolonization in the interwar period, both in the style of her imperial policy and in the character of her international alliances. The same simply cannot be said of France.

Domestic politics and institutions also account for the difference in French and British reactions to nationalist agitation. Britain had a "loyal opposition," a stable two-party system and a strong executive. France, to the contrary, was plagued by disloyal opposition from both the Right and Left, by a multiparty system and by a weak executive. Hence the French were not so able as the British to process a problem of the magnitude of decolonization. In my opinion, commentators have tended to exaggerate the shortcomings of what was pejoratively referred to as *le système,* since a stubborn colonial consensus from the Socialists to the Right contributed as much to the ineffectiveness of the political system as this, in turn, made a far-sighted policy impossible to determine and implement. Analyses of the vicissitudes of French decolonization typically present a view of the Republic's governments as "divided," "indecisive" and "immobile," and so rally to de Gaulle's earliest warnings against the deficiencies of the Fourth Republic. But as a review of both the Indochinese policy of the Blum and Ramadier governments in 1946–1947 and the Algerian policy of the Mollet Government of 1956–1957 demonstrates, it was unity, resolution and action that at these critical junctures of Socialist national leadership were the hallmarks of the regime. What typified these decisive periods of Socialist leadership was not so much the fatal logic of a political system as the fatal logic of a colonial perspective. Time and again throughout the history of the Fourth Republic, beneath the invective of political division, one finds a shared anguish at the passing of national greatness, a shared humiliation at three generations of defeat, a shared nationalistic determination that France retain her independence in a hostile world—all brought to rest on the conviction that the colonies, and especially Algeria, would remain French.

Studies that obscure this common commitment, through a gentlemen's agreement to focus strictly on the shortcomings of the system as a system, foster a sort of collective amnesia that will no doubt remain until the actors of the period have left the political scene (perhaps another decade). Where, for example, can one find in the annals of French leaders anything equivalent to the entry in the journal of Hugh Dalton, assistant to Mountbatten in negotiating the independence of India, dated February 24, 1947?

If you are in a place where you are not wanted and where you have not got the force, or perhaps the will, to squash those who don't want you, the only thing to do is to come out. This very simple truth will have to be applied other places too, e.g., Palestine.

Dalton's realism and lucidity were quite characteristic of the British. Certainly the same cannot be said for the French (as the sections from French and British parliamentary debates reprinted in this volume illustrate). It was not so much the French political system that was responsible, then, for the problems of decolonization, as it was the misperceptions of the collective mind of the political elite. This is not to deny, however, that the greater stability of the British political system made for less trouble in decolonizing, if for no other reason than that there was no particular reason to believe the loss of empire was the logical outcome of inefficient government. After the traumas of the thirties and the humiliation of the Occupation, the charges of being a *bradeur d'empire* raised much more profound self-doubt in the National Assembly than did charges of "scuttle" at Westminster.

The natural home for decolonization sentiment was the political Left. Here a comparison of the French Socialist Party with Labour in Britain reveals another important difference. To be sure, Labour hesitated, stalled and cast about on occasion for ways of granting independence that would favor future British interests. But the French Socialists could not boast a study group to bear comparison with the Fabian Colonial Bureau. Nor does the French Overseas Minister from January 1946 until November 1947, Marius Moutet, measure up terribly well to the British Colonial Secretary from late 1946 until 1950, Arthur Creech-Jones. It should be recalled that Socialists were in power in both France and England in 1947, but as the speeches reprinted later in this book attest, while French Prime Minister Ramadier was calling for votes of war credits to pursue the struggle in Indochina and staging emotional calls for support of the French army, British Prime Minister Attlee was extracting his country even more quickly from India than initial plans had projected.

These brief remarks only suggest the sort of work that still needs to be done on decolonization: the separation of different categories of analysis from national psychology to the capacities of domestic political institutions; the assignment to them of weights of relative importance based on their influence on political behavior; their coordination in an historical and comparative fashion. Case studies will of course point up idiosyncrasies in the general movement, but it should be possible to create a more dynamic and synthetic overview of the period than is now available. One thing is certain: the enterprise promises to be a fertile field for scholarly debate.

This book does not set out to offer a contribution to the history of the former colonial territories, but instead to further the study of an important aspect of contemporary European history. Part I sketches quickly the roots of decolonization in the interwar period. Parts II–IV review successively the British, French, Dutch and Belgian experiences with decolonization. Part V raises the issue of how complete this process has actually been by taking up the controversial question of neo-colonialism.

CHRONOLOGY

	Great Britain	France	Belgium & Holland	Elsewhere
1944		Brazzaville Conference.		
1945	Transjordan created.	Uprising, Sétif, Algeria. End of Mandate over Syria and Lebanon. Coup in Saigon.		Yalta Conference. Dispute over Poland. A-Bomb used against Japan. Arab League founded.
1946	Mountbatten to India.	Hostilities in Vietnam become war.		Truman Doctrine.
1947	Independence of India, Pakistan and Ceylon.	Nationalist uprising in Madagascar.		
1948	Independence of Burma. Guerrilla war starts in Malaya. Palestine independence. Serious disorders in the Gold Coast.	War in Vietnam moves past its first year, and continues. Laos and Cambodia join the French Union.		First Mid-East War. Berlin Blockade begins.
1949			Indonesian independence.	NATO formed. Communists triumph in China.
1950				Korean War starts.
1951				Libyan independence. Mossadegh nationalizes Iranian oil.

	Great Britain	France	Belgium & Holland	Elsewhere
1952	Mau-Mau uprising begins in Kenya.			Nasser to power in Egypt.
1953				Korean War ends. Stalin dies. Mossadegh falls.
1954	War in Malaya ends.	Geneva Conference ends war in Vietnam. Algerian Revolution begins.		Arbenz regime falls in Guatamala. SEATO formed. Diem wins American support in Vietnam.
1955	Mau-Mau uprising ends.			Bandung Conference. Baghdad Pact formed.
1956	Sudan gains independence. Suez invasion.	Suez invasion. Morocco and Tunisia gain independence.		Hungarian invasion.
1957	Ghana and Malaysia gain independence.			Treaty of Rome—EEC.
1958	Singapore becomes independent.	De Gaulle comes to power. Guinea becomes independent.		Kassim coup in Iraq. American troops to Lebanon, British troops to Jordan.
1959			Leopoldville riots in the Congo.	Castro comes to power in Cuba.
1960	Nigerian independence.	14 Black African states and Madagascar become independent.	Belgian Congo becomes independent.	

	Great Britain	France	Belgium & Holland	Elsewhere
1961	Sierra Leone gains independence.		Civil war against the Katanga secession.	Cuban Bay of Pigs invasion.
1962	Jamaica and Uganda gain independence.	Algeria becomes independent.	Ruanda and Urundi gain independence.	Malayan Federation forms.
1963	Kenya and Zanzibar gain independence.		Western New Guinea ceded to Indonesia.	Assassinations of Kennedy and Diem. Yaoundé Convention between the EEC and African states.
1964	Nyasaland and Northern Rhodesia gain independence.			Military coup in Brazil.
1965	Southern Rhodesia declares its independence.			U.S. occupation of the Dominican Republic.

MAP 1
The British Empire Before World War II

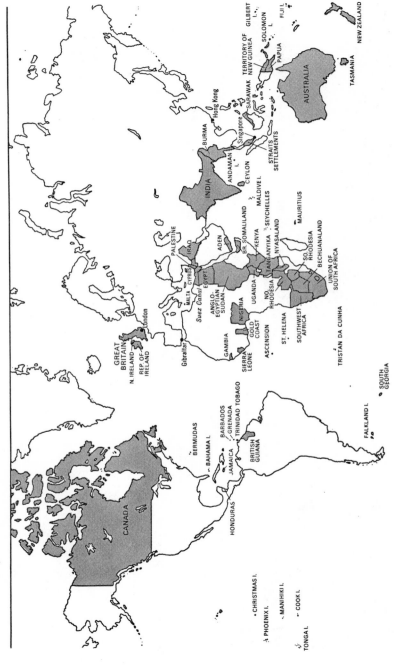

MAP 2
The French Empire Before World War II

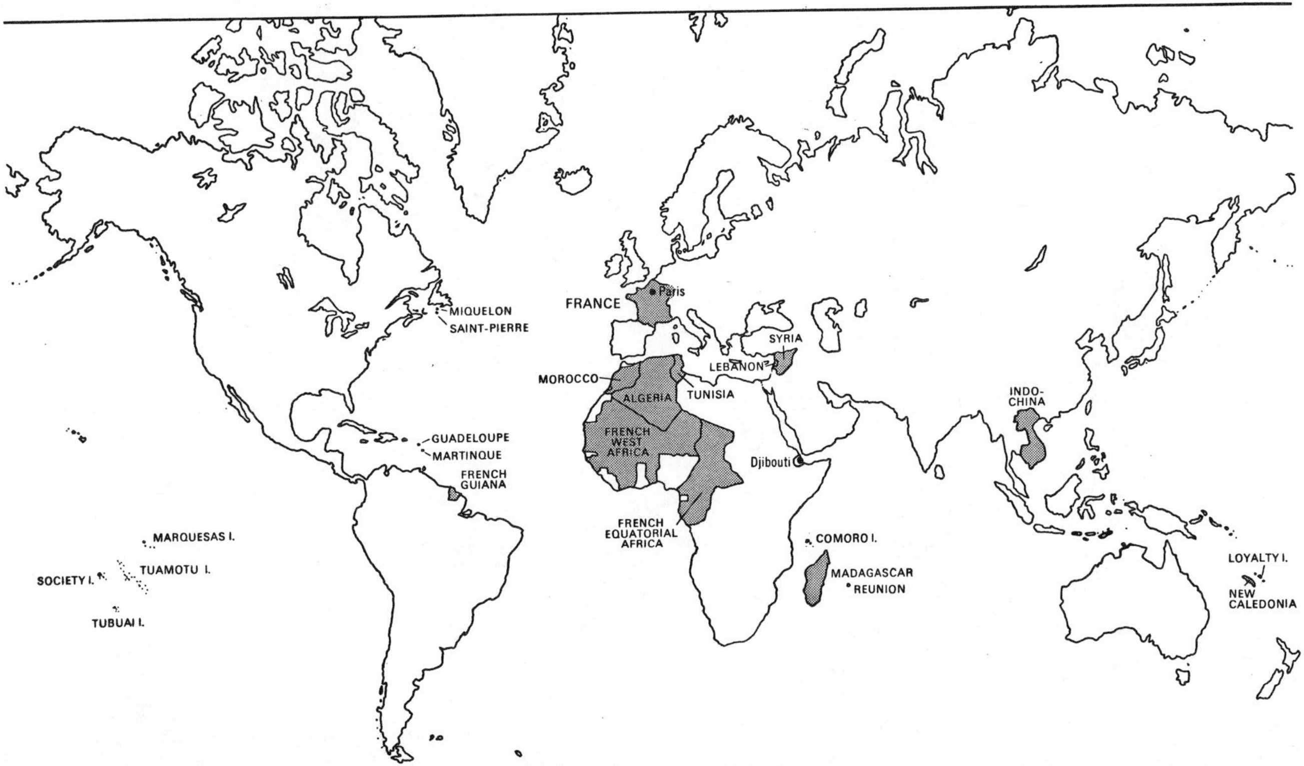

LOYALTY I.

NEW CALEDONIA

INDO-CHINA

COMORO I.

MADAGASCAR

REUNION

SYRIA

LEBANON

TUNISIA

Djibouti

PARIS

FRANCE

ALGERIA

MOROCCO

FRENCH WEST AFRICA

FRENCH EQUATORIAL AFRICA

MIQUELON

SAINT-PIERRE

GUADELOUPE

MARTINIQUE

FRENCH GUIANA

MARQUESAS I.

SOCIETY I.

TUAMOTU I.

TUBUAI I.

MAP 3
Asia in 1975

SOVIET UNION

TURKEY
CYPRUS
LEBANON
ISRAEL
JORDAN
IRAQ
IRAN
SYRIA
SAUDI ARABIA
KUWAIT
QATAR
YEMEN
UNITED ARAB EMIRATES
OMAN
P.D.R. OF YEMEN
AFGHANISTAN
PAKISTAN
INDIA
CEYLON
BANGLADESH
NEPAL
SIKKIM
BHUTAN
BURMA
MONGOLIA
CHINA
KOREA
JAPAN
TAIWAN
PHILIPPINES
LAOS
THAILAND
CAMBODIA
VIETNAM
BRUNEI
MALAYSIA
INDONESIA

MAP 4
Africa in 1975

I ROOTS OF DECOLONIZATION DURING THE INTERWAR YEARS

Rudolf von Albertini

THE IMPACT OF THE TWO WORLD WARS ON THE DECLINE OF COLONIALISM

If the wave of decolonization crested after World War II, it is nonetheless important to see its origins in the interwar period and even earlier. With the German publication in 1966 of a book whose English title is Decolonization: The Administration and Future of the Colonies, 1919–1960, *Albertini has established himself as one of the most comprehensive historians studying the decolonization process. This essay provides a sweeping yet succinct review of the decades preceding decolonization, when the forces began to assemble that would ultimately demand national independence.*

It did not escape the notice of political observers in the interwar years that the First World War had brought the "revolt of the colored man" into prominence or at least hastened its coming. So much was clear even without the speculative gaze of Spengler or the analytical elaborations of Paul Valéry. Discussions about the European forfeiture of power and prestige and the "rising tides of color" became a commonplace, although for preference the responsibility was at first placed on outside influences: President Wilson's "right of self-determination," Pan-Islam, the Russian Revolution; while German commentators stressed above all the Allies' "criminal" employment of colored troops against white ones. Today's preference is for examining individual areas of Asia and Africa and arguing in favor of an indigenous emancipation movement. A few comparative observations would therefore seem of value, for only against the wider horizon of world affairs does the emancipation of the colonies reveal its full relevance.

Europe's position in the world had reached its peak round about 1900, although the "pacification" of the African hinterland was by no means complete and it was not possible, for example, to set up the protectorate of Morocco until 1912. But with the extension of American power in Central America and the Pacific, and the rise of Japan, a new pattern took shape which was reinforced but also

Rudolf von Albertini, "The Impact of the Two World Wars on the Decline of Colonialism," *Journal of Contemporary History* (London, January 1969). Reprinted by permission of Sage Publications Ltd. Footnotes omitted.

concealed for a time by the 1902 Anglo-Japanese alliance, the colonial agreements of 1904 and 1907, and the concentration of the
Royal Navy in home waters. The fact that the spectacular victory
of Japan in 1905 and the Chinese Revolution of 1911 evoked a
powerful response in the colonial territories of Asia has been re-
peatedly stressed, but strangely, even in detailed discussion, has
never been clarified. In the years preceding the First World War, as
the colonial powers were only just moving towards a *mise en valeur*
of their possessions, the modern emancipation movements in Asia
and Arabia were taking shape, bringing to an end both the pre-
nationalist opposition of those in power before colonization, and
the more or less willing acceptance of colonial domination by a new
elite which had either come to terms with the colonial power and
was bound to it by self-interest, or had concentrated its energies on
the renewal of its own social and intellectual heritage. Nationalist
organizations and parties began to demand, if not immediate independence, at least a relaxation of authoritarian rule and an increasing share in government and administration. In India the excessive
paternalism of Lord Curzon was rewarded by demonstrations and
acts of sabotage; in Java the nationalist Sarekat Islam numbered
360,000 members even by 1912; in Indochina small elite groups
were formed under the influence of the Chinese Revolution and the
modernization of Japan. In Egypt the resignation of Cromer in 1910
marked the end of the period of uncontested British rule; significantly, in 1913 Zaghlul resigned his post as education minister and
devoted his energies to political agitation in the Legislative Assembly. In June 1912 the "jeunes Algériens" presented their demands
to Prime Minister Poincaré, asking in particular for equality before
the law of Frenchman and Moslem in accordance with the policy of
assimilation.

The outbreak of war in Europe—and this should be emphasized
—did not however lead to rebellions or unrest, nor did the national elites at once make use of it to advance radical demands. On
the contrary, the manifestations of loyalty and readiness to give military and financial aid were many and doubtless in the initial phase
genuine, perhaps because an introduction to Western culture had
forged emotional links with the colonial power despite a simultane-
ous assertion of national consciousness, perhaps because England
and France were successful in presenting a credible picture of the

war as one forced upon them in defense of freedom and justice against an autocratic Germany. German attempts to form links with the nationalists, in India and North Africa, met with only scant success. Especially striking was the attitude of Gandhi who, landing in London on 6 August 1914 on the way back from South Africa, took an active part in organizing an Indian ambulance unit and, unlike Mrs. Besant, categorically declined to make use of Indian loyalty to "extort" reforms: as late as summer 1918 Gandhi supported the British recruitment drive, even at the risk of losing the respect of the more radical nationalists and the masses.

Troops were withdrawn from India, Indochina, North and West Africa, while from Indochina to West Africa a general recruitment drive for native soldiers was opened in these areas. In the course of the war India provided 1.3 million (combatants and laborers); Indochina 150,000; Algeria 300,000; and French West Africa 200,000. This recruitment of volunteers presented at first few difficulties, no doubt because it was possible to appeal to the military tradition of certain tribes (nobody envisaged a long hard war), and because joining seemed at first advantageous. In the ensuing period, however, recruitment met with growing opposition, and open or veiled compulsion was necessary. Attempts to avoid war service, the flight of young men at the sight of recruiting agents, and even open rebellion leading to bloody punitive expeditions, are recorded in the cases of Indochina, Algeria, and Black Africa. In India recruiting had been concentrated on the Punjab, a factor often overlooked in the growing unrest and disaffection which in 1919 provoked the Amritsar massacre. The forced recruitment of camel drivers in Egypt made it easy for the nationalists in 1919 to spread agitation among the fellaheen too. The compulsory draft into the Carrier Corps in Kenya was detested: it drove whole families to seek refuge in the bush and resulted in very heavy loss of life, and at the same time gave the settlers the opportunity to recruit urgently needed African labor.

It seems to me that the significance of this more-or-less compulsory draft for the emancipation movement in the colonies has often been overrated, quite apart from the fact that the British in India and the French in North and West Africa were astute enough to treat the war veterans as a privileged group, thereby binding them more closely to the colonial power. On the other hand there can be no doubt that hundreds of thousands were uprooted from their traditional and rigidly defined society, confronted by totally new experiences and discoveries, and made socially and psychologically mobile enough to become receptive to the slogans put out by the educated elite.

A further aspect deserves consideration: political concessions and reforms were at least as much a by-product of the recruitment and mobilization of colonial troops as of the ability of nationalist spokesmen in wartime conditions to push their demands through. When France in 1916 granted the Quatre Communes in Senegal full civil rights—previously limited by provisos—together with retention of their personal status under Islamic law, and appointed the colored delegate Blaise Diagne as High Commissioner in 1917; and when Clemenceau and Leygues, presidents respectively of the two parliamentary commissions for foreign affairs, sent a letter on 25 November 1915 to the prime minister and president of the republic proposing far-reaching reforms for Algeria, in particular that of naturalization without the obligation to renounce their personal status under Islamic law, these were not reluctant responses to a nationalist challenge; they were designed to encourage recruitment by appealing to and rewarding their loyalty. The attitude of the Indians at the beginning of the war surprised the British administration and quickened its readiness for reform: hence the invitation by Lord Willingdon, Governor of Bombay, to Gokhale in early 1915 to submit proposals to him. Even before any radicalization on the Indian side, it was realized by Indian experts "that the delicate question of India's position within the Empire will (after the war) present itself from a very different angle to the British people."

However, war and the consequences of war changed the composition of the nationalist movements, which managed in a relatively short time to gain a solid footing among the masses. The "complementary" pattern of trade between colony and mother country was disrupted, industries developed or were expanded, the number of wage-earners increased sharply, the trade union movement took root. Prices rose and additional problems of adaptation at the end of the war sharpened a social ferment which found an outlet in strikes and local disturbances. The radicalization of the Congress party can be precisely traced in its choice of presidents and their opening addresses. Thus in 1917 at the Calcutta Congress Mrs. Besant pointed emphatically to India's achievements in the war—"the condition of India's usefulness to the Empire is India's freedom"—but also to the "awakening of Asia" before and during the war; England, she said, had rewarded India's loyalty with nothing but "distrust," and the Allied struggle for freedom was apparently meant to benefit only the Dominions, but not India. At the same time she was able to observe a change in the attitude of the business world represented by Tata which, annoyed at the restrictions and shortage of credit, but also at the government's refusal to compensate firms formerly trading with Germany for their losses, had given its support to the nationalist movement. India would be able to meet future Japanese competition only if she enjoyed home rule, that is, had administrative control over taxation and revenue policy. At the 1918 Congress President Malaviya enumerated Wilson's 14 Points and referred to the appointment of Sinha as India's representative at the peace conference, but did not fail to mention that Sinha was responsible to the government of India and not to the Indian people.

The British government could not let matters rest at vague promises of reform: after the surprising agreement of Congress party and Moslem League in the Lucknow Pact of 1916 and the grave Mesopotamia crisis, London found itself forced into the "Declaration on India" of 20 August 1917, which proclaimed for the first time officially that the aim of British policy in India was "responsible government" and opened the way for the 1918–1919 Montagu–Chelmsford reforms. In this dialectic of challenge and response the accelerating effect of the war is particularly noticeable. Whereas in 1912 "representative government" had been decisively rejected and autocratic rule, relaxed somewhat by the presence of representatives of Indian interests, had been considered natural and necessary for at least decades to come, by the end of the war London was committed to withdrawal from India; and though every concession might be made reluctantly, with reservations and delaying tactics, there could be no going back.

Social mobilization enabled the Egyptian nationalists as well to win over the masses and compelled England to undertake decisive reforms. London had legalized the hitherto de facto protectorate in 1914 but gave little thought in the course of the war to the country's

future, although at the time the Arabs were promised that one or
more independent Arab states would be created. Although the price
of cotton spiraled and even small landowners were able to pay off a
considerable part of their debts during the war, the forcible recruiting and requisitioning had bred distrust and hatred among the fellaheen; the wholesale price index rose from 100 in 1914 to 312 in
1920, and government employees and the lower urban middle
classes found their already low income adversely affected. This
meant that the prewar paternalism which had claimed to protect the
peasant masses from "exploitation by rapacious pashas" had lost
much of its credibility. During the serious unrest of 1919 not only
was Cairo up in arms but also the hinterland, and there were many
attacks on landowners and government officials. The change from
the prewar period was startling, even if at first the alliance between
the nationalists of upper-class origin and the masses of the townspeople and peasantry was more or less dictated by the needs of
the moment.

The Egyptians, too, naturally took up Wilson's 14 Points and were
fortified in their aspirations towards home rule or even independence. Zaghlul, as leader of the nationalist movement, referred to
them on 13 November when he met Wingate, the High Commissioner, to demand independence, under guarantees of British rights
on the Suez Canal. London's rejection of Zaghlul's request to send
a delegation to London released a wave of radicalization which led
in 1922 to the unilateral British declaration of independence. It was
none other than Lord Milner who called for far-reaching concessions when in Cairo he faced a situation which had been totally
altered in the war.

A trend towards radicalization became apparent in Indonesia also:
the membership of Sarekat Islam rose from 360,000 in 1912 to
2.5 million in 1919. The nationalist demand in October 1917 was no
longer for home rule but for independence. Left-wing socialist
groups took over the leadership but were unable to prevent the formation in May 1920 of the Communist party. The Dutch administration in May 1918 had inaugurated the People's Council, in accordance with proposals for decentralization measures made before
the war; this was intended primarily as a representative organ of the
Dutch in the colony; the Indonesians were in a minority, and in any

case the Council was purely consultative. Nevertheless it marked a new beginning, even though the proposals of the reform commission set up at the end of the war in the spirit of a "return to normalcy" were realized only in part.

Even in West Africa the war had a marked influence on the attitude of the British administration and the small class of educated Africans, although no mass movement had yet made its appearance. Here, too, economic factors require consideration: in the Gold Coast, for example, exports to Germany ceased and profits fell off accordingly, while at the same time the cost of imports rose. The Ashantis sought to raise prices by "organized holdups" and protested to the governor "against such manifest exploitation of the natives' poor resources." Governor Hugh Clifford did, it is true, make an energetic and successful stand against the plans of the Empire Resources Development Committee, which would have added still further grievances, but the educated Africans had every reason to call in the Legislative Council for the introduction of the franchise or even for self-government. The economic situation was also an important factor in the establishment of the West Africa Congress, which attempted to gain a hearing in London in 1920, and which marked the start of the emancipation movement in the interwar years.

Clifford as early as 1915 pressed for constitutional reforms, in particular an increase in the number of unofficial members of the Legislative Council, together with greater consideration for the chiefs. The relation between wartime loyalty, on which the African spokesmen based their claims, and the administration's vital need at least to give assurances for the future which went far beyond the considerations of 1914, became clear when Clifford on 2 November 1918 felt obliged to reply to the reproach of the African Casely Hayford that England was continuing to withhold the vote: "I fully agree that in the fullness of time it is possible that every part of the British Empire will be as completely self-governing as are the Dominions today." No doubt the "fullness of time" was open to interpretation, but in any case this was, by analogy with the 1917 Declaration on India, the first time that the African colonies had been placed on an equal footing with the Dominions, a status which had hitherto been constantly refused.

As Great Britain and France found themselves obliged during the war either to introduce concrete reforms at once or to lay down the principles for future decolonization—assimilation and integration in the French sphere; self-government in the British—problems peculiar to the settler colony began to take shape, although they were at first not widely recognized for what they were. In Algeria the *évolués* who favored assimilation were opposed by the closed ranks of the Franco-Algerians, who in their turn could also point to their sacrifices in the war and who in 1918–1919, in collaboration with the conservative colonialist groups in the mother country, were able to water down the reforms which had originally been generous in their intentions, and above all prohibit the grant of citizenship if personal status under Islamic law was retained. In Southern Rhodesia London was willing to concede "responsible government" rather than bear the cost of reimbursing the South Africa Company and the colonial administration, thus clearing the way for responsible government and the plebiscite of 1923. In Kenya it was felt that the colonists should be compensated for their economic hardships and military aid during the war, and in 1916 they were granted the right to vote in the Legislative Council, which later made it difficult to block the further step of an unofficial majority as a preliminary to responsible government. In other words, in the settler colonies the war propelled events in the opposite direction in the sense that a relaxation of colonial rule benefited the whites.

A further aspect deserves consideration: immediately after the war the colonial elite found that its hopes of liberal reforms had been illusory, or realized that it had overrated the readiness for such reforms. Only then did the social and psychological effects of the war make their full impact, just at the time when conservative governments faced with revolutionary forces in their own countries showed little inclination to yield to nationalist pressure. The Algeria Act of 1919 by no means fulfilled the 1915 proposals of Clemenceau and Leygues and disappointed even the moderate *évolués;* the Montagu–Chelmsford reforms were well received in India, especially by Gandhi, but they were accompanied by the Rawlatt Bills and Amritsar, which indicated the administration's opposition to reform and its belief in repression. Only when this became clear did Gandhi, who had had complete faith in England's liberal intentions, make final the break with the colonial power and give the signal for passive resistance. London's refusal to accept the Milner Report on Egypt shut the door to any remaining possibilities of an understanding with the nationalists. Liberal governors in Indochina and Indonesia gave way to conservative ones. The natural relationship of tension between colonial power and emancipation, between reaction and progress, hardened into a policy of immobility, so typical of the interwar years.

If we take Ludwig Dehio's interpretation of the Second World War as a new and final attempt to achieve hegemony in Europe, an attempt which, in a system of states already disintegrating (Holborn), inevitably took particularly destructive forms and hastened the assertion of hegemony by the flanking powers, then the recent acceleration in the process of colonial evolution and devolution can be more easily understood. This war was truly global, a conflict in which the colonial territories of Southeast Asia were the scene of decisive military action; but most important of all, the chief colonial powers suffered disastrous setbacks. France collapsed, although the Vichy government was able to hold on to a number of positions in North Africa and Indochina, and de Gaulle's Free France gained its first territorial foothold in Equatorial Africa. Great Britain suffered a shattering defeat in Singapore. In the perspective of world affairs the fall of this bastion of Southeast Asia can be seen to be of great significance, as it not only cleared the way for Japan to occupy the entire region, but also seemed symbolically to herald the collapse of the colonial system as a whole, and revealed the decline, hitherto to a great extent concealed, of England as a world maritime power.

Despite growing nationalist agitation in the thirties, national leaders once more opted almost unanimously for the Allied cause, and, with a few exceptions, showed no sympathy with the Axis powers. This was true of Gandhi and the avowed antifascist Nehru, but also of the moderate Burmese, who enjoyed a share of government and administration, of the moderate Indonesians, of Bourgiba and the Neo-Destour of Tunisia, of Ferat Abbas in Algeria, and the *évolués* in British and French Africa. Recruitment and mobilization of colonial troops again passed off with no great difficulty. The manifestations of loyalty were, however, clearly linked this time with demands for reform. The war offered a suitable opportunity for demanding autonomy or even independence, and this no longer as a mere promise to follow after the war, but effectively and at once. Refusal by the colonial powers to concede such incisive changes during the war resulted, for example in India, in a gradual sharpening of the tension with Congress and led to the 1942 "Quit India" movement, even though the possibility of a Japanese advance into India remained real. England clamped down hard but at the same time recognized that withdrawal from India was no longer to be avoided; and the question was thus reduced to the "when" and "how" of the transfer of power. The Cripps mission to India, which even envisaged that country's withdrawal from the Commonwealth, was dispatched as a move to counter the Japanese advance and in answer to American pressure.

In North Africa the Vichy government allowed little scope for nationalist movements, and de Gaulle too was for a long time reluctant to commit himself to future emancipation. After the Allied landing, however, the nationalists learned how to exploit France's weakness and the tensions within the Allied camp. During the temporary occupation of Tunisia by the Axis powers, the Sultan and Bourgiba "collaborated" and took action against France, while the Sultan of Morocco attempted with American backing to put in his claim for independence before the protectorate could be reestablished. Even more symptomatic of this trend was the change in attitude of the Algerians; Ferat Abbas dropped his plea for integration and assimilation and demanded the establishment of an Algerian state, announcing in the Algerian Manifesto of 10 February 1943 a program which, if not tantamount to a complete and open break with France, was clearly Algerian and nationalist in spirit. De Gaulle sought to counter it by granting civil rights with retention of Islamic personal status, which in reality meant implementation of the 1936–1937 popular front program.

President Roosevelt and his colleagues openly favored anticolonialism, supporting the Congress party in India and the Sultan in Morocco, and extended expressly to the colonial territories the right of self-determination embodied in the Atlantic Charter which Churchill had wished to apply only to the nations of Europe liberated from the Axis. It was only natural that the nationalists should seize upon this, and, disappointed by Churchill and by the discrepancy between Allied declarations and the effective measures taken, should rely upon future American support. The significance of American anticolonialism has, however, been perhaps exaggerated; the war alone, with all its political and social implications and repercussions, was enough to break the stagnation of the interwar years and hasten or set in motion the process of decolonization.

This was especially true in Southeast Asia where the Japanese occupation created entirely new conditions. Whereas in North and West Africa, in India and Ceylon, the colonial administration was weakened but managed to survive, in Southeast Asia it was completely destroyed, and this alone had epoch-making consequences. The unexpected collapse of the colonial power was seen as the "failure of a divine mission"; it awakened millennial expectations which were immediately identified with the expulsion of foreigners and necessarily made any rule reimposed by force appear questionable. Ties of loyalty were broken, the passive endurance of an established system of rule rejected, while on the other hand mass forces were released which lent an undreamed-of impetus to the emancipation movement. Moreover, as part of their war effort and their concept of co-prosperity, the Japanese mounted a systematic campaign of antiwestern and antiwhite propaganda and sought also with great skill to accommodate nationalist aspirations. Japanese procedure in fact varied considerably in the different regions but created similar situations. Thus the disappearance of the European ruling cadres—by retreat in Malaya and Burma, by internment in Java—and the shortage of Japanese personnel, opened the way to advancement for countless minor native officials and led at least temporarily to a collaboration of expediency with the occupying power. At the same time the "inferiority complexes" inherent in the "colonial situation" were cured and the determination to achieve self-government strengthened.

In Indochina the French administration did in fact continue, since the Japanese were content with military occupation and indirect control, but Admiral Decoux found himself obliged to employ Vietnamese in order to woo them away from the anti-French opposition movement. The Japanese replaced the languages of the European rulers by national languages and awakened hopes that independence would soon be granted. A good part of these hopes was in fact not realized, or realized only shortly before the Japanese defeat; forced labor and forced recruitment led the rural population in particular to resent Japan. In Java the nationalists released from Dutch internment took part in government only as "advisers," but they gained new opportunities of influencing the masses: anti-imperialist slogans were aimed with characteristic ambivalence both at the Allies and at Japan, and their ultimate effect was to benefit the nationalist movement. Japan set up its own mass organizations, and among other things a radio network which for the first time made the rural population politically accessible. These served to propagate the "co-prosperity" idea but were taken over by the nationalists just as Japan was preparing to consider independence and the formation of a national government, enabling the group around Sukarno and Hatta to mobilize the villages. As Japan also encouraged military training and created native armed forces in Burma, Malaya, and Indonesia, the nationalists had at their disposal a readymade instrument of power for their encounter with the returning colonial power.

At the same time the leadership of the nationalist movements passed to those radical groups which before the war had either formed an unimportant minority or had been crippled by police action. In Burma this was accompanied by a generational change: the moderate Burmese politicians and the Indian bourgeoisie who had retreated with the British were succeeded by the Thakin group under the young Aung San, a product of the extremist student nationalism of the late thirties. The group had established links with Japan and had marched with a "national liberation army" into Burma, but had then ceased its collaboration and finally fought on the side of the Allies against Japan. It thus had control of a cadre which was immediately able to take on administrative duties and assured the group of mass peasant support, so that when the Japanese capitulated, Great Britain was confronted with a fait accompli. In Indochina the Communist party of Ho Chi Minh, though small, was able to profit from the "strange alliance" and, operating from China, to consolidate a maquis position in Upper Tongking which, on the retreat of the Japanese in 1945, but just before the arrival of the French, enabled it together with other nationalist groups to declare an Indochinese Republic which, in the agreement of 6 March 1946, received from France a pledge of extensive autonomy. The attempt to get around this reluctant concession and to neutralize Ho Chi Minh's position by incorporating his republic into a French-controlled federation led in 1946 to war.

As a result of the Japanese occupation Burma's position differed fundamentally in 1945 from that of India and Ceylon, but showed great similarity to that of Java and Indochina. The deciding factor was that colonial rule had collapsed, and that when they moved to reestablish themselves the colonial powers found themselves confronted with nationalist mass organizations which, in Java and Indochina, had already declared an independent republic, and, in Burma, were in any case so firmly established that without the employment of strong military forces reconquest was unthinkable. England—short of troops and influenced by Lord Mountbatten's perceptive appraisal of the totally new situation—abandoned the idea of recovering her former empire by force; Holland and France decided to try.

In West Africa, too, decolonization was hastened or rather sparked off by the Second World War. Numerous factors, differing considerably in the various regions, had the effect of accelerating the process. The colonial administrations were maintained, and indeed the West African colonies assumed increasing importance during the war. Not only the Vichy government but also Free France stimulated the production of commodities (destined as exports to bring in currency) by forced cultivation and forced labor, thus fostering distrust and unrest which later made easier the mobilization and political indoctrination of the rural masses by nationalist spokesmen; at the same time the townspeople were hard hit by a rise in the price of imported goods. There were other reasons for discontent: in the Ivory Coast, for example, the government gave preferential treatment to the European planters, thus incurring the resentment of the African middle class. In Equatorial Africa it was necessary, after the loss of the French market, to reduce selling prices to the level of the world market in order to export, and the purchasing power of the Africans dropped. In the British territories the problems were quite different but—characteristically—brought astonishingly similar results. While exports were hindered at first by lack of shipping, and the price of cocoa for example fell, later the disruption of the Mediterranean route and the loss of Southeast Asian raw materials created a rapidly growing demand for African products which England tried to satisfy by purchase agreements, state intervention, marketing boards and other means: a real war boom brought profit to the African farmers, middlemen and business generally, thus strengthening the economic and political position of the native middle class, although here too the rising prices of consumer goods created resentment which led, among other things, to a general strike in Nigeria in 1945, and was also the prime cause of the 1948 riots in Accra, which in their turn enlarged the following of the African parties and impelled the British government to introduce decisive reforms. Factors which in the First World War had hastened the movement towards emancipation primarily in India and Egypt came to bear in the Second World War in West Africa as well. The same was true of the stationing of European troops. British West Africa—like Egypt in the earlier war—became a military depot. True, there was no fighting, but the colonies were important supply bases for English and American forces in North Africa. Airfields were built and aircraft assembled by allied troops, but with the aid of African labor; the social implications of this new kind of contact between black man and white are obvious.

Once again the part played by the veterans was considerable, if difficult to evaluate. After years of absence they were alienated from traditional society; often dissatisfied with their conditions of discharge and with insufficient opportunities for work in the towns, they formed an important element of social and political unrest in the critical phase immediately after the war, clearly discernible in, for example, the Accra riots of 1948. The national elite became more broadly based. The old notables and the few educated Africans were now replaced by younger leaders, often students, and by representatives of the African middle class—small businessmen, officials, teachers—who used new methods of organization and propaganda, founded trade unions, and began to build up modern parties. In Africa, too, wartime loyalty and service by African troops were recalled when political demands were presented. Representatives of the important student body in London and of the youth organizations in Africa started to criticize the administration sharply, especially its racial discrimination, and pressed for more rapid Africanization and the expansion of the educational system, and in the political field for swift redemption of the pledge of self-government. During a visit to London in 1943, Azikiwe, the spokesman of Nigerian nationalism, handed the colonial secretary a memorandum with the significant title "The Atlantic Charter and British West Africa," containing a claim for full independence within fifteen years. Thus challenged, London began gradually to adopt a new line: it helped to establish the trade unions, took in hand the modernization of local government, and prepared new constitutions. The details are of no interest here. What is important is the remarkable acceleration caused by the war. As late as 1938 a colonial secretary could regard centuries (!) of British rule as necessary and—apparently—possible; during the war London actually accepted an African majority in the Legislative Council (the Burns constitution for the Gold Coast, 1944–1946), thus recognizing by implication the transition to responsible government. The analogy with the situation in India in 1914–1919 needs no emphasis.

In the French sphere the initiative came much more strongly from the mother country: Free France, impelled by a revolutionary urge for renewal, attempted to break through the stagnation of the Third Republic; at the same time an effective program of reform had to be found to counter American anticolonialism. The Brazzaville conference of governors in 1944 laid down the postwar policy for Africa, the traditional concept of decolonization was upheld and the colonies, despite decentralization measures and the formation of local assemblies, were to be integrated into Greater France, with extension of civil rights and the election of African representatives to the Paris parliament. It was then that political life in French West Africa really began, since the elections necessitated parties and the new electorate had to be mobilized. The role of the Second World War as an accelerating factor was revealed perhaps even more strikingly in French West Africa than in British Africa.

Only slowly are we beginning to grasp the last 50–60 years as a kind of historical unity. We are easily tempted to isolate particular events, or to devote our attention to one single country or area— Europe, America, or Asia. The complex as a whole, but also the numerous reciprocal effects within it, tend to remain outside our field of vision.

It is historical fact that the First World War saw the collapse of the European system of states. But that was not all. It is equally well known, although detailed research is only just beginning, that the creation of armies numbering millions, the wartime economy necessitating intervention by the state and sweeping changes in production, the movement of prices and incomes, the radicalization in the labor movement and the emancipation of women—all these, among other things, stirred the bourgeois-liberal society of the pre-1914 years into movement. The interwar years appear to us today as a period of crisis and adjustment during which, although it was possible to check the wave of revolution released by the war, the new mass society achieved neither economic nor political stability: the open or latent crisis of West European democracy and the fascist-authoritarian movements in Central, East, and Southern Europe are clearly to be viewed against the broader horizon. Only in the Second World War, and not least as a consequence of that war, did the breakthrough to the welfare state follow after 1945 in the advanced industrialized countries of Europe and America, still based on the individualist-capitalist economic system, but supplemented by planning mechanisms and stabilized with the aid of an extensive machinery of state intervention.

The world wars as factors hastening the decline of colonialism should therefore not be considered in isolation, since the movement towards emancipation in the colonies was accompanied by a parallel change of structure in the colonial powers which, in the changing composition of elites and the mobilization of human masses, can be seen as an analogous phenomenon. This suggests completely new perspectives for a comparative historical approach concerned with sociological and politological issues. There has already been an interesting attempt by Professor Arno Mayer to analyze specific variants of nationalism in the years following the First World War, in which he draws attention to a similarity between the new states of Central and Eastern Europe and the states which gained independence after 1945; in both instances predominantly agrarian societies ruled by traditional elites were subjected to a rapid process of modernization, resulting in the sudden and unforeseen achievement of independence, which brought into the open national problems of integration (frontiers, minorities) as well as the conflict between old and new elites. In the absence of strongly cohesive internal forces, structural economic and social change led to a personalization of political power and to the subsequent emergence of military dictatorship as a way out of internal difficulties.

The First World War, the interwar years, and the Second World War, but also Europe and the world outside Europe, are thus drawn closer together. The emancipation of Asia and Africa should not be understood as a mere by-product of the wars in Europe, but as an integral part of the structural change in the world political constellation which had been developing since the turn of the century, characterized on the one hand by a transfer of power from Europe to the non-European world, on the other hand by a Europeanization or Westernization of this latter world.

II THE END OF THE BRITISH EMPIRE

Nicholas Mansergh
BRITAIN LEAVES INDIA

Beginning with the Battle of Plassey in 1757, the British established their control first over the province of Bengal and then, during the following century, over the rest of India (including present-day Pakistan, Bangladesh and parts of Burma). In the process, what had begun in the early seventeenth century as a series of trading posts on the Indian coast grew into one of the "twin pillars of the Empire," the most important military and economic British possession, whose defense and advancement became the fundamental concern of British foreign policy in the Middle East, Africa and Asia until after World War II. The ease with which Britain in 1947 granted India its independence was therefore altogether remarkable and remains one of the politically most foresighted moves of this century. Nicholas Mansergh is perhaps Britain's best-known Commonwealth historian, having published a number of books and document collections on Commonwealth affairs. (For reference to his work see the Suggestions for Additional Reading at the end of this book.)

The outbreak of the Second World War ushered in the last phase of British rule in India. The war's impact was twofold; it intensified the Indian demand for independence and progressively weakened the British will and capacity to withhold it. The resulting possibility, or probability, of a withdrawal of the British *Raj* sooner than had hitherto been anticipated on either side, in turn and by the natural working of the laws of politics, sharpened the struggle for the succession to power within India. Where formerly the Congress and the League had stood side by side, by March 1940 at the latest, when the Muslim League at their Lahore meeting formulated a demand for separate Muslim homelands and a separate Muslim state, they stood face to face. Where once there had been a possibility of association in independence now there was, in the idiom of a later period, confrontation.

The twin pressures of the struggles for national independence and for control of the levers of power after independence were exerted within a single context, the one at every stage reacting upon

From Nicholas Mansergh, *The Commonwealth Experience* (London and New York, 1969), pp. 295–301. Copyright © 1969 by Nicholas Mansergh. Reprinted by permission of Weidenfeld and Nicolson Ltd. and Praeger Publishers, Inc. Footnotes omitted.

the other. That context was provided at the highest political level by the policies of the British government, themselves compounded of immediate military considerations and long-term constitutional aims. First the war and then, and largely in consequence of it, the consolidation of British opinion in favor of an early transfer of power, invested those policies retrospectively with a clarity of outline that historically they did not possess. Nonetheless the record of Britain's wartime and immediately postwar advances to Indian independence on the basis of responsible government and dominion status, summarily restated, provides a necessary background to any analysis of the interrelation between constitutional advance and domestic division.

The outbreak of war underlined not so much the measure of autonomy India had so far acquired as the extent of her dependence. The viceroy, Lord Linlithgow, declared war on behalf of India without calling the leaders of the principal Indian parties, the Congress or the Muslim League, into a consultation. Constitutionally the viceroy's action was warranted by reason of the fact that the federal provisions of the Government of India Act [of] 1935 had not come into effect. But constitutional rectitude was no compensation for so grave a lapse in political judgment. The Congress, in particular, was deeply resentful; and Pandit Nehru contrasted the position of the dominions, including Ireland, free to decide in their several parliaments whether or not to declare war upon Nazi Germany, with that of an India committed to war without even so much as a reference to its representative political figures. From this inauspicious start there was to be no sustained recovery in Anglo-Indian, or more especially in Anglo-Congress relations for the duration of the war. In this there was a certain irony inasmuch as British and Congress, and indeed British and Indian, opinion as a whole, far from being in conflict, coincided substantially in respect of the causes for which war was being waged.

There were differences in the attitudes of the League and the Congress to wartime cooperation, that of the League being essentially pragmatic while the Congress characteristically defined their position in conceptual terms. They professed sympathy for the Allied cause deriving from their love of liberty and the strong anti-Fascist, anti-Nazi sentiments embodied in the prewar Congress resolutions, but maintained that despite these bonds, cooperation with Britain was precluded by India's continued dependence. India, unfree, could not fight for freedom. Such was the Congress assertion of principle. Was it reasonable to infer from it that a free India under Congress leadership would support the Allied cause in arms? The answer, and it was clearly one of potential importance in the shaping of British policy, remained debatable. In December 1939 the Congress governments in the provinces resigned rather than cooperate in a war effort directed by an alien authority. In itself and for the future this was a significant step. But it did not provide a conclusive answer about attitudes in quite different conditions. That could be founded only on less tangible and necessarily hypothetical evidence. The main body of the Congress, attentive to Jawaharlal Nehru's impassioned prewar denunciation of militarist regimes both in Europe and Asia, would presumably have favored the participation of a free India, provided it were unmistakably at her own choice and on her own terms, in the war on the side of the Western allies. But there were also the disciples of Mahatma Gandhi, already regarded with veneration as the conscience of the Congress, who accepted without qualification his doctrines of nonviolent resistance and believed them to have an absolute validity in the international, as in the domestic, field. In 1942 they were prepared with Gandhi to advocate such passive resistance to a Japanese invasion from the northeast. Nor could the British government, even assuming that it had been able to reach a conclusion reassuring to itself about the cooperation of a Congress wartime government, consider the Indian problem in its Congress setting alone. There were also the League and the princes. In terms of Britain's survival—and no less was at stake between 1940 and 1942—was there solid advantage in conceding freedom to India, even on the assumption of thereby enlisting the aid of the Congress in the prosecution of the war, if the consequences were to be the estrangement of loyal princely allies and the opening of a struggle for power within India between the Congress and the League? Even if the answer were in the affirmative, it was at best speculative and few governments are prepared to indulge in wartime speculation so risky as this. So it was that from 1939 onwards the British government were caught in a dilemma from which, despite some facile subsequent comment, there was no escape. It may well be that the chief responsibility for the existence of such a dilemma was their own, and that in wartime Britain was paying the price of the procrastinating policies of the later 1920s and early 1930s.

It is in terms of this diminishing freedom of maneuver and of the impact of the successive major crises of the war that British attempts to end the constitutional deadlock in India are to be viewed. On 23 October 1939 the secretary of state, Lord Zetland, reminded the war cabinet that when Parliament had "accepted dominion status as the goal, the feeling was that the journey was a long one, but the effect of the outbreak of the war has been to bring us hard up against the implication of dominion status for India. . . ." The nature of British wartime proposals underlined the correctness of this analysis. The first, following closely upon the fall of France, was the so-called "August offer," 1940. It proposed the immediate enlargement of the viceroy's council so as to include a certain number of representatives of the Indian political parties, but little otherwise. Further essays in constitution-making were firmly relegated to after the end of the war, though it was conceded that when the time came, and in accord with dominion precedent, any new constitution should be drafted in India. But even in this context, there was a restatement in uncompromising terms of Britain's obligations to the princes and of British inability to contemplate the transfer of their responsibility for the peace and welfare of India to any system of government, the authority of which was directly denied "by large and powerful elements in India's national life." The offer concluded with the hope that, as a result of Indian cooperation in the war, a new understanding would emerge paving the way to "the attainment by India of that free and equal partnership in the British Commonwealth which remains the proclaimed and accepted goal of the imperial Crown and of the British Parliament."

The "August offer," its modest attractions for the most part prospective and conditional, was spurned by the Congress and rejected, albeit with some judicious qualification, by the League. There followed a period of constitutional quiescence. It came to an end in 1942, that year of disaster to Allied arms in the east. On 11 March the prime minister announced in the House of Commons that "the crisis in the affairs of India arising out of the Japanese advance has made us wish to rally all the forces of Indian life to guard their land from the menace of the invader." In consequence the war cabinet had decided to send out one of their number, the lord privy seal, Sir Stafford Cripps, to India to give precision to earlier British declarations, and notably the "August offer" 1940, about dominion status for India and to convince "all classes, races and creeds in India of our sincere resolve" that "the conclusions upon which we are agreed, and which we believe represent a just and final solution, will achieve their purpose." In fact the conclusions of the war cabinet were in terms of precision, if not of principle, a decided advance upon anything hitherto formulated. At the heart of them was dominion status, with the constitution of the new Indian union to be drafted, as the Congress had consistently demanded, by an Indian Constituent Assembly in accord with dominion precedents. The new dominion was to be "associated with the United Kingdom and the other dominions by a common allegiance to the Crown, but equal to them in every respect, in no way subordinate in any aspect of its domestic or external affairs." What was contemplated, as Sir Stafford Cripps made plain on arrival in India, was dominion status without reservation or qualification. At a press conference in New Delhi he was asked whether the new dominion would be free to secede. He replied in the affirmative. He was asked whether Canada was free to secede. He replied "Of course." While these answers, when reported, gave George VI some cause for uneasy reflection, they gave, insofar as they were credited, a measure of reassurance in Delhi. However, the offer of dominion status which Sir Stafford Cripps thus expounded, while unconditional, remained prospective. Once again constitution-making was deferred till victory had been won. This was a major disappointment to Indian nationalist sentiment. There was the certainty of delay and, for many, no corresponding assurance about victory. Gandhi was alleged to have spoken of a postdated check upon a failing bank, and even if the phrase was not of his own invention—it has been attributed to K. M. Panikkar—he entertained the sentiment. Nor were Congress's feelings of frustration on the constitutional front counterbalanced by the prospect of some immediate transfer of substantial administrative responsibilities to Indian hands. At the crisis of the eastern war, the British government decided on the contrary that it must retain final control of the levers of power and direct control over defense in India. Accordingly much of what it was prepared to transfer to Indian hands was of marginal relevance to government at such a time. Moreover, while these were the chief, they were not the only causes of Congress reserve. The Cripps proposals introduced a novel principle of nonaccession, by which any province of British India which was not prepared to accept the constitution to be drafted after the war was to be enabled to retain its existing constitutional position unimpaired and outside the new Indian dominion. It was later added that the British government would be prepared to agree upon a new constitution giving the nonacceding provinces, collectively, if they so desired, the same status as the Indian union. The League had reason to welcome these concessions to its position, though it professed to feel that they did not go far enough. The formulation of the principle of nonaccession enhanced Congress suspicions of British intentions. The final outcome was rejection of the Cripps offer, first by the Congress on the specific ground of inadequate Indian control over the defense of India but clearly also for more general reasons and then by the League. The failure to reach agreement was followed by Congress endorsement in August 1942 of a "Quit India" resolution, which resulted in rebellion and led to the imprisonment of the principal Congress leaders for the remainder of the war.

The Cripps mission did not achieve its immediate purposes but it succeeded in its long-term aims. In India, and certainly no less in London, it changed the context of discussions about Anglo-Indian relations. Churchill, who had seen Cripps, the radical, socialist friend of Nehru, depart on a highly problematic mission with mixed feelings, and who was enabled to endure its failure with fortitude, remarked to the king shortly afterwards that "his colleagues and both, or all three parties in Parliament were quite prepared to give up India to the Indians after the war. He felt they had already been talked into giving up India." More precisely, there could be no going back on the offer of a constituent assembly and dominion status. And it was on this basis that negotiations were resumed after the war, first in conference at Simla and then, following the accession to office of the Labour government in Britain, by the sending of a cabinet mission consisting of Lord Pethick-Lawrence, the secretary of state for India, Sir Stafford Cripps, president of the Board of

Trade, and A. V. Alexander, the first lord of the Admiralty, to India early in 1946. There could no longer be serious doubt about the purposes of the British government. The first was to preserve the unity of India and the second to transfer power at the earliest possible moment. These dual aims were, however, conflicting. Unity might conceivably be preserved were independence deferred; independence might be conceded forthwith but at the price of unity. That much was made plain by the Indian response to the cabinet mission and its Report.

The mission examined but rejected the possibility of partition and proposed that there should be a union of India, embracing both British India and the princely states, with responsibility for foreign affairs, defense and communications. All other subjects and all residuary powers were to be vested in the provinces and the provinces were to be left free to form groups, with each group enabled to determine the provincial subjects to be dealt with in common. This three-tier structure, with its weak center, its potential groupings and its strongly entrenched provincial governments, was as far as the cabinet mission felt it possible to go towards satisfying minority sentiment while preserving a framework of federal unity. Their submissions, finally issued on 16 May 1946, in the form of a statement by the cabinet mission and the viceroy, were accepted initially but with reservations in respect of Pakistan by the League and subject to conditions by the Congress. Such qualified responses in themselves augured ill at this late hour for the prospects of unity, and the misgivings they inspired were fully realized with the failure of the viceroy's first attempts to obtain joint Congress–League participation in the interim government intended by the cabinet mission to prepare for the transfer of responsibility, or at any time in a constituent assembly to draft a constitution for India. In these circumstances the British government was compelled to contemplate the abandonment of one or other of its aims. Unity and an early transfer of power were self-evidently incompatible and it was arguable that communal antagonism was of such intensity that unity could not in any circumstances, or at any foreseeable time, survive the transfer of power. If this were so, the opportunities for transfer to a single successor authority were already in the past.

The last phase, from the autumn of 1946 to the summer of 1947, was marked by the formation of an interim government, in which Congress and League representatives in acrimonious association assumed responsibility for the conduct of Indian administration; by the summoning of the long-promised Constituent Assembly which, however, was boycotted by the representatives of the Muslim League; by the announcement, on 20 February 1947, of the "definite intention" of the British government "to take the necessary steps to effect the transference of power into responsible Indian hands by a date not later than June 1948"; by the arrival in March 1947 of Lord Mountbatten as the last viceroy and one who had welcomed the fact "that his task was to end one regime and to inaugurate a new one"; by the succeeding weeks of intense and dramatic discussion between the new viceroy and the Indian leaders, recorded for later generations by Alan Campbell Johnson in his *Mission with Mountbatten*; by the resulting final acceptance, or acquiescence, by the leaders of the Congress and the League of the inevitability of partition; by the announcement of partition and of the transfer of power to two successor dominions by the viceroy at a press conference on 4 June, at which with unfailing assurance he answered nearly a hundred questions put to him by Indian and world correspondents; by the passage through both Houses of Parliament at Westminster of the Indian Independence Act, introduced in the House of Commons by the prime minister, Clement Attlee, in a speech, which contained an apposite and moving quotation from Mountstuart Elphinstone and an allusion, deemed more felicitous then than later, to Campbell-Bannerman's parallel act of faith in restoring self-government to the defeated Boers "which bore fruit both in 1914 and in 1939"; and finally, on the midnight hour of the 14–15 August 1947, by the coming into existence of the two new dominions of India and Pakistan, with Mohammed Ali Jinnah speaking in Karachi, the new capital of a new state, of "the fulfilment of the destiny of the Muslim nation" and with Pandit Nehru in Delhi reflecting upon the long years ago when "we made a tryst with destiny" and of how the time had come "when we shall redeem our pledge."

Francis Hutchins
INDIA LEAVES BRITAIN

Accounts of the British move out of India generally stress London's control over the sequence of events that finally led to Indian independence. But as the events surrounding the "Quit India" resolution drawn up by the Congress Party in August 1942 illustrate, there was firm nationalist determination in India that the time had come for Britain to leave. As Hutchins argues, independence was not so much granted as it was taken. Professor Hutchins is author of an earlier book on India, Illusion of Permanence: British Imperialism in India.

The dismantling of European empires in Asia after World War II is frequently explained as the consequence of a weakening of European power caused by the war itself. Britain, one is often told, was no longer strong enough to hold India and withdrew as an act of political precaution. In reality, British withdrawal was the result of pressure exerted from within India. Following the war, the French returned to Indochina, the Dutch to Indonesia, and the British to Malaya, Singapore, and Burma. The British showed sufficient will in repressing a guerrilla insurgency in Malaya that was limited to one section of the population, and the French and Dutch did their best to hold onto Indochina and Indonesia. The imperial regimes were forced out of Indochina, Indonesia, Burma, and India because local pressures had become uncontrollable. What happened after the war was a result of what Asians had experienced during the war, not of what Europeans had lost by the war.

The transformations which occurred in many countries during World War II are only now beginning to come into focus. During the war momentous changes were taking place. Awareness of these changes came with startling suddenness following 1945 because of the prior monopolization of public attention by war news. In India, the war's end led to independence for India and the creation of the new state of Pakistan—events so unexpected as to lead observers naturally to attribute them vaguely to an undefined postwar ex-

Reprinted by permission of the publishers from Francis G. Hutchins, *India's Revolution: Gandhi and the Quit India Movement* (Cambridge, Mass.: Harvard University Press, Copyright © 1973, by the President and Fellows of Harvard College), pp. 1–3; 282–289. Footnotes omitted.

haustion. Reconstruction of the social history of the war years is
now beginning to make sense of these events, as it becomes clear
that Indian independence and the creation of Pakistan were the
direct results of a confrontation of social forces within India during
the war years. The British left India because Indians had made it
impossible for them to stay.

India attained independence through revolution. The midwar
Quit India movement climaxed India's nationalist revolution, which
overthrew a powerful, effective political regime. Yet the revolutionary nature of Indian nationalism might not have been recognized
even if its triumphs had not been obscured by the World War. The
reluctance to consider nationalisms such as India's as revolutionary
stems from a pooling of partial perceptions, those of many nationalists combined with those of liberal imperialists and many
social scientists. Revolutionaries need not be consciously so; they
may conceive of themselves and their goals much more modestly
or vaguely. Liberal imperialists in turn often portray the attainment
of independence as the "fulfillment" of colonial rule. From the
earliest period of British dominance in India, Englishmen had proclaimed their hopes that India would some day be ripe for independence, though it was usually assumed that this referred to an
irrelevantly remote eventuality. After the fact, however, India's independence could be described as the fulfillment of British policy by
reference to these frequently reiterated hopes. This impression was
reinforced by the fact that the Labour party happened to be in
power when India became independent. The Labour party had been
associated with the enactment of several latter-day imperial experiments with political liberalization. Depicted as methods by which
the imperial regime was laying the groundwork—consciously or un-
consciously—for its departure, these experiments were in fact efforts to forestall independence by neutralizing grievances. The
British Labour party was committed only to independence on British terms. To win independence on their own terms, Indians had
to defy their liberal well-wishers no less than their conservative
detractors. Only when independence became inevitable following
the Quit India movement of 1942 did both parties switch to efforts
to insure that the attainment of formal independence would not
affect vested interests adversely.

Some imperial regimes did take action before this had become inevitable. By conceding independence at an early date, the United States in the Philippines and Britain and France in Africa and elsewhere were able to exert greater influence on postindependence national development. In such instances it is more accurate to speak of the "granting" of independence. Not surprisingly, national elites who have been given independence have often had difficulty holding their nations together. Some countries, such as China, have resisted imperialism in a clearly revolutionary manner. Other countries have been given independence and not known what to do with it. India stands in between, having attained independence through a movement which must be called revolutionary, but which has not usually been recognized as such because of certain formal resemblances to movements which did not attain independence through their own efforts. . . .

The Quit India movement was, as Lord Linlithgow observed in a telegram to Churchill, "by far the most serious rebellion since that of 1857." The upheavals of 1857 and 1942 were in fact parallel in a number of respects. Both eradicated British authority in large areas of the country; both were most intense in many of the same areas of northern India. The differences between these two events mark the extent of the changes which had occurred over ninety years. In 1857, British rule was a struggling, makeshift affair and was challenged by the traditional social groups whose positions were being gradually eroded. The rebellion was indiscriminately xenophobic and backward-looking. The rebellion was a last stand by groups which would never again be in a position to challenge British rule. The British, moreover, were moved by the challenge to strengthen their rule, responding with renewed determination to remove the conditions which made the rising possible. In 1942, British rule was apparently impregnable; pulling British authority down by a spontaneous uprising was a much greater feat—a feat accomplished entirely without the aid of regular military forces, which in the rebellion had been supplied by mutineers from British service and the armies of several princely states. In 1942, the British Indian army and police were vastly more efficient and better disciplined forces, and the rebels were all raw amateurs. The Quit India movement was not begun or ended by the military; the movement was a violent expression of political forces whose resources included much more than the strength of arms, and which would not disappear if physically crushed. The rebels, having positive goals, employed violence symbolically, with discrimination, and hoped that some of their opponents could be persuaded to join them. The British, formally triumphant, responded to the movement with an awareness that no new effort could establish British rule on a solid footing. The seemingly similar outbursts of popular fury of 1857 and 1942 had opposite results. One led to an even firmer imposition of British rule; the other, though superficially a more futile effort, brought British rule to an end. Behind the shouting and the bloodshed, intellectual forces were at work which in 1857 left the rebels demoralized and the British more determined than ever. In 1942 the renewed clash had left the victorious British demoralized and the defeated rebels more determined than ever. Between the first outburst and the second, a revolution had taken place.

In the Quit India movement, the Indian revolution reached its climax. The revolution, conceived as an open rebellion against an apparently invincible regime, had presumed that success would be measured, not by the content of British offers, but by the strength and clarity of Indian will. Indians would be free when they acted as free men, without reference to British desires, when the appeals for generosity of the moderates and the opposition-defined defiance of the reactionaries were replaced by a confident indifference to the continuing British presence. India declared herself to be already independent, and in India's will to act independently the revolution had triumphed.

In 1942, communication between New Delhi and London was almost instantaneous; two hours was sufficient for the delivery of an urgent telegraphic message. Yet India and Whitehall were still very distant in a psychological sense, and the exchanges which took place between the viceroy and the war cabinet in London during this decisive year were characterized by a peculiarly discontinuous quality. For a brief moment at the height of the crisis of August 1942 unanimity reigned, and determination in both capitals was strong. At other times, when a mood of confidence dominated in one capital, dark pessimism dominated the other. Six months before the Quit India movement, at the time the Cripps Mission was initiated, New Delhi was brimming with confidence, while the war cabinet thought compromise might be necessary; after the Quit India movement, the war cabinet became curiously heroic, while

New Delhi was demoralized. This progression of moods was, more-over, not merely random; it led straight to the manner in which Britain vacated India in 1947.

When the Quit India movement first began to take definite shape in the summer of 1942, its import had been perceived with clarity in both London and New Delhi. Linlithgow and Amery both spoke forcefully to the effect that this was in fact a final showdown which would decide once and for all whether British or Congress pre-sumption would be shown up. On July 15, 1942, Amery asserted that "After all, we are dealing with people who are more and more advancing the claim to be considered as the alternative Govern-ment of India and ingeniously fortifying that claim step by step. At some point or other we have got to make it quite clear that *we* are the Government of India and that the claim is a bubble to be pricked."

A showdown had been welcomed, its import in the short and long run clearly perceived, and the extent of Congress vindication acknowledged. Such clarity was possible for British officials in the heat of the moment when directly engaged in battle. With the crisis past and the issue decided adversely, clarity receded. In New Delhi, the British failure to attain total victory was only indirectly acknowledged as tantamount to total defeat. In London, a recogni-tion of the truth was not repressed; in London, the failure of earlier predictions led to a new effort at clarification which was not ham-pered by an embarrassed sense of reality.

Churchill, with his usual capacity for the bold depiction of alter-natives, stated the problem simply as a choice between cutting and running or standing and ruling. The alternatives under serious consideration in the war cabinet in the aftermath of the Quit India movement were (a) to impose on India a heavy new bill for services rendered during the war and then clear out altogether, or (b) to en-gage in a grand scheme of majestic politics involving direct appeals to Indian peasants and workers over the heads of the "unrepre-sentative" bourgeois Congress.

On September 15, reported L. S. Amery, "Winston harangued us at great length about the monstrous idea that we should spend millions upon millions in the defense of India, then be told to clear out, and on top of it all owe India vast sums incurred on her behalf ...Winston's idea apparently being that...we should draw up a supplementary bill against India which may equal if not exceed the accumulated sterling balances!" At the war cabinet meeting of August 31, on the other hand, "Winston began one of his usual curious monologues about India, treating the present trouble as completely disposed of and as evidence of the fact, which he has always insisted upon, that Congress really represents hardly anybody except lawyers, money-lenders and the 'Hindu priesthood.' From this he rambled on to the suggestion that it would really pay us to take up the cause of the poor peasant and confiscate the rich Congressman's lands and divide them up. Others chipped in, more particularly Bevin, with demands for social reform."

Significantly, Churchill's heroics on the Indian question were suddenly of great interest to his more liberal colleagues. Cripps in fact composed a "Note" dated September 2 giving a detailed proposal for reform from above:

> 16. If the British Government could enlist the sympathy of the workers and peasants by immediate action on their behalf, the struggle in India would no longer be between Indian and British upon the nationalist basis, but between the classes in India upon an economic basis. There would thus be a good opportunity to rally the mass of Indian Opinion to our side.
> 17. It is most important that the Indian workers and peasants should realize that it is a British initiative which is working for them against their Indian oppressors; this would entail a proper publicity service in India.

Even the cautious Amery seemed to have been affected by the general enthusiasm. After disparaging Churchill's exaggeration, Amery admitted that "As a matter of fact, I am not sure that the time has not come . . . for a much bolder social policy."

In the privacy of the cabinet, Churchill spoke with equal drama of the strategy of cut-and-run and that of stand-and-rule, but it was clear that his instinct lay in the direction of the more heroic course. His instinct was out of place; he had, however, stated the alternatives with greater abruptness than the government of India were capable of. Linlithgow and his advisers were too painfully implicated in the Indian situation to permit a forceful penetration to the core of their dilemma. They too preferred a grand manner, but felt at the same time the utter impossibility of undertaking such a course. Before the Quit India movement, the viceroy had been eager to move ahead to scatter the Congress and rally the moderates, but had been restrained by a realization that his actions were subject to being overruled by a cabinet which included Cripps and Attlee. After the Quit India movement, the viceroy was forced to shift his apprehensions in the opposite direction. Now the greatest obstacle to grand new initiatives did not seem to be parliamentary timidity, but Indian intransigence. Before the Quit India movement, his concern had been whether Parliament would back him up. Now the viceroy's chief concern was that the cabinet and British public opinion in general would not fully grasp the seriousness of his situation and the difficulty he would face in merely holding on to power, let alone undertaking new initiatives.

The "gravity and extent" of the disorders "we have so far concealed from the world for reasons of military security," Linlithgow cabled, with the result that "opinion at home may think . . . this business has not been so serious as, in fact, it has."

The persistence of popular support for the Congress now appeared to be a "most intractable problem." The British could not circumvent the Congress by direct appeals to the masses; the masses, to the extent to which they were not controlled by the Congress, were even more hostile to the British than the Congress. Churchill had posed the necessity for a sharp break with the status quo in order to force the issue in one direction; the consequence was to force the issue in the other direction. Churchill said "Rule or get out." The viceroy was unable to do either. Churchill's heroics forced the British to choose, and the viceroy informed them that one of their supposed options was now closed.

The wrenching events at the war's end registered the changes which had been wrought during the war. Churchill's now exclusively Conservative government concluded that their election prospects might be enhanced by a rapprochement with Congress leaders and sanctioned the calling of the Simla Conference, for which Nehru, Azad, and other Congress leaders were released from prison. The Simla Conference of June 1945 was as abortive as Churchill's election bid, but, as Azad has observed, the conference "marks a breakwater in Indian political history. This was the first time that negotiations failed, not on the basic political issue between India and Britain, but on the communal issue dividing different Indian groups." For the first time, the British made no effort to take creative advantage of India's diversity. Divisions did not thereby disappear. The conference nonetheless signaled the fact that, even before the decisive Labour victory of July 1945, the British, having failed to create a political India to accord with the hierarchical pomp of the just-completed capital city, were now eager to quit.

The released Congress prisoners were everywhere greeted by jubilant throngs. The massive indignation expressed at the British effort to stage treason trials for Indian officers who had fought with the Japanese further indicated the meaning which Indians intended to give to the wartime era. It quickly became apparent that the British not only could not influence the future course of Indian politics, but could not even insure law and order for the time being. Indians in British service, many of whom had been secretly sympathetic during the Quit India movement, were now openly so. Maulana Azad noted that, "Wherever I went during this period, the young men of the Defense forces came out to welcome me and express their sympathy and admiration without any regard for the reaction of their European officers." In Calcutta "a large gathering of constables and head constables surrounded my car. They saluted me and some touched my feet. They all expressed their regard for Congress and said that they would act according to our orders." The Naval Mutiny of February 1946 demonstrated that the Congress were already the de facto rulers of the country. Twenty ships in the Bombay harbor, as well as all the shore batteries, were taken over by Indian sailors, training their guns on the white troops rushed to Bombay to recapture the harbor. "Almost all of the Royal Indian Navy's 75 or more ships and 20 shore batteries on the subcontinent were affected." Only Congress intervention brought the strike to an end. The Congress secured guarantees against victimization from the British and reassured the sailors that only technicalities now remained before their formal assumption of power. The Congress had the loyalty of the public and the services to command, and the British were given only a brief respite to honor their promise to depart.

Gandhi's demand that the British should unilaterally Quit India was in fact the demand on which the British government acted in 1947. And the basis for their withdrawal was, to a considerable extent, an acceptance of Gandhi's demand that India be left to anarchy. The initial announcement of withdrawal was unconditional and time-bound; Britain would go by June 1948, whether a "stable" window-dressing regime had been manufactured in the meantime or not. If no national government had been agreed upon by that date, the government proposed to hand over sovereign power to the several provinces. This might in fact have occurred and ushered in a period of loose federalism comparable to the immediate postrevolutionary American situation under the Articles of Confederation, had Wavell remained viceroy. Wavell drew up a plan of staged military withdrawal from India, called by the inspired title "Operation Ebbtide," but could make no headway in forming a stable national government. Lord Mountbatten's sudden arrival, and his sudden decision to settle things on the basis of the establishment of two successor states, to be free within a matter of weeks, represented a temporary return of the British zeal for a departure premised upon a "settlement" rather than anarchy.

The letter of instructions Prime Minister Attlee gave Mountbatten in 1947 urged him to work out a settlement which would preserve Indian unity *if possible;* British dedication to unity was no longer a device for postponing Indian independence, but merely an expression of nonbinding preference. The important part of Mountbatten's charge was that he should work out a settlement acceptable to the parties concerned. The "parties concerned" were the Congress and the Muslim League. The parties whose interests were now to be sacrificed if necessary included the princes, the Sikhs, and the Untouchables—all those groups which, along with the Muslims, Churchill had been fond of enumerating as the "composite majority" that supported British rule. Discretionary power to protect the weak which the British had for so long insisted on retaining in their own hands as a check on party tyranny was no longer an issue. "Sovereignty" had passed into Congress hands and the British realized that they would have to act fast if they were to persuade the soverign Congress to make any concessions whatsoever before their formal power lapsed. The development of Muslim consciousness in the years since 1940 had made the Pakistan demand one which would have had to be dealt with by any Indian ruler. There was no necessary reason, however, why it had to be dealt with before British withdrawal. The only justification for doing so involved an assumption that the British would deal with the demand more justly than a successor government, which would, nonetheless, have to live with the situation which the British would leave after making a settlement. Mountbatten stated that his first consideration in urging a quick settlement was that this "would be likely to make for lasting goodwill between the United Kingdom and the successor Governments in India"; Mountbatten said nothing of the relationship likely to exist between the successor governments themselves. Sovereignty was handed over to two successor regimes, in recognition of the need for politically effective control of the tense situation in the country. The details of the partition scheme were withheld pending the working out of a just settlement by British authority. The two new governments were thus given full responsibility without full authority. As a result, neither government was satisfied with the settlement or prepared to defend it. Nothing was settled except the fact that arbitrary direct power had been transferred to two new governments.

Significantly, much better success resulted from British handling of the Sikhs, Untouchables, and princes, where anarchy was once again the order of the day. These groups were simply abandoned. The leaders of the Muslim League and the Congress were men whose goodwill was worth having, in Mountbatten's opinion, while other groups remained as negligible as the Muslim League and the Congress had themselves once seemed. "The Provincial Muslim and Provincial Sikh political leadership," Mountbatten commented, "was in the hands of unbalanced and seemingly unintelligent men." Minorities were no longer to be protected; they were told to look for protection to the new sovereign power. The princes were treated no differently; they were told that they were now free, as British paramountcy had simply lapsed. The British announcement that the princes should now consider their solemn covenants with the British scraps of paper had the effect which Gandhi had anticipated: the princes, faced with hard realities and deprived of the opportunity of maneuvering for advantage which an external power provided, quickly came to terms. Where trouble persisted, it was a consequence of the partition of the subcontinent and the opportunity to maneuver with reference to a new third party.

The abandonment of the princes to the fond clutches of the totalitarian Congress was, as Tory statesmen pointed out, dishonorable. It dishonored the memory of a mistaken policy from which the nation now wished to dissociate itself. It dishonored the attempt to sustain vestiges of a mistaken policy for the purpose of coddling the national myth that mistakes could never have been made. It damaged the nation's credibility, shaking the world's faith that Britain would continue to uphold the same mistaken policy in other areas. It made possible, on the other hand, fresh thinking about the nation's place in a changed world, and a healthy acceptance of the nation's limitations and fallibility. Britain only learned to live with the world after she gave up the idea of conquering it.

Debates of the House of Commons
PRIME MINISTER ATTLEE ON INDIA, MARCH 15, 1946

On March 15, 1946, Prime Minister Clement Attlee (1883–1967) announced to the House of Commons the eventual independence of India and the departure of a cabinet mission charged to lay out the ground rules for the transfer of power. Attlee's Labour Party had come to power the preceding July and remained in office until the fall of 1951, thereby overseeing the initial phase of British decolonization. It is interesting to compare this text with a March 1946 speech of French Socialist Prime Minister Ramadier printed later in this book concerning the French decision to return to Indochina.

Prime Minister Attlee: ... I have had a fairly close connection with this problem now for nearly 20 years, and I would say there have been faults on all sides, but at this time we should be looking to the future rather than harking back to the past. This alone I would say to hon. Members, that it is no good applying the formulae of the past to the present position. The temperature of 1946 is not the temperature of 1920 or of 1930 or even of 1942. The slogans of an earlier day are discarded. Indeed, sometimes words that seemed at that

From *Parliamentary Debates of the House of Commons*, Volume 420, pp. 1418–1423.

time to Indians to express the height of their aspirations are now set on one side, and other words, other ideas, are substituted. Nothing increases more the pace of the movement of public opinion than a great war. Everyone who had anything to do with this question in the early days between the wars knows what an effect the war of 1914–1918 had on Indian aspirations and Indian ideals. A tide which runs slowly in peace becomes in wartime vastly accelerated, and especially directly after a war, because that tide is to some extent banked up during the war.

I am quite certain that at the present time the tide of nationalism is running very fast in India and, indeed, all over Asia. One always has to remember that India is affected by what happens elsewhere in Asia. I remember so well, when I was on the Simon Commission, how it was borne in upon us what an effect the challenge that had been thrown out by Japan at that time had had on the Asiatic people. The tide of nationalism that at one time seemed to be canalized among a comparatively small proportion of the people of India—mainly a few of the educated classes—has tended to spread wider and wider. I remember so well, indeed, I think we put it in the Simon Commission Report, that although there were great differences in the expression of nationalist sentiment between what are called the extremists and the moderates, and although in many circumstances there might be such a stress on communal claims as might seem almost to exclude the conception of nationalism, yet we found that Hindu, Muslim, Sikh or Mahrattah, the politician or civil servant—among all of them that conception of nationalism had been growing stronger and stronger. Today I think that national idea has spread right through and not least, perhaps, among some of those soldiers who have given such wonderful service in the war. I should like today, therefore, not to stress too much the differences between Indians. Let us all realize that whatever the difficulties, whatever the divisions may be, there is this underlying demand among all the Indian peoples. . . .

The right hon. Gentleman stressed the great part India played during the war. It is worthwhile recording that twice in 25 years India has played a great part in the defeat of tyranny. Is it any wonder that today she claims—as a nation of 400 million people that has twice sent her sons to die for freedom—that she should herself have freedom to decide her own destiny? My colleagues are going to India with the intention of using their utmost endeavors to help her to attain that freedom as speedily and fully as possible. What form of Government is to replace the present regime is for India to decide; but our desire is to help her to set up forthwith the machinery for making that decision. There we are met sometimes with the initial difficulty of getting that machinery set up. We are resolved that machinery shall be set up and we seek the utmost cooperation of all Indian leaders to do so. . . .

India herself must choose what will be her future Constitution; what will be her position in the world. I hope that the Indian people may elect to remain within the British Commonwealth. I am certain that she will find great advantages in doing so. In these days that demand for complete, isolated nationhood apart from the rest of the world, is really outdated. Unity may come through the United Nations, or through the Commonwealth, but no great nation can stand alone without sharing in what is happening in the world. But if she does so elect, it must be by her own free will. The British Commonwealth and Empire is not bound together by chains of external compulsion. It is a free association of free peoples. If, on the other hand, she elects for independence, in our view she has a right to do so. It will be for us to help to make the transition as smooth and easy as possible.

We should be conscious that the British have done a great work in India. We have united India and given her that sense of nationality which she so very largely lacked over the previous centuries. She has learned from us principles of democracy and justice. When Indians attack our rule, they base their attack, not on Indian principles, but on the basis of standards derived from Britain. I was very struck the other day in the United States, at a dinner where I met a number of distinguished Americans, including a very distinguished Indian, where the talk was turning on the way in which principles worked out here have been applied on the continent of America. It was pointed out that America had a great heritage from Britain. My Indian friend said to me, "You know, the Americans sometimes forget there is another great nation that has also inherited these principles and traditions, and that is India. We feel that we have a duty, a right and a privilege because we also bring to the world and work those very principles that you evolved in Britain.''

I am well aware, when I speak of India, that I speak of a country containing a congeries of races, religions and languages, and I know well all the difficulties thereby created. But those difficulties can only be overcome by Indians. We are very mindful of the rights of minorities and minorities should be able to live free from fear. On the other hand, we cannot allow a minority to place a veto on the advance of the majority.

We cannot dictate how these difficulties may be overcome. Our first duty is to get the machinery of decision set up. That is the main purpose of my hon. Friends and the Viceroy. We also want to see set up an interim Government. One of the purposes of the Bill which has been discussed today is to give the Viceroy a greater freedom in order that in the period that shall elapse while this Constitution is being worked out, we may have a Government commanding the greatest possible support in India. I would not like to fetter the Viceroy's discretion in any way with regard to the allocation of portfolios.

There were a number of points my right hon. Friend mentioned with which I should like to deal. There is the problem of the Indian States. In many Indian States great advances have been made in democratic institutions, and a most interesting experiment is now going forward in Travancore, under the guidance of the distinguished statesman, Sir C. P. Ramaswari Aiyar. Of course, the feelings in British India in regard to nationalism and the unity of India cannot be confined by the boundaries that separate these States from the Provinces. I hope that the statesmen of British India and of princely India will be able to work out a solution of the problem of bringing together, in one great polity, these disparate constituent parts. There again, we must see that the Indian States find their due place, there can be no positive veto on advance, and I do not believe for a moment that the Indian princes would desire to be a bar to the forward march of India. But, as in the case of any other problems this is a matter that Indians will settle themselves.

I am very well aware, as we all are, of the minority problems in India, and I think that Indian leaders are more and more realizing the need for settling them if India is to have a smooth passage in future years. I believe that due provision will be made for that in the Constitution, and my right hon. Friends, in their conversations, will certainly not neglect the point. We must, however, recognize that we cannot make Indians responsible for governing themselves and, at the same time, retain over here responsibility for the treatment of minorities and the power to intervene on their behalf. We are mindful, too, I can assure the right hon. Gentleman, of the position of the Services—the men who have done great service to India—and the position of their families. I think India should be sensible of the responsibility she has towards those who have served her, and I think that a Government which takes over, so to speak, the assets of our Government will also have to take over the liabilities. . . .

In conclusion, may I stress again the crucial nature of the task before us? This problem is of vital importance not only to India and the British Commonwealth and Empire, but to the world. There is this immense nation, set in the midst of Asia, an Asia which has been ravaged by war. Here we have the one great country that has been seeking to apply the principles of democracy. I have always hoped myself that politically India might be the light of Asia. It is a most unfortunate circumstance that, just at the time when we have to deal with these great political issues, there should be grave economic difficulties and, in particular, very grave anxiety over India's food supply. The House knows that His Majesty's Government are deeply concerned in this problem, and my right hon. Friend the Minister of Food is at the present time in the United States with an Indian delegation. We shall do our utmost to help her. At the present moment I do not think I should say anything on the social and economic difficulties to which the right hon. Gentleman referred except this: I believe that those economic and social difficulties can only be solved by the Indians themselves, because they are so closely bound up with the whole Indian way of life and outlook. Whatever we can do to assist, we shall do. My right hon. Friends are going out to India resolved to succeed and I am sure everyone will wish them "God speed." . . .

CHURCHILL VERSUS ATTLEE OVER BURMA, DECEMBER 20, 1946

On December 20, 1946, Attlee again addressed the House of Commons, this time to announce the eventual independence of Burma and to detail the shape of the machinery to effect it. Winston Churchill's interruption of this declaration befitted his position as leader of the Conservative opposition and as the great exponent of British imperial sentiment. Shortly after graduation from Sandhurst, Churchill (1874–1965) served with the army in India, with Kitchener on the Nile and in the Boer War. His widely read correspondence from these posts and his reputation for bravery gained him a seat in Parliament in 1900. Twice Prime Minister, Churchill will also be remembered for his splendid histories, of which the best known are A History of the English-Speaking Peoples *and* Marlborough: His Life and Times. *Here he gives expression to his regrets at the passing of the British Empire.*

Prime Minister Attlee: ... In a statement made to this House on 20th January, 1931, at the time of the decision to separate Burma from India, it was stated that His Majesty's Government wished it to be understood that the prospects of constitutional advance held out to Burma as part of British India would not be prejudiced by the decision to proceed with the separation of Burma from India. Since that time great steps forward towards self-government have been made in India and developments in the same direction have taken place in Burma. In the latter case, however, the matter has been greatly complicated by the Japanese invasion and occupation, from which Burma emerged after the surrender of the Japanese in a condition of great chaos and without any settled Burmese Government. In the White Paper which was subsequently issued by the Government and agreed to by this House, a plan was set out whereby it was hoped that Burmese self-government could be rapidly achieved.

Recent developments in India have led the Burmese people to desire to expedite their own advance to self-government and their leaders have expressed some impatience with the apparently slow development of the White Paper plan. In these circumstances, His Majesty's Government think that that plan requires reconsideration

From *Parliamentary Debates of the House of Commons*, Volume 431, pp. 2341–2353.

and that the Burmese leaders should be given the fullest opportunity of putting forward all the suggestions which they may wish to make with a view to their discussion.

His Majesty's Government do not regard the White Paper plan as unchangeable in the light of developing circumstances. Their desire is that the Burmese people should attain their self-government by the quickest and most convenient path possible. His Majesty's Government further take the view that the pledge of 1931 must be fully carried out. In particular, I would repeat, so far as Burma is concerned, what I have already said with regard to India. We do not desire to retain within the Commonwealth and Empire any unwilling peoples. It is for the people of Burma to decide their own future, but we are certain that it will be to their interest, as it will be to ours, if they decide to remain within the Commonwealth and we sincerely hope that they will arrive at such a decision. Likewise, we consider that the new Constitution for Burma should be settled by nationals of Burma and we believe that arrangements to this end can be made as a result of the forthcoming elections, without the necessity for holding fresh elections for a Constituent Assembly, on the analogy of what has already been done in India where the Constituent Assembly is based upon the ordinary provincial elections. . . .

Mr. Churchill: It was said, in the days of the great Administration of Lord Chatham, that one had to get up very early in the morning in order not to miss some of the gains and accessions of territory which were then characteristic of our fortunes. The no less memorable Administration of the right hon. Gentleman opposite is distinguished for the opposite set of experiences. The British Empire seems to be running off almost as fast as the American Loan. The steady and remorseless process of divesting ourselves of what has been gained by so many generations of toil, administration and sacrifice continues. In the case of Burma it is hardly a year since, by the superb exertions of the Fourteenth Army and enormous sacrifices in life and treasure—sacrifices in British blood and in Indian blood—the Japanese were forced to surrender, destroyed, or driven out, and the country was liberated. And yet, although barely a year has passed away, there is this extraordinary haste that we should take the necessary measures to get out of Burma finally and forever. The same formula, the right hon. Gentleman says, will be used as was used in the case of India, with the same extensions he put on to that formula when the Indian Mission was sent out, eliminating the—

Mr. Speaker: Order. There is no Motion before the House.

Mr. Churchill: With great respect, Sir, I thought we were entitled to make some observations on this very important statement made by the Government. . . . If you, Sir, give this new Ruling on the subject, which is a departure from the practice which has been in force both in the last Parliament and in this, I have no choice but to submit, and I shall not attempt further to comment upon this lamentable and deplorable event and announcement at this moment, but I ask the Government if they will move the Adjournment of the House.

House adjourned.

Mr. Churchill (Woodford):   I was not proposing to embark upon a formal or full-dress Debate upon the evacuation or abandonment of Burma. This, it seems to me, must be a subject for discussion upon another occasion. All that I was intending to do was to mark, for the nation and the country at large, the significance of the statement which the Prime Minister rattled off so quickly and so smoothly as if it were an ordinary matter or routine. It should be realized that a very important and far-reaching declaration has now been made by the Prime Minister, and we should consider what its consequences will be.

As I said on another occasion, it is less than a year since the Japanese were expelled or destroyed. There have been no adequate elections, no representative assembly formed, and nothing that could be said to be a representative or settled view of the people there. Those people are only now returning, with great difficulty, as the Government have pointed out, and as was pointed out in the White Paper issued last year, to their ruined homes in many parts of that country, which were ravaged by the Japanese. Yet we are told that we must accelerate the process of our departure as much as possible, that special measures must be taken, and these gentlemen invited from Burma to come over here and discuss with the Government the peaceful transference of power and the rapid departure of the British. Before they come, before they would even condescend to come, a declaration has to be made in terms which place this matter in the same state as what is happening now in India.

This must be realized. We have held Burma since 1885. We have followed its affairs with attention. My father was the Minister responsible for the annexation of Burma. During that time, great progress has been made in that small country. There are 17 million people, mostly, or a very large proportion of them, primitive people. Good progress has been made. We defended them as well as we could against the Japanese invasion, but we were not successful. It was only after the tremendous campaign of three years of heavy fighting that the Japanese were driven out, and the country was liberated from the invaders' hands. In those circumstances it would have been reasonable to allow law and order to be established, and the people to settle down on their farms and in their habitations. Then we could have resumed consideration of the question of self-government, to which we had definitely pledged ourselves, but all in due course, and in due time. Again, by the unfortunate form of the Prime Minister's declaration to which the right hon. Gentleman has now given vent, and which has taken its place as an operative declaration, the intermediate stage of Dominion status is, to all intents and purposes, eliminated, just as it was in India. In eliminating that interim stage in India it was said: "This makes no difference, because Dominion status implies the right to contract out of the British Empire."

The proper stages are of the utmost consequence. If, in India, we had proceeded under Dominion status, and had established a Government based upon Dominion status, that Government could then have addressed itself to the question whether to use what I call the escalator Clause or not. A very different situation would then have arisen. There would have been an opportunity for the friends of this country who desire that we should stay, and who appreciate the blessings which British rule has conferred upon those regions, to rally. They would have had a chance to decide whether, upon a basis of full Dominion status, they would be partners in the British Commonwealth of Nations or not. The elimination of that stage, the short-circuiting of that process, has the effect, and could only have the effect, of repulsing all loyalties, the abandoning of friends, and compelling everyone in India to face the fact that the British were going. The result is that no fair chance has been given to the people of India to express themselves, in a calm atmosphere and under proper conditions, upon the question whether, having obtained full self-government, they would wish to leave the British Commonwealth of Nations or not.

This evil process, which has been attended by disasters of which at present we are only on the threshold, and which will to a large extent occupy or dominate the mind and attention of the present Parliament in the months and years to come, is now quite needlessly extended to Burma. I cannot see why this should be done, unless it is to try to induce the Burmese representatives to come over here and discuss this matter with us. This haste is appalling. "Scuttle" is the only word that can be applied. What, spread over a number of years, would be a healthy and constitutional process and might easily have given the Burmese people an opportunity of continuing their association with our congregation of nations, has been cast aside. We are seeing in home affairs the unseemly rush of legislation, disorganizing our national life and impeding our recovery, legislation thrust upon Parliament at break-neck speed, hon. Members debarred from taking part in Debates by matters being transferred from the Floor of this House to other parts of the building. We see the same haste which, I suppose, will be paraded as vigor. "Labour gets things done!"

As regards divesting ourselves of these great possessions of the British Crown, and freeing ourselves from all responsibility for the populations—primitive and often divided—who have hitherto looked to British justice and administration for the means of leading their ordinary lives in peace, I thought it necessary at the earliest moment to dissociate myself and those who sit on this side from the course of action which the Government are taking. I said the other day about India that we take no responsibility for the course the Government take; they must bear the responsibility. I see it was said in another place that I was suggesting that should the Conservative Party be returned to power, we would reverse this process. I think it would be utterly impossible to reverse it. The words that have come from the lips of the right hon. Gentleman today, supported as they are by the overwhelming majority of this House—unrepresentative of the balance of forces in the country—are irrevocable. He has in fact shorn Burma away from the British Crown by what is being done. That, at least, is a matter of which notice should be taken, if it be only passing notice, even in this period when we are getting so accustomed and indurated to the process of the decline and fall of the British Empire.

The Prime Minister (Mr. Attlee): I have always thought of the right hon. Gentleman as a great historian, but he seems to have forgotten some recent history. When he talks of India, he seems to have forgotten the Cripps Mission; he seems to have forgotten the declaration made in his own interim Government by Mr. Amery, and our declaration has gone no further than that. He has also forgotten that when I made my statement on India in this House, there was no opposition in this House, there was no opposition in the country. I think he was the only objector. He has so often found himself alone on these matters—

Mr. Boyd-Carpenter (Kingston-upon-Thames):   He is generally right.

The Prime Minister: I think he has not been right on these matters. Perhaps he has here one supporter, but he had very few supporters right through the long period in which we were dealing with what he said was the right process, that slow, constitutional advance that he suggested, which he opposed at every step. When he says it is the right way to go first by Dominion status, did he accept Dominion status in those days? No, he opposed it. The fact is that he opposed every step in advancement.

Mr. Churchill: The right hon. Gentleman was reproaching me for not stating all history in a short exposition, but he is quite wrong when he says that I opposed every advance in India. The 70 gentlemen who acted with me in the five years of that Parliament accepted fully the Simon Report offering Provincial Government. Where we differed was in the attempt to build up the Central Government. He should not omit that, because the Simon Commission of which he was a Member, but which was spurned by the Government of the day and sidetracked for a much more ambitious scheme, would never have recommended that. We stuck to the main line of the Simon Report and the right hon. Gentleman must not suggest that that was a reactionary document.

The Prime Minister: No. I am very well acquainted with the Simon Report, and I am very well aware that we envisaged there a federal structure for India. Why we were unable to do anything with regard to the set-up, was because it was quite uncertain at that time as to whether the Princes would come in. The whole position was changed by the Princes coming in, which gave a reason why there should be further extension. I am well aware that the right hon. Gentleman was in this long before; he was in the Government of Minto and Montagu. You cannot put the clock back in this case. There is a necessary advance in public opinion, and it is much more dangerous to lag behind, than to keep up with the movements of public opinion in these countries. I should have said that in these matters this country had not been too fast but too slow. If the right hon. Gentleman is going back into history, I must refer to one of the unfortunate things, the failure to deal with the Irish question for years and years, until the right Gentleman himself and his Government had to act in what I think he would call a policy of scuttle at the end of the last war.

In the matter of Burma, it is undoubted that at the time Burma was separated, the Burmese were assured that their constitutional advance would go *pari passu* with that of India and, as a matter of fact, the problems are not so difficult in Burma. There is not that terrible communal trouble which there is in India. The declaration we have made is not one in which we say to Burma, "Go out of the British Empire." On the contrary, we believe they will stay in. We invite them to stay in, but we say that we do not compel people to stay in and I believe that is the right attitude. It was the attitude adopted towards India by the right hon. Gentleman's Government in the declaration made by Mr. Amery. I see no reason why the Burmese should be treated worse than the Indians in this respect.

CHURCHILL VERSUS ATTLEE OVER INDIA, FEBRUARY–MARCH, 1947

On February 20, 1947, Prime Minister Attlee made a further report to the House of Commons on his Government's progress in withdrawing Britain from India. Churchill's rejoinder to this announcement on March 6, 1947, criticized many aspects of the move and gloomily concluded it to be a "hurried scuttle." "Many have defended Britain against her foes. None can defend her against herself."

From *Parliamentary Debates of the House of Commons*, Volume 433, pp. 1395–1398, and Volume 434, pp. 663–678.

The Prime Minister (Mr. Attlee):   I desire to make a statement on Indian policy.

It has long been the policy of successive British Governments to work towards the realization of self-government in India. In pursuance of this policy an increasing measure of responsibility has been devolved on Indians and today the civil administration and the Indian Armed Forces rely to a very large extent on Indian civilians and officers. In the constitutional field the Acts of 1919 and 1935 passed by the British Parliament each represented a substantial transfer of political power. In 1940 the Coalition Government recognized the principle that Indians should themselves frame a new constitution for a fully autonomous India, and in the offer of 1942 they invited them to set up a Constituent Assembly for this purpose as soon as the war was over.

His Majesty's Government believe this policy to have been right and in accordance with sound democratic principles. Since they came into office, they have done their utmost to carry it forward to its fulfilment. The declaration of the Prime Minister of 15th March last which met with general approval in Parliament and the country, made it clear that it was for the Indian people themselves to choose their future status and constitution and that in the opinion of His Majesty's Government the time had come for responsibility for the Government of India to pass into Indian hands. . . .

It is with great regret that His Majesty's Government find that there are still differences among Indian Parties which are preventing the Constituent Assembly from functioning as it was intended that it should. It is of the essence of the plan that the Assembly should be fully representative.

His Majesty's Government desire to hand over their responsibility to authorities established by a constitution approved by all parties in India in accordance with the Cabinet Mission's plan, but unfortunately there is at present no clear prospect that such a constitution and such authorities will emerge. The present state of uncertainty is fraught with danger and cannot be indefinitely prolonged. His Majesty's Government wish to make it clear that it is their definite intention to take the necessary steps to effect the transference of power into responsible Indian hands by a date not later than June, 1948. . . .

His Majesty's Government will negotiate agreements in regard to matters arising out of the transfer of power with the representatives of those to whom they propose to transfer power.

His Majesty's Government believe that British commercial and industrial interests in India can look forward to a fair field for their enterprise under the new conditions. The commercial connection between India and the United Kingdom has been long and friendly, and will continue to be to their mutual advantage.

His Majesty's Government cannot conclude this statement without expressing on behalf of the people of this country their goodwill and good wishes towards the people of India as they go forward to this final stage in their achievement of self-government. It will be the wish of everyone in these islands that, notwithstanding constitutional changes, the association of the British and Indian peoples should not be brought to an end; and they will wish to continue to do all that is in their power to further the well-being of India.

This concludes the statement on policy.

Mr. Churchill (Woodford): When great parties in this country have for many years pursued a combined and united policy on some large issue, and when, for what seemed to them to be good reasons, they decide to separate, not only in Debate but by Division, it is desirable and even necessary that the causes of such separation and the limitations of the differences which exist should be placed on record. This afternoon we begin a new chapter in our relations across the Floor of the House in regard to the Indian problem. We on this side of the House have, for some time, made it clear that the sole responsibility for the control of India's affairs rests, of course, with His Majesty's Government. We have criticized their action in various ways but this is the first time we have felt it our duty as the official Opposition to express our dissent and difference by a formal vote.

Let us first place on record the measure of agreement which lies between us, and separate that from the differences that now lead us into opposite Lobbies. Both sides of the House are bound by the declaration made at the time of the British Mission to India in March, 1942. It is not true to suggest, as was done lately, that this decision marked a decisive change in the policy of the British Parliament towards India. There was a long story before we got to that. Great Britain had for many years been committed to handing over responsibility for the government of India to the representatives of the Indian people. There was the promise of Dominion status implicit in the declaration of August, 1917. There was the expansion and definition of Dominion status by the Statute of Westminster. There was the Simon Commission Report of 1930, followed by the Hoare-Linlithgow Reforms of 1935. There was the Linlithgow offer of 1940, for which, as head of the Government in those days, I took my share of responsibility. By this, the Viceroy undertook that, as soon as possible after the war, Indians themselves should frame a fully self-governing Constitution. All this constituted the preliminary basis on which the proposals of the Cripps Mission of 1942 were set. The proposals of this Mission were not, in fact, a departure in principle from what had long been growing up, but they constituted a definite, decisive and urgent project for action. Let us consider the circumstances in which this offer was made.

The violent irruption of Japan upon East Asia, the withdrawal of the United States Fleet to the American coast, the sinking of the *Prince of Wales* and the *Repulse,* the loss of Malaya and the surrender of Singapore, and many other circumstances of that time left us for the moment without any assured means of defending India from invasion by Japan. We had lost the command of the Bay of Bengal, and, indeed, to a large extent, of the Indian Ocean. Whether the Provinces of Madras and Bengal would be pillaged and ravaged by the Japanese at that time seemed to hang in the balance, and the question naturally arose with poignant force how best to rally all Indian elements to the defense of their native land.

The offer of the Cripps Mission, I would remind the House, was substantially this: His Majesty's Government undertook to accept and implement an agreed Constitution for an Indian Union, which should be a Dominion, framed by an elected Constituent Assembly and affording representation to the Princes. This undertaking was subject only to the right of nonacceding Provinces to receive separate treatment, and to the conclusion of a treaty guaranteeing the protection of religious and racial minorities. The offer of the Cripps Mission was not accepted by the political classes in India who alone are vocal and to whom it was addressed. On the contrary, the Congress, led by Mr. Gandhi and Mr. Nehru, did their utmost to make a revolt intended to paralyze the perilous communications of our Army in Burma and to help the fortunes of Japan. Therefore, the National Coalition Government of those days made a large series of mass arrests of Indian Congress leaders, and the bulk were kept in prison until the end of the war. I was not myself present in the Cabinet when these decisions were taken. I was at Cairo preparing for the operations which opened at Alamein, but I highly approved of the action which was taken in my absence by the then Deputy Prime Minister, the present Prime Minister, who sits opposite, and which I think was the only one possible on that occasion.

Therefore, it is quite clear that, whatever was the offer of the Cripps Mission, it was not accepted. On the contrary, it was repudiated by the parties to whom it was addressed. . . .

. . . Both sides of this House are bound by this offer, and bound by all of it, and it is on the basis of this offer being an agreed matter between the parties, and on that basis alone, that our present and future controversies arise. If I am bound by the offer of Dominion status and all that it implies, the Prime Minister is equally bound, or was equally bound, to the conditions about agreement between the principal communities, about the proper discharge of our pledges about the protection of minorities and the like. The right hon. Gentleman has a perfect right to change his mind. He may cast away all these stipulations which we jointly made, and proceed only with the positive side of the offer. He has the right to claim the support of his Parliamentary majority for any action he takes, but he has no right to claim our support beyond the limits to which we are engaged by the Cripps declaration. . . . I am only trying to lay down the basis on which we can agree to differ—the basis of 1942 and the present time. Before this latest pronouncement of theirs, His Majesty's Government had already departed from the Cripps Mission declaration of 1942, and they had departed from it in three major aspects. First, they had eliminated the stage of Dominion status. The Cripps Mission expressly said that the objective was the creation of a new Indian Union which would constitute a Dominion associated with the United Kingdom and the other Dominions by common allegiance to the Crown, but equal to them in every respect, in no way subordinated in any aspect of domestic or external affairs. . . .

. . . If the Dominion status procedure had been involved, in my view, the new Indian Dominion would have been perfectly free to leave the Commonwealth if it chose, but full opportunity would have been given for all the dangers and disadvantages to be surveyed by responsible Indian Ministers beforehand, and also for the wishes of the great mass of the Indian people to be expressed, as they cannot be expressed now. It would have been possible to insert in the Dominion Constitution the necessary safeguards for minorities, and for the fulfillment of the British pledges to the various elements of Indian life, notably the Depressed Classes. This would have been a part of the agreement between the Indian Union and Great Britain, and would have been embodied in the necessary British legislation on the lines of the British North America Act, to which the great free Dominion of Canada has always attached importance, and still does. So the second departure from the Cripps Mission declaration was the total abandonment by His Majesty's Government of all responsibility for carrying out its pledges to minorities and the Depressed Classes, as well as for fulfilling their treaties with the Indian States. All these are to be left to fend for themselves, or to fight for themselves as best they can. That is a grave major departure.

The third departure was no less grave. The essence of the Cripps Mission declaration was that there should be agreement between the principal Indian communities, namely, in fact, the Muslims and the Hindus. That, also, has been thrown overboard. But I state, as it is my duty to do when we take a step such as we are going to take tonight, of great formality and solemness, that it is the Government who have broken away from the agreement which has been reached between parties, and has so long subsisted between parties, and that it is not we in the Conservative Party who have, in any way, gone back on our faithful undertaking. To these departures from our principle, there must be added a formidable list of practical mistakes in handling the problem during that past year since the Cabinet Mission was sent out. Some of these mistakes may have been made by the Government, and some of them by the Viceroy, but they are both jointly responsible for all. . . .

. . . Such was the situation before the latest plunge which the Government have taken was made, and it is this plunge which, added to all that has gone before, makes it our duty to sever ourselves altogether from the Indian policy of His Majesty's Government, and to disclaim all responsibility for the consequences which will darken—aye, and redden—the coming years. . . .

I do not think that the 14-months' time limit gives the new Viceroy a fair chance. We do not know what directives have been given to him. No explanation of that has been provided. Indeed, we are told very little. Looking on this Indian problem and having to address the House upon it, I am surprised how many great gaps there are in information which should be in the full possession of the House. We are told very little. What is the policy and purpose for which he is to be sent out, and how is he to employ these 14 months? Is he to make a new effort to restore the situation, or is it merely Operation Scuttle on which he and other distinguished officers have been despatched? The Prime Minister should deal with this and should tell us something of the purpose behind all these movements. Parliament has its powers, but it may use them wrongly and unwisely if it is not given information which, in all other periods that I have known, would have been placed at its disposal—except, of course, in time of war when we must not tell the enemy what we intend to do.

Everyone knows that the 14-months' time limit is fatal to any orderly transference of power, and I am bound to say that the whole thing wears the aspect of an attempt by the Government to make use of brilliant war figures in order to cover up a melancholy and disastrous transaction. One thing seems to me absolutely certain. The Government, by their 14-months' time limit, have put an end to all prospect of Indian unity. I myself have never believed that that could be preserved after the departure of the British Raj, but the last chance has been extinguished by the Government's action. How can one suppose that the thousand-year gulf which yawns between Muslim and Hindu will be bridged in 14 months? Here are these people, in many cases, of the same race, charming people, lightly clad, crowded together in all the streets and bazaars and so forth, and yet there is no intermarriage. It is astounding. Religion has raised a bar which not even the strongest impulses of nature can overleap. It is an astounding thing. Yet the Government expect in 14 months that there will be an agreement on these subjects between these races. . . .

Let the House remember this. The Indian political parties and political classes do not represent the Indian masses. It is a delusion to believe that they do. I wish they did. They are not as representative of them as the movements in Britain represent the surges and impulses of the British nation. This has been proved in the war, and I can show the House how it was proved. The Congress Party declared noncooperation with Great Britain and the Allies. The other great political party, to whom all main power is to be given, the Muslim League, sought to make a bargain about it, but no bargain was made. So both great political parties in India, the only forces that have been dealt with so far, stood aside. Nevertheless, the only great volunteer army in the world that fought on either side in that struggle was formed in India. More than three and a half million men came forward to support the King-Emperor and the cause of Britain; they came forward not by conscription or compulsion, but out of their loyalty to Britain and to all that Britain stood for in their lives. In handing over the Government of India to these so-called political classes we are handing over to men of straw, of whom, in a few years, no trace will remain. . . .

I have for some time pressed upon His Majesty's Government that, if they are unable to carry out their pledges in Palestine or keep order there, they should return their Mandate, or, at any rate, invoke the aid of U.N.O. to help them in their work; and that, after six or seven months' delay—a needless delay—they have actually done. Now, is it not difficult to resist the feeling that the same train of reasoning applies on a far greater scale and with much stronger force to India? We are told that we cannot walk out of Palestine because we should leave behind us a war between 600,000 Jews and 200,000 Arabs. How, then, can we walk out of India in 14 months and leave behind us a war between 90 million Muslims and 200 million caste Hindus, and all the other tribulations which will fall upon the helpless population of 400 million? Will it not be a terrible disgrace to our name and record if, after our 14-months' time limit, we allow one-fifth of the population of the globe, occupying a region nearly as large as Europe, to fall into chaos and into carnage? Would it not be a world crime that we should be committing, a crime that would stain—not merely strip us, as we are being stripped, in the material position—but would stain our good name for ever?

Yesterday, the President of the Board of Trade and other speakers brought into great prominence our physical and military weakness. How can we keep a large Army in India for 15 or 20 years? He and other speakers stressed that point; and, certainly, it is a very grave point. But he might as well have urged that in our present forlorn condition we have, not only not the physical strength, but not the moral strength and will power. If we, through lack of physical and moral strength, cannot wind up our affairs in a responsible and

humane and honorable fashion, ought we not to consider invoking
the aid or, at least, the advice of the world international organization, which is now clothed with reality, and on which so many of us,
in all parts of the House, base our hopes for the peaceful progress,
freedom, and, indeed, the salvation of all mankind? . . .

I thank the House for listening so long and so attentively to what
I have said. I have spoken with a lifetime of thought and contact
with these topics. It is with deep grief I watch the clattering down of
the British Empire, with all its glories and all the services it has rendered to mankind. I am sure that in the hour of our victory, now not
so long ago, we had the power, or could have had the power, to
make a solution of our difficulties which would have been honorable
and lasting. Many have defended Britain against her foes. None can
defend her against herself. We must face the evils that are coming
upon us, and that we are powerless to avert. We must do our best in
all these circumstances, and not exclude any expedient that may
help to mitigate the ruin and disaster that will follow the disappearance of Britain from the East. But, at least, let us not add—by
shameful flight, by a premature, hurried scuttle—at least, let us not
add, to the pangs of sorrow so many of us feel, the taint and smear
of shame. . . .

A. P. Thornton
THE DECLINE OF BRITISH POWER
IN THE MIDDLE EAST

*Britain managed far less well in the Middle East than in India. Here the
Palestinian question presented insuperable obstacles to settlement while
the Suez fiasco in the fall of 1956 constituted an unusual blindness in
British political vision. Although written nearly 20 years ago, Professor
Thornton's account of this period remains one of the most lucid on record.*

A. P. Thornton, *The Imperial Idea and Its Enemies* (London and New York, 1958),
pp. 376–378; 380–390; 397–400. Reprinted by permission of Macmillan, London and
Basingstoke, and St. Martin's Press. Footnotes omitted.

He documents that the passing of empire was not so smooth for the British as is sometimes maintained. Among his other works are Doctrines of Imperialism *and* For the File on Empire.

. . . To Curzon and to all imperialists, it had been the *Raj* that stood as the symbol for British power. But in a flush of enthusiasm this had been given away to others. What was left to take its place? There was, indeed, something: a last barbican of Empire, perhaps, but one where Britain's was a famous name and her preponderance was real. It had to be admitted that the forces of the British Empire had not been sufficient to "win the war," either in Europe or in the Far East. No equivalent of Wellington or Nelson had arisen from the British ranks to rout the villain on land and the villain at sea. In one theater alone had British action been genuinely decisive, in both the strategical and political fields. This theater was the Middle East, and Montgomery, Middle East victor, was the only British general whose status and prestige were everywhere admired. (The annual Alamein reunion dinner in the Albert Hall in London was the only celebration of its kind, a popular and democratic event.) Enthusiasms nourished by the excitements of war died without putting up much fight, and a lot of cold water helped to chill the fire of slogans concerning the finest hour when we stood alone, and to blur the figures on the Royal Air Force's Battle of Britain scorecard: but from these misfortunes the record of the "desert victory" remained free. The world of the Middle East remained a sphere of the old-style British imperial power, and still managed to arouse old-style British imperial emotions.

In doing so the area performed a function of some value. Bastions of British power were now so few. With the British economy itself underpropped by American money; with the Western Approaches under the command of an American Admiral; with the North Atlantic Treaty Organization dependent for its life on American strategy and weapons; with the American Sixth Fleet the principal power in the Mediterranean; with the American A- and H-bombs the chief deterrents of war with the Soviet Union; with the failure to shore up imperial power in Southeast Asia, Malaya, Indochina, and Indonesia; with Australia learning the lessons of Japanese bombs on Darwin and constructing a defense pact with

New Zealand and the United States without benefit of British participation at all (1950); with Hong Kong existing on sufferance of Communist China, and with Asian members of the Commonwealth pursuing policies of neutrality for what they were thought to be worth,
symbols of power were hard to discern. Some emotion might be
expended on Gibraltar, about which Spain was again restive: while
the island of Cyprus, hardly heard of since Disraeli's achievement
of 1878, was to become an imperial controversy by force of circumstance. Labour colonial policy busied itself in accelerating a program already laid down, of granting self-government to colonies
adjudged likely to make some decent use of it, and it was Africa, a
continent still unthreatened by any outside power, that witnessed
the greatest development of this. . . .

But the harmony of view between Left and Right in colonial affairs proper was not reflected in the Middle East, where it was still
necessary for Great Britain to have, and to be prepared to own to,
an imperial policy proper. It was difficult to get matters into focus,
for what Ramsay MacDonald had once called "the confusions of an
imperial inheritance" had always been more pronounced in the
Levant than anywhere else. It was all very well for Bevin to declare
that he aimed to substitute another policy by proper negotiation.
Agreed, methods of negotiation could be improved, and now that
the war was over it was not right or fitting that we, democrats all,
should order Governments about and displace Prime Ministers with
others more amenable. (After all, this was the kind of thing that
went on behind the Iron Curtain.) But how could the policy itself
be changed? Changed to what? What other policy was there?
Attlee in 1946 could comprehend perfectly why it was that Egyptian
nationalism should be determined to get the British to clear their
troops out of Cairo, but at the same time he could bring no sympathy to the Egyptian assertion that Egypt had her own imperial
rights in the Sudan. Bevin's negotiations with Sidky foundered on
this very point: the Sudan was still, as Austen Chamberlain had expressed it, a trust of a particularly sacred nature, and if British imperialism had ever had a shop-window, it was surely in the Sudan,
brought in fifty years from absolute anarchy to relative prosperity
and absolute peace. Similarly, Bevin (and Eden with him) might believe that they had good grounds for thinking that the Arab League,

hastily constructed before the war's end, would act as a protégé force for Great Britain, something like Brigadier Glubb's Arab Legion in the British-subsidized Transjordan—but this was never true, and before ten years had passed a day was to come when it was no longer true of Glubb's Arab Legion either.

The Indian Army, underprop of British might in the Middle East, had gone. Some other must be found, and fashioned. Genuine bases must be established. The soldiers were to wander, sometimes in imagination, sometimes in reality, from the Canal Zone to Kenya, from Cyprus back to Haifa, searching, somewhere along this inner circle, for security for the British Empire, for the protection of its communications and the safeguarding of its supplies of oil, two-thirds of which now came from the Middle East and 68 million tons of which passed through the Suez Canal in 1955 (1938's figure had been 5 million). It was a task which had to be done, as it turned out, in the teeth of a nationalism that was at once self-righteous, militant, and incompetent, and it was not surprising that it was done with an equivalent degree of self-righteous incompetence.

Lynchpin of any settlement in the Middle East was, of course, agreement with Egypt. At the end of the war Egypt was, as in 1919, a vast military camp. Under the terms of the treaty that Eden and Nahas had signed in 1936, Britain was entitled to keep in Egypt a maximum of 10,000 troops, confined to the zone that bordered the Suez Canal. The delay in withdrawing what Nahas called the carefree khaki hordes—over 80,000 of them—caused Egyptian nationalist opinion to harden against the retention of even the agreed 10,000. The example set by Syria and the Lebanon, who with considerable dexterity and deft manipulation had succeeded in ridding their countries entirely of the French, had been carefully noted in Cairo. The Attlee Government, resolved to treat Egypt as an ally, and to consider the *"alliance* with Egypt as one between two equal nations having interests in common," proposed in May 1946 a withdrawal of all British forces from Egypt, and to settle "mutual assistance in time of war or imminent threat of war in accordance with the alliance." But Churchill adjourned the House: the presence of British troops in Egypt was something that served not merely a British purpose, or an Anglo-Egyptian purpose, but an imperial purpose and a world purpose. "It is to keep the Canal open that we require troops on the spot."

Attlee in 1954 threw this back at him when Churchill, again Prime Minister, presided over the Government that did finally agree to take British troops out of the Canal Zone. The day had gone when we could put bases in other people's territory when the people did not want them. That had been as abundantly clear in 1945 and 1946 as it now was, even to the Tory imperialists, in 1954. Labour policy was right all the time, and it was a pity for the Tories' own reputation and *amour-propre* that they had not decided to recognize this when there might have been some grace in their doing so. Of course, there was an immense difference between Churchill in office and Churchill in opposition. When he came into office he had to face realities: he had to take responsibility instead of indulging in merely factious attacks on those who were bearing responsibility. Attlee turned the knife in the wound, for Labour had not forgotten how Churchill had always held that Labour was not fit to govern, and had no idea what responsibility consisted of. "We have borne for years these accusations, freely thrown about, of 'scuttle.' " If it was true that to keep the Canal open we required troops on the spot, was not Nasser winning a more famous victory at Suez than Musaddiq over the Anglo-Iranian Oil Company at Abadan? Even now the Tories did it all with a bad grace, and their spokesman Antony Head led off with the rueful remark that it was always unpalatable to national pride for a proud and great nation to take a step which looked as though she was being forced by duress to do something which she had been shouted at to do for a long time. Even now they had no policy worth speaking of. In 1954 they were doing what Labour, the anti-imperialists, the scuttlers, had refused to do in 1946, and were selling the Sudanese down the river. They still declared that the Suez Canal was a great imperial lifeline, but seemed ready—as their own "Suez Group" back-benchers charged them—to hand it over to the fates and the furies.

Here was genuine bitterness, genuine spleen, made the sourer because both sides recognized that the security of the Middle East was a genuine British interest, and neither side had any idea how best to safeguard it. In 1946 Bevin's alternative to a Suez base was a base in Palestine: in 1954 Eden's alternative to a Suez base was a base in Cyprus. Palestine had blown up in Bevin's face, and it was confidently expected that Cyprus would do the same in Eden's. It was (surely?) pointless and dishonest for Eden to keep declaring, as he did during this rancorous debate of July 1954, that the main base for war would remain in Egypt. At once Waterhouse, die-hard leader of the Suez Group imperialists, asked him, "What happens if these provisions are broken, as they may well be broken? Are we going to reenter forcibly?" Obviously such a step would be out of the question: to Waterhouse it was plain that we were taking a step that was absolutely irrevocable so far as the Canal went. He believed that we were really losing our will to rule—and on this Hansard noted a cry of "Oh" from honorable Members.

The Radicals on the Labour benches—and there were now not so very many—pushed this point home. Crossman conceded that if this Suez agreement was the beginning of a new relationship with Egypt and the forces of nationalism in the Middle East, and not merely a scuttle out of Egypt into Cyprus, there was some hope for us in the Middle East—but there was none if the whole thing was merely a symbol of imperialism grown weaker. For eighteen months or more the Suez Group Tory rebels—aided by "the rebel on the Front Bench," Churchill himself—had delayed meeting the inevitable, and coming to terms with President Nasser. Churchill, Crossman accused, had kept 80,000 men in the Canal Zone and had spent £100 million in order to transform what might have been a magnanimous action "into the scuttle of imperialists who fail to keep up their imperialism." . . .

While she found it possible to reach, even after painful hesitation, not only an understanding of but to give full political recognition to such a movement as Indian nationalism, she persisted in putting Middle Eastern nationalisms into an entirely different category. India, after all, could afford what more sensible men might describe as aberrations, for India was not threatened (or not yet, anyway) by any outside power. This could certainly not be said of the Middle East, now not only a strategic but a great economic goal for the predatory. Russia showed signs, signs that increased as the postwar decade passed (until eventually she was supplying arms to the Arab world indiscriminately), of returning to that old sphere of influence where once the name of Tsar Nicholas I had been one to conjure with in the Holy Places. The Middle East could therefore not be allowed by the Western Powers to become a kind of no-man's-land, for plainly the area was not cut out for the role. Understanding of nationalism therein could not be carried too far, certainly not to any political abdication such as had been the outcome in India: as in Colvin's day in 1882, the presence of nationalism must be taken into account as a political factor of significance, but not of such significance that it could be allowed to tip the balance. For, if a Western power-relationship were not successfully maintained, an Eastern power-relationship would be successfully established.

The Middle East, then, could not be allowed to go by default. British and French opinion accused the American Government, which seemed to think in concrete terms of oil and cash readily enough, but of nothing more profound, of so letting it go—to the United States' own ultimate detriment. What was required was that the United States should cultivate a Middle East imperialism of her own—although let her by all means call it merely her Middle Eastern policy. The real problem—the one that ought to have been hammered out together by like-minded statesmen together in Washington, London, and Paris, but the one that, before 1957, never was—was how best to establish the power-relationship so that it made as many friends and as few enemies as possible. Was the task an impossible one? Very well, then, it was an impossible one: let us proceed. The Western powers could not bring themselves to talk of client-states and satellites, but these were what they were always looking for in the Middle East. When, ultimately, it seemed that the Arabs, long the protégé of the one imperial power and long the subjects of the other, were turning against all the policies that Britain and France were putting forward, Britain and France in their turn swung back again, *faute de mieux,* to look with favor on the Jews. Were the latter, beleaguered in the Levant as they were, worthy of a new, more positive patronage? It was Israelite *efficiency* in the sphere of power-politics that, as the twentieth century ended its fifth decade, seemed likely to win new friends for Zionism, of a type the movement had not previously enjoyed.

No British Government had been actively friendly to Zionism since the fall of the Lloyd George Coalition in 1922. The Colonial Office had included the Jews, naturally, among the many subject-races whom it had to govern impartially and well, and successive governments in Britain had done their best to carry out a legacy of obligation in the Levant without examining the principles on which they were trying to operate. Arabs were clients and so were Jews. This might have been very well had either client been able to recognize in Great Britain the honest broker she professed herself to be. But it was not possible that either could do so. The inroads made by the Zionist nationalist and imperialist movement into their own Arab world made Arabs aware of the political potentialities of the twentieth century's great movement, self-determination, in a way in which, outside of Egypt, they had not realized before, since the "Arab revolt" of 1915–1918 had been primarily dynastic in its impetus. The weapon which the Jews were using to such effect might prove as useful in Arab hands—and Arabs, after all, were far more numerous. The British protection of Zionism entailed a British neglect of those Arab aspirations which they had been the first to foster. The British, always (as was known) sensitive to a charge of failure in duty, could here be caught off balance. And so it proved —although it was to be the Jews who first took advantage of Britain's uneasy stance.

The presence of these two irreconcilable elements bedeviled British imperial policy in the Middle East to its ultimate point, collapse. The situation was at no time improved while for nearly thirty-five years British statesmen, bemused by the doctrine of continuity in foreign policy, continued to deny in public that there were any irreconcilables at all. Yet what, in its essence, did the policy of supporting the establishing of a Jewish "National Home" in Palestine entail? It entailed the furthering the invasion of Palestine by immigrants, while at the same time providing for the protection of the native population against the consequences of this invasion. "A national home," George Antonius has remarked of this process, "can only be established for one people in the country of another by dislodging or exterminating the people in possession." Lloyd George admitted as much in the evidence he gave to the Peel Commission investigating in 1937 the causes of the Palestine rebellion: "the possibility of a Jewish commonwealth in which the Arab population would be in a minority was in fact contemplated." To that, fulminated the *Round Table,* the only honorable answer was that our pledges to the Arabs were never consistent with a Jewish majority in Palestine as a whole, and thus no valid promise implying this could ever have been given.

The outbreak of the Palestine rebellion of 1936–1939 thus differed in intensity from the other Arab rebellions against Western dominance—those in Egypt in 1919, in Iraq in 1920, in Syria in 1925—in that the intensity of the Palestine Arabs' detestation of imperial policy was itself so much the greater. For neither Egypt nor Iraq nor Syria had undergone an actual invasion by aliens, and although there were alien governments in those countries they were not in fact so irrevocably rooted there that an aspiring nationalist might not look forward with some confidence at least to the day when his country would be free of them. But no one could hold such an opinion or dream such a dream in Mandated Palestine. Arabs, controlled by the British, were forced to suffer the entry into their midst of the Jews, whose intention (for they saw little reason to conceal it) was to establish a foreign state in their territory, either oppressing their Arab subjects or expelling them completely. British Governments continued to deny that any such thing would be allowed to come to pass, but could never answer the Arab argument that such a thing would certainly come to pass unless the British chose to stop the process which was so clearly facilitating it. The advent of Hitler to power in Germany made the whole issue more acute: Jews began to pour in, and as a result 20,000 British troops spent from 1936 through 1939 in Palestine endeavoring to keep order among people who had no wish that order should be kept. A Royal Commission (Peel's) came to the bold conclusion that the Balfour Declaration was in fact unrealizable, and that the only solution was to partition Palestine. The Arabs thought this anathema: for if the Jews were given a legalized base in the area they would assuredly use it as a military base, and make off, in no very long run, with the whole of Palestine, and doubtless with whatever other surrounding districts they claimed were owing to them through two thousand years of history.

Two years later the British Government tried to meet the Arab point, and issued the celebrated White Paper of 1939, which abandoned partition and caused a certain lull. The British announced their intention of setting up, within ten years (1949), an independent state of Palestine in which Arabs and Jews should share in the government in a manner that would guarantee the interests of both communities.

Although they entered their formal objections, the Arabs were not too displeased about this statement of British intention. Partition had been abandoned, and with it the wicked Balfour Declaration. Independence, of a kind, would be along in ten years' time. So long, then, as the British Government stuck to these guns, all might yet be well. But Zionism had no intention of letting this or any subsequent British Government stick to any such guns. The White Paper of 1939 served notice on the Jews that Great Britain had now definitely refused to carve out any "national home," or Zionist state, by force of British arms. The desired end, therefore, could now only be attained by force of Zionist arms. These would first have to be turned against the British, upholders of the obstructing Mandate, and then against the Arabs—not an enemy that was hated, but an inevitable enemy nonetheless. The Arabs made an error, in that they did not grasp that such was the Zionist outlook, and such the Zionist blueprint for the future. That the Jews could grow strong enough and confident enough to displace the British, the "country power" in the Middle East, and seize Palestine for themselves seemed, in 1939, an impossibility, an Arabian nightmare. But by 1945 it was not an impossibility at all. . . .

British authority had broken down, and it was first to the Palestine Arabs that the British Government sought to turn to rescue it from the impasse: Bevin despaired of the Jews, who were talking "in terms of millions." But the Arabs were disorganized, and could do nothing either for the Foreign Office or for themselves. It was in February 1947 that Bevin first referred the Palestine issue to the United Nations. A board comprising eleven nations, among them Canada, India, and Australia, investigated the tangle, and based their conclusions broadly on the evidence that had already been compiled in the Report of the Peel Commission issued in 1937. They recommended that the Mandate should be ended, that Palestine should, after all, be partitioned, and that both a Jewish state and an Arab state, later to be confederated, should be formed. The British Government, stormed at from all sides, jeered at by Churchill still for their "manifest incapacity," undermined by President Truman's open support for the machinations of the Zionist lobby in Washington, accepted this recommendation, and thus returned to the position that Sir Edward Grey had once idly sketched out—that there should be some kind of international authority in Palestine. On 15 May 1948 the Mandate ended its sad life. War broke out in Palestine at once, for the Arabs were resolved to prevent the carrying-out of the United Nations' resolutions. At the United Nations Assembly at Lake Success the British at once opposed the placing of any sanctions on the attacking Arabs.

This was a gesture of despair, unlikely to win friends. It won none. Throwing up the cards in Palestine, whatever else there was to be said for it, was hardly the way to win Arab friendship. In the only place where Arabs were prepared to concede that Great Britain had indeed some imperial duties—namely, to keep the Jews at bay in Palestine—she had failed to carry them out. Shortly afterwards, during 1951 and 1952, in a state not Arab at all, it seemed also to be proved that Britain lacked the nerve and the power to defend her own legitimate oil interests in Persia. The Arab world cohered: Ibn Saud, and his son after him, made his peace with the Hashimites, and with the pleasant consciousness of American friendship behind him, prepared to wait on the sidelines while the Egyptians sought to play the dominant role in the drama of Middle East nationalism. Egypt did not play the part with any particular skill, but she could hardly fail to score the necessary points.

For the debacle that the Arab League had suffered in its war with the new state of Israel in 1948 had increased to boiling-point the Arab bitterness against the British. Anglo-Egyptian relations in particular, which had been lurching downhill since the Bevin-Sidky agreement of 1946 had been abandoned, now sped vertically downwards at a spectacular pace, despite all the conciliatory actions that were taken by the British Government: the re-equipment of the Egyptian forces by modern arms, the supply of jet planes, the release of sterling balances, the suggestion that the old imperial relationship should be buried in a new—namely, in a Middle East Defense Organization based on the pattern of the North Atlantic Treaty Organization. In October 1951 the Egyptian Government unilaterally abrogated the Anglo-Egyptian Treaty of 1936, and bottom was reached during the murderous hours of Black Saturday in Cairo on 26 January 1952. The revolutionary junta government which deposed Farouk that summer was enabled, while the British policy of conciliation continued, to pull off two remarkable feats at British expense: the agreement of 12 February 1953, largely negotiated by Neguib, which provided for a type of self-government in the Sudan which (at any rate at the outset) was free from both British and Egyptian pressures; and the agreement of 19 October 1954—Nasser's doing—whereby the British promised to leave the Suez Canal base in Egyptian hands, while retaining the right to return in emergency. The British evacuated the base as promised by June 1956.

But emergency occurred, for the next month Nasser commandeered the Suez Canal as an Egyptian waterway. By 5 November the British were parachuting back again, in an attempt to reestablish a naked power-relationship, since all else seemed to have failed. In this venture the Jews found themselves promoted, once more, as agents of Western imperialism: for it was an Israeli punitive raid in force into the Sinai peninsula, 100 miles from the Canal, that was used as a screen for their own activities and intentions by the British and the French. It was a venture that failed as it was bound to, as its British instigators had entirely miscalculated the number of enemies that imperial ideas of this particular kind now mustered. One cannot comment on the object of the policy, as it is not yet known. What Britain intended to do with a subjugated Egypt, deserted by a Nasser as discredited as once Arabi had been, is anyone's guess. Certainly another Cromer would have been as hard to find in the mid-twentieth century as another docile Egyptian Prime Minister.

Much has already been said about the "Suez adventure," and more will be. Its interest here is its emotional symbolism. Eden as Premier was true to the sentiments he had expressed when a young back-bencher in 1929: the Suez Canal was too vital an artery of the British Empire to be left to the mercy of the goodwill of the Egyptians. The imperialist is a single-minded man, and despite Eden's long career in European politics as a dexterous diplomat, balancing, compromising, squaring off conflicting interests, he never saw any reason to change his mind on this point. The emotional support that his action engendered in the country stood on much the same basis: if our entire history in the Middle East since 1882 was not to be made ridiculous, how could we allow ourselves to be "pushed around" by Egyptians? A Balfour Declaration about Jews might be jettisoned without many tears being shed by the British democracy:

but the Suez Canal? Did we not build it? (No.) Did Disraeli not buy it? (No.) Had we not fulfilled our duty to the world in our guardianship of it by keeping it always open to the world's commerce, even in time of war? (No.) Were not the Egyptians grateful for all that we had done for them, particularly during the Second World War? (No.) Was not Nasser as sinister a figure, in his rather cardboard Egyptian way, as Hitler? (No.) And anyway, did not a Tory Government, headed by so patently sincere a figure as Eden, really have a better grasp of British interests in the Middle East than all its captious critics?

John Hatch
THE DECLINE OF BRITISH POWER IN AFRICA

After occupying Egypt in 1882, Britain participated in the so-called "Scramble for Africa." To her expanding holdings in the South centered on the Cape Colony, Britain added rich trading areas around the Niger River in West Africa and consolidated her hold over the territory of present-day Ghana and Sierra Leone. To the East, Britain secured the areas we today call Kenya, Uganda and the Sudan, thereby protecting the Nile and the Suez Canal and so the approach to India. Other territories came to her as a result of Germany's defeat in World War I. Professor Hatch, author of several books on African history, reviews British policy toward West, East and South-Central Africa while at the same time keeping in view the larger historical and economic considerations affecting British decisions.

If the imposition of British imperial rule on Africans in the late nineteenth century had been dramatically sudden, the dissolution of colonial governance came with even more spectacular abruptness. Within twenty years following the conclusion of the Second World War virtually the entire British African empire had been dissolved.

John Hatch, *The History of Britain in Africa: From the Fifteenth Century to the Present* (New York and London, 1969), pp. 239–246; 249–251; 255–265; 270–277. Reprinted by permission of Praeger Publishers, Inc. and Andre Deutsch Ltd. Footnotes omitted.

The relationship between Britons and Africans, which at the beginning of that war had appeared more deeply rooted in the soil of imperialism than ever, experienced its second violent reversal within seventy-five years. It is still too early to discern the outlines of its new character.

The most remarkable aspect of this *bouleversement* was that it took place at a time when the gap between British and African strength was wider than ever before. During the course of the war Britain had participated in the discovery of means to split the atom, providing her with a source of power never previously possessed by man. Moreover, despite expenditure of her treasure, she had expanded her manufacturing and industrial capabilities beyond her prewar achievements even if she had yet to realize their potential. Britain had also emerged victorious from a war in which, despite the eventual participation of the United States and the Soviet Union, she had stood alone at a crucial time against the collective resources of Europe organized against her by the Nazis and Fascists. One might therefore have assumed that her imperial *élan,* backed by greater power to enforce her dictat, would have enabled Britain to reinforce her grip on the Empire.

We may be too close to the events to assess judicially the reasons for history confuting this expectation. But we must at least attempt to analyze some of the elements, however incomplete the conclusion.

In the twenty-year period of decolonization which followed the war the colonies certainly had neither the economic nor military power to challenge British hegemony. What they did possess, however, was the ability to force Britain to choose between progressive decolonization and a series of colonial wars. It was already clear by the end of the war that the Indian subcontinent would revolt if complete self-government were not offered quickly. Perhaps Britain could have defeated the Indians militarily, but only by involving herself in a long and costly war fought against the entire weight of international opinion. French and Dutch colonial wars in Asia revealed that even in the age of atomic bombs the nationalist forces of poor countries could cause imperial powers acute embarrassment and undermine metropolitan economies. British experience in Malaya and later in Kenya, even when fighting with some international sympathy, taught the same lesson.

It may be argued that if this rationale had been applied in the nineteenth century the British Empire in Africa would never have been built. There is some truth in this assertion, although, despite the resistance shown by some Africans, large areas of Africa were annexed without active opposition. But the more opposite fact is that Britain's strategic, economic and political interests had radically changed since the nineteenth century. Independence for India in 1947 removed the paramount strategic necessity of controlling the sea lanes which the development of air power had, in any case, reduced in importance. British concern in overseas trade and investment remained concentrated on the industrialized countries, while the important resources of the African colonies were already controlled by British companies which could expect to continue their operations after political control had passed into local hands. In both international and domestic fields the political atmosphere had become heavily laden with anti-imperialist elements.

In order to understand British attitudes towards decolonization, both her conscious and subconscious motives, we need to examine the country's economic and political situation in the mid-twentieth century. The central factor was that Britain had now finally lost her nineteenth-century economic preeminence. We have already seen how, in the latter part of the nineteenth century, British industrialists had begun to lose the momentum gained in the earlier part of the century. They had failed to recognize the opportunities for new forms of production to replace traditional products in which they were being overtaken by America and Germany. The First World War seriously dislocated British production and, although it removed German competition for a time, it also enabled the Germans to return in the 1930s with a rebuilt, modernized industrial machine. The absence of German competition and Britain's privileged imperial position obscured the harsh realities for the first half of the interwar period, but the world crisis again exposed them. Even though imperial preferences again helped to cushion the shock and although some diversification was accomplished during the 1930s, by the outbreak of the war [the] British had once more been overtaken by the Germans, while the Americans were almost out of sight.

The consequences of the Second World War to Britain's economic position were even more drastic than the First. To pay for her efforts she had to sell overseas capital assets worth a net amount of nearly £5,000 million, more than she actually held in 1939. Although this "net sale" does not indicate that all these assets actually left British ownership, those which did not were offset by foreign debts incurred in order to pay for the war—many of them forming part of the sterling balances owed to colonial countries for goods provided to Britain on credit. And industrial production had again been diverted from constructive paths in order to supply the needs of war.

The Second World War finally exposed the demise of Britain as a great power in the economic world. It is true that this fact was once again slightly disguised by the removal of Germany and, this time, of Japan, too, from international competition. But both were back in the forefront of international industry by the 1950s. They returned with modernized structures rebuilt out of the ashes. Few people deceived themselves about the reality of Britain's decline this time. Dependence on American aid during the war had prepared most observers for an inevitable continuation of assistance in rebuilding the economy after the war. Now it was to be Britain which would seek injections of external capital if her industries were to be regeared to supply her postwar needs.

Thus, in one way, Britain in the mid-twentieth century had exchanged places with the America of a century before. She might have opened up an even wider gap between the standard of life of her people and that of her African subjects, but to maintain that standard she would now need American dollars, and to gain them she possessed the enormous advantage of colonies which earned dollars. In Africa cocoa and gold from the Gold Coast, copper from Northern Rhodesia, joined Malaya's tin and rubber as the sterling area's main dollar earners. During the decade following the war the colonial share of the sterling balances rose from 12 percent to 32 percent, from £450 million to nearly £1,300 million. Their value also suffered from devaluation in 1949; while although they were to become available to the new states after independence, for the time being they could not be used by the colonies concerned to buy the dollar goods needed for development and earned only about 3 percent interest.

Some people may have been deceived into believing that Britain was back again on the road to economic power when overseas investment showed a remarkable postwar recovery. In the ten years after the war it attained the prewar monetary figures, although the income derived from it was never to reach the percentage of national income reached in the 1920s and, of course, could not aspire to the pre-1914 heights. But two aspects of this investment boom tell another story. While the monetary figures were impressive, the net figure was much smaller than the gross. For the period 1946–1954, for instance, gross overseas investment produced an income which averaged 3.85 percent of the national income; but the net income showed an average of only 1.65 percent. The difference arose from the amount of overseas capital entering Britain.

The consequences of this factor can be seen from another angle. During the same period net property income was never large enough to pay for more than 14 percent of British imports. In fact, that figure was only reached in 1950 and only in one other year did it attain double figures. Yet, even in 1938, after several years of disinvestment, it was 19 percent. Moreover, during this postwar period imports were running at a lower volume level than in 1938. The conclusion is clear. Not only had Britain to rely on exports to pay her import bill to a far greater extent than ever before—90 percent by 1949 compared with 56 percent in 1938—but the investment of foreigners in Britain was largely offsetting the income obtained from her own overseas investments. The days of *rentier* Britain, with her imports and national income substantially subsidized from earlier investment, were obviously over.

The nineteenth-century positions of Britain and America had now been reversed in another direction. Not only were Americans investing in Britain, but it was now America that insisted on free international trade. The Atlantic Charter guaranteed "access on equal terms to trade and raw materials" and, despite Churchill's concern for Empire agreements, the only qualification the British delegation could get the Americans to accept was that such free trade should be "with due respect for existing obligations." The Lend-Lease contract, the Keynes Loan, the General Agreement on Tariffs and Trade and Marshall Aid all undermined imperial preferences by insisting on convertibility of sterling (vainly, as it transpired), a halt to discriminatory protection and reduced restrictions on dollar imports. (This American pressure also played a part in persuading the

Labour government to dismantle the wartime government economic controls which could have helped to plan the economy.) It was now American technological supremacy which stood to gain from free trade, although Americans, unlike the nineteenth-century British, were not so self-confident as to abandon their own protective system; they were living not in the single world economy of the nineteenth century, but in a world divided between Communist and capitalist blocs.

The result was that America threw her weight into the anti-colonial balance, always on condition that the regimes which succeeded colonial rule could be trusted to remain in the capitalist camp, and were prepared to keep the rules now laid down by the dominant sectors of American capitalism. For, like the British in the previous century, America regarded empires as a restraint on the trade she knew she could dominate if restrictions were removed. Thus, from the declaration in the Atlantic Charter that America and Britain respect "the right of all peoples to choose the form of government under which they will live and they wish to see sovereign rights and self-government restored to those who have been forcibly deprived of them," America took an active part in giving moral aid to anti-colonial movements and in persuading her allies that the days of imperialism were past. In vain did Churchill protest that colonies were not covered by this clause. Americans sought a postwar world in which imperial practices discriminating against her trading potential were abolished. Her position as the world's supermarket and credit controller gave her an irresistible power of persuasion, as Britain and France were to learn abruptly over the 1956 Suez invasion.

It might be expected that Britain and the other European imperial powers would resist American pressures to undermine their colonial empires. To some extent they did so. The Dutch and French fought particularly bitter colonial wars in Asia and the British in Malaya, while the American qualification to her anti-colonial attitude was clearly seen in the case of British Guiana. When Britain's decolonization policy provided an opportunity for a communist-socialist government to take office, the Americans fully supported British efforts to remove it.

But in Africa the situation was more ambiguous. Once the choice

had been made to give India independence rather than face a
costly imperial war, a strong case could be made for considering
a similar policy for the Gold Coast and possibly for Nigeria. It was
not simply that postwar disturbances in West Africa presaged anti-
colonial conflict there; American and British overseas capital had
become equivocal as to where their interests lay in the future development of British Africa.

It is important to examine the character of postwar British external investment if we are to understand its influence on the government's colonial policy. This character was already changing
during the interwar years. Instead of being largely composed, as
before the First World War, of small *rentiers* investing in government stock, it was the large combines which increasingly dominated overseas capital. Moreover, it was largely from the public
sector that capital sales were secured during the war. The impact
of the war itself accelerated this process. Thus, during the period
1938–1948 sales of private overseas capital totalled £650 million of
the £3,000 million held, whereas £1,050 million of the £1,500 million
public holdings were sold. And in the five years following the war
£4,300 million was added to the private sector compared with only
£350 million to the public. It is also significant to note that the general direction of investment remained in the same channels as before: business investors were still much more interested in the
developed than the developing countries. During this five-year period
more private capital was invested in South Africa than in all the
colonies combined. Although the opportunities in Europe had now
been almost exhausted, the U.S.A., Canada, Australia and the
Rhodesias, added to South Africa, still attracted the bulk of investment. The proportion invested in underdeveloped areas even declined after the war, despite the fact that Middle East oil now
accounted for nearly half the total to these developing countries.

So the main investing interests in the postwar period still regarded the colonial empire, and particularly the African section of
it, as no more than of peripheral concern. They were more involved
in restoring Britain's position in the international fields of banking,
investment and trade, concentrating on those countries where
development had already taken place. Often they were engaged in
buying a share of international combines. They saw the importance

of avoiding further expense and dislocation from unnecessary wars and of averting international hostility in a world atmosphere which had become increasingly chilly towards imperialism—and particularly cold in the most important environment, America.

The main investors directly involved in Africa were now combines, of which the Unilever subsidiary, the United Africa Company, is a good example. As we have already seen, this had become a vertically integrated organization, collecting raw materials, processing them, and also selling consumer goods in the local market. It was therefore important for these combines to maintain control of raw material production, but equally important to remain on good terms with local leaders. Not only did they aim to increase dividends —and succeed in doing so—but, taking a longer-term view, to plow back a proportion of their profits. It was from this process that an important section of increased investment was derived. This again depended on good relations with local representatives. These large corporations operated as quasi-political units. In contrast to the earlier small investors they controlled such a proportion of colonial incomes as to hold an independent position within a colony, responsible to neither imperial government nor local nationalists. As colonial power was threatened they recognized that their future depended on sympathetic relations with anti-colonial leaders and parties; and the nationalists also had to accept the fact that it was unlikely they would be able to develop their economics without some kind of alliance with the alien economic giants. . . .

While this attitude held generally true in West Africa, the situation was somewhat different in the white-settled lands in the east and center of the continent. Here the expectation was that Europeans would become the successor rulers to Whitehall. There were a few qualified exceptions—in Central Africa the Booker interests and the Rhodesian Selection Trust saw the light earlier than others —but most British businesses fully expected East and Central Africa to follow the example of South, rather than of West Africa. This did not mean that the great corporations were any more inclined to throw their weight into the preservation of imperial rule than their colleagues in the west; but it did involve them in the tortuous path first, of participating in the efforts of Europeans in Kenya, Uganda, both Rhodesias and Nyasaland to remove Colonial

Office rule so as to establish independent, white-controlled governments, and then suddenly changing direction in order to keep their
place on the road now clearly leading to African independence. It
was, however, the trade and investment prospects of the successor
regimes which attracted them rather than the preservation of British
political authority. By this time they realized anyway that Britain
could only retain colonial power by engaging in wars as disruptive
as that in Algeria.

The economic environment, then, was ripe for decolonization.
Without the changed character of Britain's economy and the new
direction taken by her major economic interests British political
control over Africans would have not been concluded at this time.
As we have seen, the gap in military power between Britain and her
colonial subjects had never been so wide.

Yet, equally, whatever the environment, if there had not also been
a virile movement among Africans to rid themselves of colonial rule,
decolonization would not have followed the course that it did. Although the British forces supporting colonial rule were in retreat,
they had not reached the point of flight seen, for instance, in Belgium after 1957.

There is no simple description for the outlook of Africans after
the Second World War. Their feelings are commonly termed "nationalist," but, with very few exceptions, they had never lived in
nation states. They had certainly never been governed as nations
under colonial rulers. They had been subject peoples, governed
by institutions and officers whose final authority lay in Westminster.
It is true that a form of diarchy had increasingly arisen as colonial
councils, under governors, had been accorded greater powers.
Such local governments stimulated some ambition for statehood,
but as the units of administration hardly ever coincided with social
or cultural entities, the achievement of nationhood was a different
matter. The fact was that Africans, to a much greater extent than
their colonial cousins in Asia or the Caribbean, had little, if any
national heritage to which they could nostalgically refer. They had
strong localized traditions and cultures, but, with few exceptions,
these had never been politically organized into nation states even
before colonization. One of the usual and most potent forces capable of mobilization in the cause of decolonization was therefore
almost entirely absent from Africa.

Yet there is no doubt that anti-colonial emotions gripped many Africans. We have seen earlier that some Africans had never accepted the colonial status. Opposition to the imposition of alien rule was widespread from its inception and continued in an active and often violent form well into the First World War. Of even deeper import, however, were the efforts made by Africans to plan their own social and political future. The Fante Confederation of the 1870s provided an early example. The Aborigines' Rights Protection Society of 1897 organized defense of land rights in the Gold Coast. Professor Du Bois, an American Negro, took the lead in stimulating pan-African ideals and initiated a number of conferences to develop them from 1900 onward. In 1918 a Gold Coast lawyer, J. E. Caseley Hayford, founded the National Congress of British West Africa which sought African participation in colonial governments and some form of unity between the four West African territories ruled by Britain; for a few years it became active in both the Gold Coast and Nigeria. In the following decade the West African Youth League strove even more forthrightly to achieve unity in British West Africa. As increasing numbers of African young men went to study in London and other British cities, political theories and their application to the African scene became a constant subject of discussion. The emphasis during the interwar period was usually on gaining greater representation in the colonial institutions set up in their homelands and on the need to create a wider African consciousness. The West African Students' Union, founded in the mid-twenties, provided the liveliest forum for these discussions. During the same period, too, Herbert Macaulay, grandson of Nigeria's first African bishop, founded the Nigerian National Democratic Party. Its object was to press for self-government within the British Commonwealth, but although it was able to gain some publicity in Lagos during the periodic elections to the Legislative Council, it never succeeded in attracting serious support outside Lagos. . . .

Over most of Africa during the interwar years the movement against colonial rule appeared incipient rather than openly challenging. The masses were still almost entirely engaged in traditional agriculture. Their frustrations were expressed through schismatic or messianic religious sects rather than in political organization. Among a small proportion of Africans outside the subsistence economy, however, three groups or classes had begun to emerge, first and most clearly in West Africa. There were the traditionalists, chiefs and their henchmen, who usually worked with the colonial authorities; there was a professional, business element, sometimes related to chiefly families, usually with close connections with Britain, intent on reforming the existing structure and securing a better place in it for themselves; thirdly, there were the beginnings of an urbanized leadership, whose contacts in Britain were usually with left-wing politicians, who were just starting to recognize that the logic of their adoption of political democracy must lead to an attack on colonial rule itself.

The effects of the Second World War were to strengthen the position of the third group, greatly expand their numbers and extend their outlook to territories previously slumbering under unchallenged British rule. It was from this group, sometimes temporarily allied to the middle class, that was to come the leadership against the roots of colonial rule.

In the Second World War, as in the First, thousands of Africans were to witness white men killing each other by the most horrific means scientific minds could devise. They listened to the propaganda and counter-propaganda, realizing that the "Christian civilization" brought to them from Europe soon discarded its teaching on the supreme value of Truth when its various communities quarrelled with each other. Now they also saw that the Europeans were vulnerable when an Asian, nonwhite nation, Japan, captured the British, French, Dutch and American empires in Asia. They also found that their French-speaking brothers were involved in the bitter quarrels between two rival French governments, Vichy and de Gaulle, both seeking support from French Africans. They heard or read of the passionate debates in South Africa and Rhodesia as to whether it was safe to arm black men; on the other hand, many of them saw a country ruled by black men for the first time when they participated in the liberation of Ethiopia from Italian rule and the restoration of the Emperor. They learned in Burma and India that other colored subjects of the British Empire were organizing for total independence, for the complete removal of British rule. In short, the Second World War destroyed the European mystique on which so much of imperial rule depended.

Africans may have felt that in Nazism they were fighting a philosophy aimed at their own dignity and human identity as well as helping to defend their imperial masters; but the concept of innate racial superiority could never survive the war experience among Africans, even if Europeans were less ready to accept the logic. The fact that by the end of the war the East African forces numbered 228,000 and West African 146,000 shows that the experience was considerable. The war also bequeathed an Africa different in significant respects from the prewar continent. This time important campaigns had been fought right across the northern part of the continent itself. Mobilization of war supplies had been organized in many African countries. Roads, railways, harbors and airfields had been either newly built or greatly improved. Production in both agriculture and industry had been considerably increased to supply the insatiable maws of war. Towns and cities had grown enormously as a result and having gained this momentum, urbanization was maintained after the war. Lagos, for instance, which had been a small town of some 75,000 inhabitants in 1914, had grown to 230,000 by 1950 and to 675,000 by 1962, and during the same period Accra's population increased from 20,000 to 135,000 to 325,000. Enugu, a village of only 15,000 residents in 1939, had grown to a sizeable town of 35,000 by 1945 and to 60,000 in 1953. Similar patterns were to be seen in Nairobi, the Northern Rhodesian copper towns, in Salisbury, and Bulawayo. Urbanization brought release from the disciplines of tribal life, and an exchange of ideas between people from different communities. Social life became more diverse and stimulating, many cafés and bars were opened, public transport had to be provided, new types of houses supplied, and new household goods produced. Expanded town life naturally stimulated the local market; it also led urbanized Africans to organize modern social associations on a serious scale for the first time. Trade unions were established, some with the help of the British trade union movement, an activity encouraged by Britain's new Foreign Secretary, Ernest Bevin, and his protégé, Arthur Creech Jones, who became Colonial Secretary. (Though it was to become significant that the unions established under the aegis of the TUC were always strongly advised by that body to remain aloof from politics.) Ex-servicemen's associations, market women's groups, sports clubs, religious and educational bodies, all provided increasing experience in organization for the growing number of Africans in the towns. Newspapers proliferated, giving increased opportunities for debate and argument in their columns, and by the end of the war, with prices high, shortages of goods, returning servicemen unable to find work, there was plenty to debate and many issues inviting organized pressures.

By the end of the war, too, not only was a little of the wealth produced by increased economic activity beginning to rub off on to a few African shoulders, but the consequences of prewar educational opportunities were becoming apparent. In the immediate postwar years, for instance, nearly 120,000 children were at school in the Gold Coast, over 600,000 in Nigeria, over 250,000 in Kenya and about 170,000 in Northern Rhodesia. These might be very small percentages of the total child population; but as literate individuals in African society they had a particular significance for the growth of political consciousness. Immediately after the war university colleges were established in the Gold Coast, Nigeria, Uganda and the Sudan. These institutions, though often conducted on British classical lines, offered extended opportunities, previously only supplied by Fourah Bay in Sierra Leone, for higher education and the experience of student debate and organization.

It was in these turbulent circumstances that the first serious African political organizations were founded. In the Sudan the Graduates' General Congress, formed in 1937, raised the cry for self-determination soon after the war ended. The Congress divided in 1945 between the Ashiqqua party supporting Egypt and the more conciliatory Umma. Azikiwe and Macaulay, influenced by the radical attitudes of Nigerian students, formed the National Council of Nigeria and the Cameroons in 1944. In the same year the Nyasaland African Congress was set up, mainly by civil servants and chiefs. Two years later the Northern Rhodesians federated their welfare societies throughout the country in defense against the political ambitions of the European community; the federation was later to graduate into a Congress. In Kenya a new organization, the Kenya African Union, was established in 1944 and secured backing from Luo and Kamba as well as from the Kikuyu although the latter remained its largest supporters. Nineteen forty-seven saw the formation of Dr. Danquah's United Gold Coast Convention.

Almost all these organizations aimed to represent as broad a cross-section of the population as possible and usually demanded some form of "self-government." They owed much of their inspiration to the Indian Congress, often adopting the same name, and seeking support in a similar way from as many different sectors of society as possible. Usually they were federal-type organizations, linking together a variety of separate bodies without provision for an individual membership of their own. Their response was to a general sense of resentment against alien rule and a desire to secure increased representation for indigenous inhabitants in established colonial institutions. Usually they were led by a mixture of professionals and intellectuals who had contact with left-wing circles in Britain. They had, with the notable exception of Azikiwe, as little conception of the roots of imperialism or of the future structure of their countries as had their friends in Britain.

These organizations were an African reflection of the prevalent attitudes towards imperialism among Fabians and Labour Party colonial experts in London. When Arthur Creech Jones was appointed Colonial Secretary in 1946 he became the official representative of this outlook. Passionately devoted to the cause of colonial reform, he nevertheless accepted the general bipartisan approach to colonial policy assumed in Britain to be essential for continuity of policy. Under the influence of Lord Hailey, Britain's trusteeship approach was now extended into the field of social development. Hailey, Oliver Stanley from the Conservative Party, and Creech Jones, all accepted that in the postwar world Britain had a responsibility to ensure better living standards and social services for her colonial subjects. This would entail the imperial government exercising greater influence over the policies of the colonial governments in the colonies, taking the initiative in London and providing some of the funds for development. It also implied that "good government" and social progress should take precedence over "self-government" or any serious attack on the economic controllers of colonial economies.

This outlook was particularly fitted to Labour's postwar perspective of welfare reformism. It found a ready response from leaders like Ernest Bevin and the trade union cohorts whom he represented, always suspicious of intellectuals obsessed by politics who had no concern with the bread-and-butter needs of either colonial subjects or British workers! In any case, Bevin was speaking for many in the Labour Party when he told the House of Commons, "I am not prepared to sacrifice the British Empire, because I know that if the British Empire fell . . . it would mean the standard of life of our constituents would fall considerably." Creech Jones, despite his sincere desire to reform the Empire, rejected the idea that a Labour Colonial Secretary had the responsibility of introducing socialism into the colonies. He declared that it was "contrary to the spirit of British policy to force people into particular molds because a Secretary of State or his particular party thinks it good for them." ...

On the political front the prescription was for gradual advance in indigenous representation as social and economic conditions improved and a class of politicians and administrators emerged replete with British habits, attitudes and values. Creech Jones revealed his outlook by an address in Cambridge in 1948 when he declared, "Our conception of African development is based on Western political philosophy, and as far as we can see at present, that of the African leaders is based on the same ideas." It was assumed that "natives" in the colonies would acquire British administrative routines if they were provided with an example for long enough. The exercise of political democracy, first through local government and then at the national level, would be taught by the same colonial officials. The fact that democracy might involve conflict between organized social classes—as had occurred in Britain—was too dangerous a thought to be contemplated. After all, this was not how the official classes regarded British politics; the "Establishment" ruled the country, while the politicians played their game of musical chairs according to the accepted rules. It was not surprising, therefore, that when the Colonial Office defended the Gold Coast Burns' constitution against an official commission's verdict that it was "outmoded," it aggrievedly pointed out that the constitution had been approved by press, public and Legislative Council. What the colonial officials failed to perceive was that it was no longer sufficient to claim legitimacy because some black faces had replaced white. In situations like that of the Gold Coast, traditional chiefs and British-trained lawyers were no longer acceptable as representatives of the people, even though they were black; nor would institutions be acknowledged as democratic because of the skin color of those occupying their benches. ...

Even before the new constitutions paved the way for popular elections, circumstances began to develop which invited mass organization. Postwar discontents erupted into revolt of various types in several colonies during the 1940s. In the Gold Coast there were strikes in the mines, a boycott of foreign stores, protest marches from ex-servicemen, and twenty-one were killed in subsequent riots. In Nigeria one of Azikiwe's newspapers was fined for sedition, while strikes and threats of strikes revealed the new militancy of trade unions. In Buganda discontent broke out against the feudal outlook of the aristocrats who ruled the country. In Kenya Kikuyu land grievances against their neighboring white farmers mingled with resentment against lack of employment in the towns. These spontaneous discontents provided ready ammunition for the nascent political parties, for it was not of a character which appealed to the conservative, middle-class leadership. In any case, it could only be capitalized by the organization of urban masses in West Africa and a combination among the same kind of people along with the peasant farmers in the East. This was a task beyond the capacities of the wealthier, upper-middle-class professionals and merchants who led the older type of organization like the United Gold Coast Convention; it could only be accomplished by the lower-middle-class cadres recruited by an Nkrumah to mobilize mass support behind a program of action. "Self-government now," easily translated into "freedom now," provided the kind of rallying cry which could appeal to mass audiences. Strikes, boycotts, non-violent demonstrations, could readily be organized under the attractively simple slogan of "positive action." When Nkrumah and his lieutenants went to gaol charismatic martyrdom completed the pattern.

Yet the influence of Britain was still strong. The Gold Coast revolution was quickly transformed into a gentlemanly agreement. Whether the Colonial Office officials could see the realities of the colonial scene or not, Sir Charles Arden-Clarke, governor of the Gold Coast, certainly could. Although Nkrumah was in prison at the time of the 1951 elections, the governor released him as soon as it was clear that his CPP had secured the support of the electorate. Arden-Clarke recalled his situation in a reminiscent article: "My choice was fairly simple: if I did not release him we would not even make a start with working the Constitution; and if I did release him, he would find it very difficult to refuse to work the Constitution or give it a trial, even though it might be called 'bogus and fraudulent.' So he was released. He came up to see me, and I asked him to form a Government." Nkrumah's response to the governor's action was equally appropriate to the best British manners. "I would like to make it absolutely clear," he declared on his release, "that I am a friend of Britain. I desire for the Gold Coast Dominion status within the Commonwealth."

Ghana's attainment of responsibility for her own domestic affairs set the whole of West Africa inexorably on the road to independence. As soon as it was proven that Africans could control a modern state machine—and why should it have been thought that Africans were any less capable of doing so than anyone else?—West Africans were accepted into the same stream of British policy which had previously swept Canada, Australia, New Zealand and South Africa into statehood. British interests were no more threatened by black faces in Christiansborg Castle than they had been by pink in Canberra, Ottawa or Pretoria.

A few minor delays occurred in the 1950s, usually occasioned by communal fears. The approach of independence in Ghana provoked a revival of traditionalist pride in Ashanti. Three-way suspicions between Hausa-Fulani, Ibo and Yoruba, forced the Nigerians to experiment with various types of federal constitution, postponing their independence until 1960. In Sierra Leone tensions between the tribal communities of the hinterland and the more sophisticated Creoles on the coast, together with suspicions between the Mende and Temne tribes delayed independence there until 1961. Gambia tried to sort out her relations with surrounding Senegal and had to convince herself and the British that she was large enough to become an independent state. But by 1951 the die was cast; franchises were to become universal (except for Northern Nigeria's sex discrimination); parties would fight elections—the CPP in Ghana, the SLPP in Sierra Leone, the NCNC, Action Group and NPC in Nigeria; victorious parties would form governments; their governments, supported by majority parties in the legislatures, would ask for sovereignty and the British parliament would pass independence acts. As the Sudan had gained independent status by the same means in 1956 and the Somali Protectorate was due to join her brother Somalis in 1960, political decolonization in non-settler Africa was now inevitable.

Political independence, of course, did not bring imperialism to an end. Unilever's United Africa Company, which at the end of the war was responsible for a third of all Gold Coast and Nigerian imports and exports, did not leave with the proconsuls. The company might find it more expedient under African government to bequeath the retail trade to the locals, but only to transfer its investment into the production of consumer goods, cold storage, assembly of vehicles, drinks, cement, etc. In fact it often found that African governments were more sympathetic than their colonial predecessors. As they hoped to protect local production, which the colonial rulers had refused to do, and as UAC, as part of the huge Unilever combine, had such a strong bargaining power, marketing opportunities could actually increase after independence. It was sufficiently strong to maintain its low-wage policy and even to insist on importing many of the materials it processed for the African market rather than use local products. . . .

The victory of decolonizing forces in West Africa did not necessarily presage parallel developments in the rest of British Africa. It was certainly clear by now that the political rule of the British would be ultimately withdrawn from the whole continent, but the timetable was uncertain and the character of the successor regimes obscure. East and Central Africa consisted of colonies of white settlement and until the beginning of the 1960s passionate arguments continued as to whether the principles applied in West Africa were appropriate to Kenya, Uganda, Tanganyika, Nyasaland and the Rhodesias. At least until 1959 the British Conservative Party pursued a policy towards these countries more closely approximating to that in the pre-Union Cape Colony than to the attitude which was bringing independence to West Africa.

Two central issues governed the outcome of this debate. First, it had to be seen whether the white settlers with political pretensions, those in Kenya and the Rhodesias in particular, could mobilize sufficient force to assert political power over their African populations. They were given the chance, though—with the exception of Southern Rhodesia—they never secured unreserved support from the imperial government. Until the mid-1950s the 60,000 Europeans in Kenya were allowed to advance towards the same position as had been assumed by their cousins in the Cape Colony and Southern Rhodesia. It was not expected that Europeans in either Uganda or Tanganyika would be strong enough to imitate them, but it was thought that a federation of the three territories might sustain "good" and white government for the whole region if the Kenyans proved themselves.

The Mau Mau rebellion ended this dream. Frustrated by land dis-crimination, unemployment, interference in tribal traditions and the cold-shouldering of Kenyatta's KAU, the Kikuyu, together with some Meru, Embu and Kamba, broke into violent revolt. Their warfare was conducted by medieval, quasi-mystical tactics to secure modern ends. The oath-taking ritualistic methods employed had little in common with the tactics of political parties in the rest of the con-tinent; their objectives—removing discrimination, land reform, urban employment—were very similar.

The significance of the Mau Mau, however, was that it proved that the Europeans of Kenya were too few to meet the challenge of modern African political protest. Tom Mboya and his colleagues demonstrated their capacity to organize political activities even un-der the restrictions of the emergency. And Mau Mau itself could only be contained by the use of British military strength. The situa-tion was therefore clarified by the rebellion. Europeans in Kenya were not strong enough to rule the country without continued British support. If they were left alone they would face the growing pres-sures of African political protest. Their history showed little evi-dence of ability to abdicate voluntarily; so another war could be foreseen. In these circumstances Britain saw it as her interest to mediate while there was still time. For a few years British Conserva-tive politicians tried to compromise by introducing various types of "multiracial" political balances. When they found that these would not appease the Africans, who used them only in order to increase their pressure, capitulation to the principle of popular democracy as practiced in West Africa was inevitable.

The second factor was the degree to which Britain was able and willing to use her resources in order to impose her policies on re-calcitrant colonies, but the Suez invasion settled the issue and showed that the days of gunboat colonial policy had passed. In fu-ture Britain would support the successful forces in her colonies, even if she had to wait some time before being able to identify them.

In the meantime Julius Nyerere was proving in Tanganyika that Nkrumah's strategy could succeed in the vastly different environ-ment of East Africa. He based his approach on the power of a mass party, organized throughout the country. Leading it with firmness, tact and good humor, together with the use of his special advantage at the United Nations as representing a Trust Territory, he steadily pressed a retreating Colonial Office towards granting independence. He had little trouble with his Europeans, less than a third of Kenya's community and perhaps somewhat abashed by their neighbors' experience with Mau Mau. In fact, he showed those Europeans and Asians with foresight that their security depended on popular democratic government. In teaching this lesson and securing the cooperation of leading Europeans and Asians, Nyerere certainly eased the transition towards African government in Kenya.

Nyerere's quiet revolution also helped to kill the idea of a white-governed East African Federation. Uganda had been so agitated at the prospect that the Kabaka of Buganda, the most powerful traditionalist monarch, rebelled against British authority and was exiled in consequence. Though delayed by internal disputes, the revulsion against white rule thus expressed ensured that Uganda, once she could find the means of developing a national consciousness superseding communal and traditionalist loyalties, would follow the Tanganyikan example. So white-settler rule, whether territorial or federal, was decisively rejected throughout East Africa. As British policy was now firmly marching along the decolonization road, the only alternative was African government based on popular election.

This verdict was facilitated by the fact that no major economic interests were involved in preserving European hegemony in East Africa. White farmers and businessmen, Asian traders and small industrialists, absorbed most foreign investment. Mining of soda in Kenya, copper in Uganda and diamonds in Tanganyika, never involved the large combines. This factor prevented the white-settler lobby at Westminster ever gaining serious support in the City, which, in any case, was surely convinced after the mid-fifties that European rule in East Africa could only be imposed at the cost of further expensive wars. It also enabled post-independence African governments to show what could be achieved in controlling foreign capital, at least where the large corporations were not operating. The Uganda Development Corporation dominated industrial output in that country, while Nyerere ensured that about 70 percent of Williamson's diamond profit accrued to his treasury. His 1967 Arusha declaration, proclaiming a policy of nationalization in banking, insurance, commerce and some industry, accompanied by austerity and anti-corruption measures, demonstrated a determination, unparalleled in Africa, to exercise African control over the country's economy and to develop social justice amongst his own people. His example was partially followed the next year by Kaunda in Zambia. If the massive corporations were little interested in East Africa, the picture in Central Africa was in complete contrast. Here were to be found Anglo-American and the Selection Trust in copper, Imperial Tobacco, Dunlops, Booker Brothers, Stewart and Lloyd, Metal Box, Turner and Newall, British Oxygen, De Havilland, and many others. In the five years following the war £150 milllon was added to the prewar £50 million British investment in the Rhodesias, while the public debt holding rose from £10 million to £100 million. The Rhodesias certainly became a profitable field for British investment in the postwar period. Northern Rhodesia provided the classic example of a colonial mining enclave. Between 1937 and 1956 output rose from £12 million to £115 million, dividends and royalties from £5.5 million to £34 million. The country's exports, almost entirely composed of copper, provided over 80 percent of her money income, while payments leaving the country varied between a quarter and a half of her export revenues.

Southern Rhodesia, on the other hand, was a white-settled colony, having been ruled first by the British South Africa Company and then, after 1923, directly by the white settlers. Her exports, a third of them tobacco, provided between 40 and 60 percent of her national income. Transfer of profits and dividends again played a prominent part in export earnings, though not as large as in the northern territory, while much of the domestic savings from the white settlers were channelled to London rather than being invested in economic development in the territory.

Yet, despite this large-scale economic interest in the Rhodesias, the political issue remained the same as in East Africa. Could the white settlers, numbering between 200,000 and 300,000 compared to under 100,000 in East Africa, control the governmental machine against the political pressures of the Africans? If they could, capitalist interests and politicians would be prepared to support them as they had in South Africa. If there were risks of serious disturbance, especially of a form requiring British military assistance, allegiances would have to be reconsidered.

It seemed at first that the Europeans were sufficiently powerful to establish a modified form of South African regime. The white Southern Rhodesians, ruling a conquered African population, had demonstrated the possibility. They had maintained political stability and developed a growing European market as immigrants poured in from Britain after the war, attracting considerable investment. But the settlers were greedy. As immigration increased, pressure rose on the social amenities suitable for the comfortable colonial-style life which attracted Europeans. Materials, skilled labor and services were scarce. The whites looked enviously, as they had before the war, at Northern Rhodesia's copper wealth.

The scheme for federation of the two Rhodesias and Nyasaland which was put into operation in 1953 made good capitalist sense for the settler community. Southern Rhodesia had greatly benefited from the war through expenditure by the forces and enforced import substitution in manufactures. If copper profits could be restrained from expatriation through taxation, the two Rhodesias could accumulate capital, as the South Africans had done, to build up their own manufacturing industries, thus becoming economically self-sustaining. Even many members of the British Labour Party believed that federation would be good for the economy of Central Africa. What they did not realize was that it depended on the maintenance of cheap African labor in the mines, where white trade unionists were fighting for the retention of the racial differential, and that it represented the white capitalist alternative to African government which alone could harness wealth production to the people's needs.

Conservative politicians, aided by divided views within the Labour Party, fought hard up to 1959 to preserve the federation. They were even prepared to prejudice peaceful political advance in East Africa lest it might undermine European hegemony in the Rhodesias. As late as March 1959, Lord Perth, from the Colonial Office, was telling Rhodesians that "so far as our general colonial policy is concerned, a halt is being called to the rapid advance of colonial territories to independence. For Tanganyika, for example, we are proposing a long-term program." This speech was made less than three years before Tanganyika's independence and in the midst of the few months which finally killed the multiracial concept in East and Central Africa.

Federation became the Achilles' heel of European Central Africa. What the Europeans had not realized was that Britain was bound to

John Hatch

allow some political rights and provide for certain electoral systems in her protectorates, Nyasaland and Northern Rhodesia, in concert with her general colonial policy. These were bound to stimulate African political activity and the growth of parties; even the restricted, highly qualified federal franchise would have the same consequence. And, although the Europeans might be able to hold the line in the Federation and in Southern Rhodesia, they could hardly expect to do so in the northern territories. There were simply not enough Europeans, while the presence of the Colonial Office in Lusaka and Zomba, with its responsibility to Westminster, would open up channels of debate constantly eroding white supremacy.

So, from a state of quietude before the argument on federation opened in 1951, the morrow of federation found Nkumbula and Kaunda in Northern Rhodesia, Nkomo in Southern Rhodesia and Banda, Chiume and Chipembere in Nyasaland, organizing modern political parties. At first they were of the congress type, but as electoral opportunities in the federation and the territories widened, each party began to organize its branches, determine a constitution, debate policies and strengthen its machinery. The Europeans had ignored the lesson taught by South Africans: that any political rights accorded to the masses must foster political organization, eventually fatal to an oligarchy.

So when the trial of strength opened in 1959 the outcome in Nyasaland and Northern Rhodesia was inevitable. Emergencies might be declared in Southern Rhodesia and Nyasaland; Africans might be killed; leaders like Kaunda, Banda and Nkomo might be imprisoned. As had been found in the rest of British Africa, this only led to martyrdom and in its turn to that charismatic leadership which represented the last nail in the federal coffin. The white community had shown, as in East Africa, that it could not govern without provoking conflict and relying on British help. Henceforth it was doomed to be abandoned by British interests. They quickly turned to making their peace with African leaders destined to become successors to the British governors and to Huggins, Welensky and their white colleagues who had failed to hold the succession. As in East Africa, feeble attempts might be made to stave off the inevitable or to modify the shock, but 1959 saw the defeat of the federal concept and of the white oligarchy which had gambled on its success; the conclusion of federation in 1963 was no more than a funeral four years after the death. The independence celebrations in Malawi and Zambia in 1964 marked the conception of new national lives. The strength of African organization within the British colonial context had successfully challenged European hegemony, forcing it to display its weakness to those most concerned to measure its capacity for preserving that form of stability likely to provide safe conditions for investment.

The collapse of federation and the founding of Malawi and Zambia still left open the issue of Southern Rhodesia. Here the situation was quite different, for the Europeans had been in political control for over forty years and had preserved the basic elements of stability. They had learned only part of the South African lesson, allowing their Africans minimal rights and ruling them as conquered subjects. What remained to be seen was whether the rupture from Zambia would seriously weaken the Rhodesian economy and if contact with the north had stimulated the African population to political organization capable of challenging white hegemony. In the meantime, other factors entered the scene. Rhodesia was left as the residual problem of the British African Empire. With the remainder of her African dependencies now independent states (Bechuanaland became the independent state of Botswana, Basutoland became Lesotho, in 1966; Swaziland followed in 1968), Britain had to calculate whether her interest lay in appeasing the Rhodesian Europeans or in preserving her relations with black Africa. In the event she did neither, ineffectually refusing to recognize the 1965 Rhodesian unilateral declaration of independence, but failing to convince the Africans that she was genuinely trying to replace white oligarchic rule by black democracy. Both the political and the economic future of Rhodesia lay poised in the balance; on the one hand, European Rhodesia had become entirely dependent on the support of the South Africans and Portuguese; on the other, she was refused recognition by the rest of the world, despite the pressure of British Conservatives, some closely linked with Rhodesian business. Meanwhile, guerrilla fighters began to infiltrate across her borders, the standard bearers for the inevitable eventual attack of black Africa on the white southern redoubt.

Harold Macmillan
THE WINDS OF CHANGE

Conservative Prime Minister Macmillan visited South Africa early in 1960, and there delivered his famous "winds of change" speech warning that black nationalism would spread from British West Africa to the East and South-Central territories. The speech is here annotated by Macmillan as it appears in the latest of his five volumes of memoirs.

The meeting took place in a historic building—the Chamber of the old Cape Colony Parliament. The audience amounted to some two hundred and fifty, of which ninety were members of the Senate and the rest of the House of Commons. I sat on a platform with the Prime Minister, the Opposition leaders, the Speaker and one or two other officials. On entering the door there was a polite ripple of applause. Although I had given Dr. Verwoerd an indication of what I intended to say, it was clear that, having merely seen the main outlines, the full effect of the actual text and especially of certain phrases came to him as a surprise, and perhaps a shock. I began by speaking of the pleasure that my wife and I had had in our travels through Africa and of the privilege to be visiting South Africa in 1960, the year of "Golden Wedding of the Union."

> *In the fifty years of their nationhood the people of South Africa have built a strong economy founded upon healthy agriculture and thriving and resilient industries....I have seen the great city of Durban, with its wonderful port, and the skyscrapers of Johannesburg, standing where seventy years ago there was nothing but the open veldt.*

I turned next to Britain's part in this development—nearly two-thirds of the overseas investment outstanding in the Union at the end of 1956 was British. Our economies were now largely interdependent, Britain supplying one-third of all South Africa's imports and buying one-third of all her exports. I spoke of the contribution that South

Africa had made to our common cause during the war and of the technical assistance which she was offering to the less well-developed parts of Africa in time of peace.

I then broached the topic which has caused this speech to be regarded as something of a watershed in African affairs—the emergence of nationalism in the African continent.

Ever since the break-up of the Roman Empire one of the constant facts of political life in Europe has been the emergence of independent nations. They have come into existence over the centuries in different forms, with different kinds of Government, but all have been inspired by a deep, keen feeling of nationalism, which has grown as the nations have grown.

In the twentieth century, and especially since the end of the war, the processes which gave birth to the nation states of Europe have been repeated all over the world. We have seen the awakening of national consciousness in peoples who have for centuries lived in dependence upon some other power. Fifteen years ago this movement spread through Asia. Many countries there of different races and civilizations pressed their claim to an independent national life. Today the same thing is happening in Africa, and the most striking of all the impressions I have formed since I left London a month ago is of the strength of this African national consciousness. In different places it takes different forms, but it is happening everywhere. The wind of change is blowing through this continent, and, whether we like it or not, this growth of national consciousness is a political fact. We must all accept it as a fact, and our national policies must take account of it.

With what some of the critics regarded as a malicious deftness but which was really intended to soften the impact I continued:

Of course, you understand this better than anyone. You are sprung from Europe, the home of nationalism, and here in Africa you have yourselves created a new nation. Indeed, in the history of our times yours will be recorded as the first of the African nationalisms, and this tide of national consciousness which is now rising in Africa is a fact for which you and we and the other nations of the Western World are ultimately responsible. For its causes are to be found in the achievements of Western civilization, in the pushing forward of the frontiers of knowledge, in the applying of science in the service of human needs, in the expanding of food production, in the speeding and multiplying of the means of communication, and perhaps, above all, the spread of education.

Where would these new emerging nations align themselves—with the West or with the Communist East? What guidance would they receive from the independent members of the Commonwealth?

It is a basic principle of our modern Commonwealth that we respect each other's sovereignty in matters of internal policy. At the same time we must recognize that in this shrinking world in which we live today the internal policies of one nation may have effects outside it. We may sometimes be tempted to say to each other "Mind your own business," but in these days I would myself expand the old saying so that it runs: "Mind your own business, but mind how it affects my business, too."

We realized, I told my audience, that what we in the United Kingdom did in the Commonwealth countries now reaching independence must inevitably have consequences for the Union. We would act with full knowledge of the responsibility we had to all our friends; but equally in our own areas we must each do what we thought right; and that must, in our view, include offering the opportunity for an increasing share in political power and responsibility.

I went on to discuss the special problems of countries inhabited by several different races, pointing out that this applied not only to Africa but also, for instance, to Malaya, inhabited by both Chinese and Malays. The United Kingdom's attitude, I said, was expressed by the Foreign Secretary, Selwyn Lloyd, when he spoke at the United Nations General Assembly on 17 September 1959.

These were his words: "In those territories where different races or tribes live side by side the task is to ensure that all the people may enjoy security and freedom and the chance to contribute as individuals to the progress and well being of these countries. We reject the idea of any inherent superiority of one race over another. Our policy therefore is nonracial. It offers a future in which Africans, Europeans, Asians, the peoples of the Pacific and others with whom we are concerned, will all play their full part as citizens in the countries where they live, and in which feelings of race will be submerged in loyalty to new nations."

I recognized that the members of the Union Parliament had to face problems very different from those which confronted the parliaments of countries with homogeneous populations but I added:

As a fellow member of the Commonwealth it is our earnest desire to give South Africa our support and encouragement, but I hope you won't

mind my saying frankly that there are some aspects of your policies
which make it impossible for us to do this without being false to our own
deep convictions about the political destinies of free men to which in
our own territories we are trying to give effect.

I went on to speak of the impossibility, whether for men or nations,
of living in isolation.

What Dr. John Donne said of individual men three hundred years ago is
true today of my country, your country, and all the countries of the world:
"Any man's death diminishes me, because I am involved in Mankind.
And therefore never send to know for whom the bell tolls; it tolls for thee."

It was in this conviction of the interdependence of nations, I told
my audience, that I had made my journey to Moscow in 1959. It was
in this belief that I had encouraged contacts between individuals
and contacts in trade between the Western and the Communist
world. "I certainly do not believe," I said, "in refusing to trade with
people because you may happen to dislike the way they manage
their internal affairs at home." I went on to express my disapproval
of the attempts being made in Britain to boycott South African
goods. It could only have serious effects on Commonwealth relations.

The independent members of the Commonwealth do not always agree on
every subject. It is not a condition of their association that they should
do so. On the contrary, the strength of our Commonwealth lies largely in
the fact that it is a free association of independent sovereign states, each
responsible for ordering its own affairs but cooperating in the pursuit of
common aims and purposes in world affairs. Moreover these differences
may be transitory. In time they may be resolved. Our duty is to see them
in perspective against the background of our long association. Of this at
any rate I am certain—those of us who by grace of the electorate are
temporarily in charge of affairs in your country and in mine, we fleeting
transient phantoms on the great stage of history, we have no right to
sweep aside on this account the friendship that exists between our coun-
tries, for that is the legacy of history.

And I ended:

Let us resolve to build, not to destroy, and let us remember always that
weakness comes from division, strength from unity.

The speech lasted for nearly fifty minutes, and as soon as I sat down Dr. Verwoerd thought it necessary to include in an official vote of thanks an impromptu defense of his policies, putting the case, as he expressed it, "for justice for the white man." The first reactions, however, in the local Press were much less hostile than I expected, and it was not until the news came of the reception of the speech in Britain and throughout the world that criticism combined with a good deal of self-pity and resentment began to develop.

III THE END OF THE FRENCH EMPIRE

Tony Smith

THE FRENCH COLONIAL CONSENSUS AND PEOPLE'S WAR, 1946–1958

The reaction of the French Fourth Republic to the pressures for decolonization was quite different from that of the British. Commentators generally fault the French political system for this failure, saying that its divisions made a clear, forceful policy impossible to develop or apply. This essay argues, to the contrary, that a policy did exist and that it was not the system that made policy formulation impossible. Rather, it was a "colonial consensus" that made success impossible and so ultimately wrecked the political system. The problem, then, is to locate and interrelate the key beliefs of the "collective mind" of the French political elite and to explain their origin and their persistence from the experiences of these leaders.

With the moral enthusiasm born of the Renaissance as well as with the practical realism born of the defeat, France sought immediately after World War II to reinforce her domination over her overseas territories by evidence of a new spirit of reform. On the one hand, the French clearly perceived threats to their continued imperial rule. Their recent and serious defeat at the hands of Germany, the occupation by foreign powers of their colonial possessions in the Levant, the Far East and North Africa, the new rhetoric of anticolonialism heard from the United States and the Soviet Union, and the markedly increased political sophistication of local native elites were well recognized warnings that the future character of the Empire was in question. On the other hand, however, the French were apparently persuaded that the loyalty of the colonies during the war was evidence of the basic solidity of the Empire in the immediate and that native elites would see good reasons of interest stemming from the character of postwar international relations for staying within the redefined French community in the future. De Gaulle set the example of how to conduct a policy of imperial preservation, showing that France must act firmly as well as generously, that although change was necessary, it would be effective in maintaining French rule only where there was a sure sense that it was

Tony Smith, "The French Colonial Consensus and People's War, 1946–1958," *Journal of Contemporary History,* October 1974, Parts II and III. Reprinted by permission. Footnotes omitted.

being brought about to this end. Fortunately for France, national and international duty would once more coincide: continued sovereignty abroad called for reform while reform properly administered would contribute to the maintenance of sovereignty. In the process, the interests of both the colonial peoples and the French would be advanced.

The honeymoon period from 1944 through the first months of 1946, showed some impressive accomplishments. Following the recommendations of the Brazzaville Conference, public authorities checked the worst of past abuses (such as forced labor and special legal codes for natives) and took the first concrete steps toward encouraging the political maturity of the colonial peoples by providing for their representation at the Constituent National Assembly, talking of a future French "federation" (soon to be called the French Union), and projecting increased competence to local political assemblies. The men who succeeded de Gaulle subsequently demonstrated their loyalty to his injunction to be firm in colonial matters as well. Between August 1946 and August 1947, they made this clear to the Vietnamese at Fontainebleau and Haiphong, to the Moroccans with General Juin, to the Madagascans with the repression of April 1947, and to the Algerians by the tone of the new Statute of Algeria.

Enlightened as these reforms appeared at the time in comparison with the colonial practices of the Third Republic, they nonetheless lagged substantially behind the demands being made by certain key colonial nationalists. In the Levant even before the end of the war, independence movements cooperated with by the British had defeated de Gaulle's dogged efforts to maintain special French claims on Syria and Lebanon, under mandate to Paris since the First World War. In Madagascar, Morocco and Tunisia, nationalists had submitted programs calling for independence to the French authorities by 1946. But it was in Algeria and Indochina that nationalists were advancing the most significant demands, for Algeria was by far the most important of France's colonial possessions while the Indochinese appeared the best able to put French policy immediately to the test. Except for parts of Black Africa, slogans of "change within order" and "reform in order to preserve" enlisted little enthusiasm outside metropolitan France.

Despite these contradictions in position, a brief moratorium from the last months of the war through the beginning of the summer of 1946 allowed the various parties involved time to clarify their own stand and that of their interlocutors. The nationalists were, to be sure, calling for independence, but even the Vietnamese were willing to negotiate the timing and character of such an event. For their part, the French were retreating behind the vague but implicitly liberal formula of "independence within the framework of the French Union" whose character the Constituent Assembly (first elected in October 1945, reelected in June 1946) would specify.

It was negotiations with the Vietminh at Fontainebleau in July–August 1946 over the future status of Indochina which first galvanized official French opinion both on this specific issue and on the general question of the French Union (then before the Constitutional Commission of the second Constituent Assembly) to insist that France retain undisturbed sovereignty over the Empire. The decision was crucial, for although de Gaulle had announced the preceding August that France would preserve her position in Indochina (thereby reiterating the terms of the Declaration of March 24, 1945, relative to Indochina, which provided for the effective balkanization of the area under the authority of Paris), and although the French had launched a coup in Saigon on September 23, 1945, to remove the city from Vietminh control, de Gaulle's successors had initially moved more cautiously. Thus the Agreement of March 6, 1946, providing for the return of 15,000 French troops to Tonkin for a period of five years, recognized "the Republic of Vietnam as a free state having its government, its parliament, its army and its finances and forming part of the Indochinese Federation and the French Union." Aside from the obvious ambiguity of the formula "free state . . . part of the Indochinese Federation and the French Union," the negotiators agreed that a future meeting should work out the terms of what the concluding clause called "the diplomatic relations between Vietnam and foreign states, the future status of Indochina and economic and cultural interests."

Even before Fontainebleau, the first Dalat Conference called by the High Commissioner of Indochina d'Argenlieu and the terms of the agreements reached by rulers of Laos and Cambodia with the returning French armies suggested that France was in no mood to equivocate on the reestablishment of her sovereignty in Southeast Asia. Fontainebleau confirmed this. In essence, the French position at this two-month conference represented a choice for the Declaration of March 24, 1945 over the recently concluded and much more liberal provisions of the Agreement of March 6, 1946. Vietnam would be neither united nor independent. Cochin China would continue to be separate from the two northern Ky of Annam and Tonkin while the French negotiators defined the political, military and economic obligations of the Ho Chi Minh Government within the Indochinese Federation and the nascent French Union in such a manner that French sovereignty over the area would in practice be virtually incontestable.

Within days of the close of the Fontainebleau Conference the National Assembly obliged the Constitutional Commission to revise its proposals for the future French Union in such a fashion that this body could never put the imperial authority of Paris in doubt. By the end of September 1946, therefore, the presumed happy marriage between reform and continued French sovereignty in the overseas territories had ended. Not de Gaulle's departure from power (as his supporters loudly maintained) but the inability of his formula for change within order to contain colonial nationalism posed a terrible dilemma for the French. Should they, on the one hand, continue to be liberal and accept the inevitability of the Empire's dissolution, or should they, on the other, shelve reforms which would only facilitate nationalist agitation in favor of assuring the maintenance of the Empire? With the choice for the latter alternative, the rhetoric of reformism—genuine as it was only a short time before—was readied to be debased into a legitimizing mask for colonial "pacification."

Full-scale hostilities finally commenced between the Vietminh and the French in the winter of 1946, only three months after the close of the Fontainebleau Conference. The aging Socialist leader Leon Blum was Prime Minister of France for a short while once again. In an important speech before the National Assembly on December 23, he declared:

> The old colonial system which established possession by conquest and maintained it by constraint, and which aimed at the exploitation of the peoples and the lands conquered, is today out of date. . . . According to

our Republican doctrine, colonial possession reaches its final goal and finds its true justification only the day it ends, that is to say, the day when the colonial people have been made able to live fully free and to govern themselves. The reward of the colonizing people is then to have raised sentiments of gratitude and affection in the colonized people, to have created the interpenetration and the solidarity of thought, culture and interest which will permit each to unite freely with the other. Once this [present] crisis is surmounted, our goal will remain exactly the same. . . . We must faithfully take up the work now interrupted, that is, the organization of a free Vietnam in an Indochinese Union freely associated with the French Union.

But first of all, peaceful order, the necessary base for the execution of contracts, must be restored.

Virtually all the essential aspects of republican colonial doctrine were hereby announced in the first hour of trial. With this speech, Blum rallied to de Gaulle's formula for the future of Indochina under French sovereignty—membership in the Indochinese Union and the French Union—justified it in terms of French humanistic pretensions and supported it with a call to arms.

In January 1947, another Socialist, Paul Ramadier, succeeded Blum as Prime Minister. In his investiture speech, Ramadier made it clear that France would not tolerate rebel aggression against what he called "the historic work of eternal France." On March 18, during a debate over Indochina, Ramadier unilaterally denounced the Agreement of March 6, 1946 (in essence this had already been effected by the Fontainebleau and second Dalat Conferences) claiming that the Constitution of the Fourth Republic now abrogated the earlier accord. Henceforth for Vietnam it was a question of "independence within the framework of the French Union. . . . Today it is no longer a matter of the framework of the treaty of March 6." And France would fight:

We cannot accept peace and order being disturbed. We must protect the lives and possessions of the French, the foreigners and our Indochinese friends who have shown their confidence in French liberty.

Let it be known, he concluded, that "France must remain in Indochina, that her replacement there is not open, and that she must continue her civilizing work." *

---

* See the Ramadier speech reprinted later in this volume—Ed.

Ramadier was also in power when the lackluster Statute of Algeria was finally adopted by the National Assembly in August 1947. During the interwar years a fragmented Muslim political elite had developed in the "three North African departments" and began increasingly to press for independence as the Nazi threat subsided. The Statute was an attempt to redefine the political character of Algeria, providing a remedy to "legitimate" Muslim grievances but assuring the continued rule of France there. The logic of the confrontation in Algeria was such, however, that the two principal groups concerned by the Statute, the settler and Muslim communities, declared it unacceptable and in short order the French administration sabotaged it. In the first elections to the newly constituted Algerian Assembly in April 1948, a Socialist Governor General and a Socialist Minister of the Interior oversaw the systematic rigging of the ballots. Protesting Communist deputies took the case for annulment of the vote to the National Assembly, the Assembly's Commission of the Interior, the Council of the Republic, and the Assembly of the French Union. In each instance, bureaucratic subterfuge managed to provide a disguise behind which the majority of the deputies could kill the Communist motion. Over the six years intervening between the first "good joke" (bonne blague) election, as it was called in Algeria, and the outbreak of the Revolution in November 1954, the practice became established tradition. In 1951, the Communists tried once again to invalidate these proceedings by protesting the Algerian vote to the second legislature of the National Assembly. In August, the Assembly by a vote of 316 to 55 dismissed their motion and accepted the officially reported returns. Among the Socialists voting for the validation of these procedures (as politically inept and dangerous as they were ethically indefensible) were Guy Mollet, Christian Pineau, Jules Moch and Edouard Depreux.

This is not, of course, to say that the Socialists were primarily responsible for the failures of postwar French colonial policy. Rather the point is to mark the limits of parliamentary division by establishing the character of a Socialist commitment to the decision that France should remain fast throughout the Empire. There was, to be sure, important opposition within the Party to the leadership's colonial posture while the Party as a whole stood to the left of the colonial consensus (particularly after the first years of the Indochinese War). But there is ample evidence that the major concerns of the SFIO bound them to, rather than divided them from, the parties to their right. The best illustration of this is the colonial policy of the leader of the left-wing Socialists (in the forties) Guy Mollet, who in January 1956 became the first Socialist Prime Minister since Ramadier's resignation in 1947.

It is important to recall that during the election campaign of December 1955, there was a decided mood of confidence on the French Left and Center-Left that the victory of the so-called Republican Front, associating primarily Guy Mollet and Mendès-France, would bring peace again to Algeria. The conflict there was already more than a year old, and the serious incidents at Philippeville in the department of Constantine the previous October had brought home to the French the gravity of the struggle. In March, the Socialists had refused to vote Prime Minister Faure emergency powers for use in Algeria claiming that his policy of force was inappropriate to the character of the problem. During the election campaign, articles in the two Republican Front periodicals *l'Express* and *Le Populaire* made the Algerian question the chief issue of debate and elaborated a liberal critique of Faure. Headlines denounced the forces of "reaction," warning against both settler pressure groups and the colonial bureaucracy while calling for negotiations with qualified nationalist leaders instead of French puppets like Ben Arafa and Bao Dai. The Republican Front promised, on the contrary, to stop this "blind repression unworthy of France." As Mollet put it two weeks before the balloting:

> The first duty of the government that will be formed after the election will be to restore peace to North Africa. What we must do before all else is to stop lying, to stop repeating the same errors of Indochina, Morocco and Tunisia. Of course we must protect the Algerian populations, but we must stop this blind and imbecile repression.

Yet it was precisely the Mollet Government which committed the Fourth Republic irreversibly to the repression of the Revolution. Shortly after his investiture, Mollet made a trip to Algiers where he assured the settler community of the unequivocal support of the metropole (demonstrated immediately by rescinding the nomination of General Catroux as Governor General). Subsequently, he called up the reserves, committed the conscript army to the "pacification" effort, arranged for the delegation of important civilian powers to the military in Algeria and acquiesced in their arrogation of yet more authority (the most blatant example of which was the Army's arrest of Ben Bella) thereby strengthening Algiers at the expense of Paris. In addition, Mollet denounced "defeatism" at home, increased domestic censorship, purged dissenters from his Party, covered the use of torture by the Army in Algeria and, in the most startlingly clear demonstration of his incomprehension of the problems in North Africa, sanctioned the invasion of Suez in order thereby to quell the Algerian uprising. Throughout the entire process, Mollet maintained a steady barrage of reformist rhetoric designed to assure the Muslim population (and thereby the conscience of Jacobin France) that Algeria's continued existence under French rule was in their own best interest. Thus Suez marked the fulfillment of Mollet's "international duty." In regard to Algeria, he declared:

> ... The Socialist concern is to spare the dependent peoples the nationalist phase [of historical development]. We believe that a people can see its desire for emancipation and its will to be free from all oppression satisfied, without at the same time giving in to a reaction of isolation and retreat which characterizes nationalism.

Or again, he contrasted the benefits of French rule to those of "an independence which would have as its certain consequence an economic and social regression and a political regression to a dictatorship or to the quasi-feudal regime of one of the Arab States. Would this be progress?" On the terms of a settlement he was adamant (as his decision to invade Suez best evidences): Algeria would remain French. Even after he had left power, Mollet was to remain a guiding spirit in the attempts to draw up a political reform bill for Algeria. The ultimate product of these labors was the ill-starred loi-cadre of 1957. As he put it in his investiture speech:

> The world expects much of France, of her traditional generosity, of her daring to walk the path of great, worthwhile changes. This role will be fully assumed only if we show ourselves equally daring and generous towards the overseas peoples.... We will show to these people who are our friends that, faithful to her liberating mission, France will lead them to freedom.*

---

* See also a speech of Mollet's partly reprinted later in this volume—Ed.

Mollet's actions were not the consequence of some personal failing, as is sometimes alleged, but the logical development of a train
of thought of far more general currency on the French non-Communist Left. Thus one of the most striking aspects of this entire
charade was that even Mollet's most outspoken critics—men like
Mendès-France and André Philip—shared his same basic assumptions. As late as 1957, most of these leftist leaders, still blinded by
their patriotism to the realities of a conflict nearly three years old,
continued to believe that Algeria could be made secure for France.
Their disagreement with Mollet was over means, not over ends. Reform coupled with force could still produce the "psychological
shock," a term current in these circles at the time, necessary to
bring the Muslim community to the side of the French. Since 1955,
there had been a veritable deluge of articles in Center-Left publications such as *La Nef, l'Express* and *Esprit* on the virtue of different
schemes like "federalism" intended to grant significant political reform in the colonies while assuring a continued French presence
there. These projects made far more sense in regard to Africa south
of the Sahara, as the Defferre reforms of this period illustrate, than
they did to Algeria where political mobilization and consciousness
was much more advanced. The remedy to the conflict, then, was not
to call for more reforms but to see beyond reformism to the possibility of independence.

After 1945, France found she could not be both democratic and
sovereign in Algeria as she had hoped. Caught between their scru-
ples and their ambitions, the French tried to effect a compromise in
Algeria by way of reform. But as the Statute of Algeria demonstrated
as early as 1947, modest reforms would only anger the Muslims and
alarm the settlers. Neither democratic nor totalitarian resolutely in
their "three North African departments," the French failed to institu-
tionalize either of the two forms of rule which have survived the test
of twentieth-century mass political mobilization. Instead their presence was characterized by a lethal mixture of liberality, which allowed discontent to organize in labor unions and political parties,
authoritarianism, which in ignorance and fear refused to satisfy the
demands it had allowed to collect by arresting nationalist leaders
and tricking elections, and neglect, which (true to the pattern familiar under the Third Republic as well) was the favored road to pursue where no one position on a problem could be consistently

adopted. It was this untenable contradiction, far more than repression alone, which set French rule off from that in South Africa and which explains an important part of the Revolution's origin and success. In their clumsy efforts successively to repress, to allay, or worst of all perhaps to disregard Muslim hostility through stratagems of self-deception, the French failed to deal at all effectively with the increasingly conscious and organized native leadership first of the interwar period and then after World War II.

Years before the Revolution began the contradiction between reform and continued sovereignty opened. Obliged to choose, the French opted first for fraud then for force in deciding to maintain their sovereignty at the expense of their liberalism. Simultaneously, reformism began to make up in stridence for what it still lacked in substance. In the process, self-deception became the Republic's trademark. How appropriate, then, that after months of feverish debate and the fall of the Bourgès Government over it, the most spectacularly misconceived formula for governing Algeria in 128 years of French rule—the loi-cadre of 1957–1958—should have become law, only to be annulled 15 weeks later by the collapse of the Fourth Republic.

If we put aside explanations for the French colonial imbroglio which center on the character of the political system, rational calculations offer some basis for understanding why France tried so persistently to maintain her sovereignty over Algeria. The experience of 125 years of French rule had created of this area less than 500 miles south of Marseille a colony unequalled in terms of trade, political bonds and demonstrated strategic worth. The actual size of the country—four times that of France—had only symbolic importance since most of it was mountain or desert waste. But Algeria was France's largest colonial trading partner and the significance of North Africa as a base for military operations during World War II served to put its strategic worth beyond question. Of great importance in addition was the political weight of Algeria's settler community—one million strong, some 12 percent of the local population —which had rooted itself in Paris and in the colonial bureaucracy in Algiers long before the difficult problems of decolonization arose. The French could claim with some justice that they had moral obligations to the Muslim and settler communities as well. All these arguments ultimately converged, however, on a single point: the loss of Algeria meant the irrevocable decline of France to second-power rank. Prime Ministers Mendès-France, Faure and Mollet each declared in turn that this historical development was intolerable and would not be accepted.

Here was the first important link in a series of agreements which fatally united republican France's definition of the national interest to that of the military-colonialist alliance: the preservation of Algeria under French sovereignty was beyond negotiation. When the Governments of the Fourth (and eventually the Fifth) Republic appeared to be defaulting on their acknowledged responsibility, other more "healthy" segments of the society which had seen this happen before in the thirties and again over Indochina had the right—indeed the obligation—to fulfill the nation's duty to itself. The chief intellectual proponent of such extralegal action was Jacques Soustelle, noted scholar of pre-Columbian America, close associate of General de Gaulle, Governor General of Algeria from early in 1955 to February 1956, parliamentarian and brilliant polemicist in defense of the cause of French Algeria. What is so remarkable about Soustelle's speeches and writings—and what makes him in my opinion the most instructive thinker on the tormented mind of France during this period—is not so much his extremism and vituperation as the resonance his diagnosis found so often in the ranks of republican France. As he stated it frequently, the end of France as a "Euro-African power" meant the end of France as "a power, period":

> *Algeria lost . . . would equal in depth and consequence the most horrible defeats in our history . . . it is clear that if France lets herself be backed into a situation where she is led to abandon Algeria, it is not only Algeria which would be lost, it would be Africa. And in losing Africa, France would lose at the same time her future. I fear that if such a misfortune should befall us, then France, plunged into a humiliation which would embitter her against herself and others, leaving her open to all the temptations of xenophobia, distrust and despair, might fall into the worst of adventures.*

Soustelle's charge was even more basic yet. It was not simply that the loss of Algeria would remove France definitively from the ranks of the great powers, *but that this move would be an act of her own doing:*

In reality, the drama is not that of Algeria. It is that of decadence. . . . To abandon Algeria is to condemn France to decadence; to save Algeria is to call a halt to this terrible process of degradation, is to return to our country, to its people, to its youth their chance and their future.

The Gaullist strains in such statements are unmistakable. Indeed no man better illustrates republican France's parentage of the extremist Algérie française movement than Jacques Soustelle. In this same vein, however much the partisans of French Algeria might lay the *outbreak* of the insurrection to the connivances of foreign capitals like Moscow and Cairo, their account of the Revolution's perseverance centered on the ineptitude of the Fourth Republic to lead a successful struggle and, more basically, on the inability of a decadent bourgeoisie to rally in its own defense. A content analysis of the political images generated by colonialist extremists shows them viewing themselves as resolutely masculine, tough and decided, while depicting the supporters of the Fourth Republic as effete Frenchmen who lacked the backbone and spittle to make Algeria theirs.

The point is key, for far too often republican France seemed to give its assent, fearing that these accusers in giving voice to their own most secret fears might be right, that a "nation of cowards" was losing the glorious heritage of France. The examples of the thirties, World War II and Indochina were there for all to see. Catastrophe had come from a divided paralyzed government unable to provide the leadership the country so desperately needed. And it was happening once again. Government crises, incessant quarrelling when a government was in power, errors committed, acts undone—the responsibility for the debacle in Algeria could squarely be pinpointed on a system of rule. As Mollet put it in describing the popular reaction to the military insurrection against civilian authority when it finally came in 1958:

The police, Army and administration were in rout. Organize this vast and profound reaction? Of course this is what we wanted to do. Throughout an entire night, representatives of the free labor unions came through my office. The result of our consultations was clear: the working class, not because of softness but because of incomprehension, would stay quiet. They were not ready to fight for this disqualified form of government, this impotent Republic.

The argument is a familiar one by now; French failure lay not in what it proposed that the future of Algeria be, but in the political system which was charged to carry this decision out. Yet as may be recalled, Mollet entered office with a mandate to end the war, with a large backing in the National Assembly, with the determination to give top priority to the Algerian question, and with an opposition which was relatively weak and divided. The shortcoming of the Fourth Republic lay not so much in its divisions and weakness at this particular point in time but rather in its united decision to keep Algeria French. The failure of the Fourth Republic, as Mollet saw it, was its inability to hold on to Algeria—not in its inability to let go. This explains in part the persistence of the reformist mentality. Instead of seeing that his *policy* was at fault for the lengthening war, he assumed that the fault lay with his *regime,* "this disqualified form of government, this impotent Republic":

> *...The rebels knew that the Governments of the Fourth Republic were particularly fragile; they counted, moreover, not only on the fatigue and the discouragement of our people, but also on the moral aid, if not material, that they were accorded by the Communists and a number of partisan propogandists or naive advocates. For my part, I believe that nothing did so much as these internal divisions among the French to reinforce the most intransigent among the FLN.*

Just as both the colonialist alliance and the leaders of republican France believed in their respective fashions that the *perseverence* of the Revolution depended on the weakness of the French State, so they both held outside predators seeking to claim the Empire as part of the spoils of World War II responsible for the *origin* of postwar colonial unrest. The French were extremely sensitive to British maneuvers, especially in the Middle East, while they both distrusted American intentions toward Indochina and North Africa and resented their reliance on American economic and military aid. But their special distrust was reserved for what they consider the machinations of international communism and its latest ally pan-Arabism. As early as 1947, de Gaulle reintroduced the charge of Communist sponsorship of local disruptions into North African politics in a speech at Algiers in October. In so doing, he was revitalizing a theme as old as the French Communist Party. Increasingly, however, pan-Arabism had become the scapegoat for disorders in Algeria, though its close affiliation with Moscow was generally recalled. The result was Suez. The high-flown justifications, the transparent lies, the irony of a Socialist Government commandeering an expedition in defense of this sacred enclave of capitalist imperialism throw into sharp focus the irreality of French thinking about Algeria. For as General Challe who led the French forces attests, Paris "sought the conclusion of the Algerian problem at Suez." Hence Suez was "an episode linked to Algeria both in timing and strategy, by its motives and consequences." According to Mollet, the fundamental rationale of the French action was an "anti-Munich reflex" which he claimed was common to the majority of Frenchmen when faced with the menace of Nasser. An interesting report, produced by Herbert Luethy and David Rodnick at the time of the invasion, suggests that Mollet was correct to believe a considerable number of his fellow countrymen agreed with him. To end the troubles in Algeria, the French must first settle what they called the "Egyptian preliminary" (*préalable égyptien*). As Socialist Resident Minister Lacoste summed up this mood, "One French division in Egypt is worth four in North Africa."

Leuthy and Rodnick document the prevalence of another important theme as well which this present study suggests is basic to an understanding of the period: the French had had enough of international reversals. After World War II, the Levant, Indochina, Tunisia and Morocco, they had decided to make a stand in Algeria. Their national pride would retreat no farther. Alexander Werth coined a widely used phrase to describe this period of patriotic fervor: "National-Molletism." Concerns such as these were what made the extremist colonial group the Secret Army Organization (OAS) first of all French and only quite secondarily "fascist." Thus behind the persistence of the reformist rhetoric which mistakenly maintained that France could be both liberal and sovereign in Algeria, just as behind the invasion of Suez, lay the basic terms of the colonial consensus. And the consequence of this consensus, in turn, was the inability of the Fourth Republic effectively to deal with the issue of decolonization. It is this consensus which must be understood to grasp the vicissitudes of the political system, just as the system must be understood to grasp the vicissitudes of the consensus.

The logic of the consensus grew from the lessons a generation of men had learned from the bitter experiences of the thirties, World War II and Indochina. Time and again, weak and divided governments had not faced up to the challenges of the world and the country had suffered humiliating defeat. Hence the prevalence throughout the life of the Fourth Republic of appeals to Frenchmen to unite, to will victory in order that it be theirs. "The fault is not in our stars but in ourselves that we are underlings," said Cassius to Brutus as he urged him to imprudent action in Shakespeare's *Julius Caesar*. So Colonial Minister Moutet put it before the Constitutional Commission in August 1946:

> *Does France really consider herself as uniting 110 million souls or rather does she wish to retire into herself, considering herself only as a people of 40 million? Will France be a great power or will she not?*

Hence Soustelle's Jacobin credentials were quite in order when he juxtaposed "a great multi-cultural and multi-racial France" to a France without Algeria, to a France "faint-heartedly pulled inside her hexagon . . . the choice of a cowardly bourgeoisie." Elsewhere he championed France's need for spiritual lebensraum:

> *France needs a "Far West!" She has one: it is her "Far South." Instead of closing herself cowardly into her European territory in search of petit bourgeois comforts, she would draw from Africa the taste of great spaces and bold undertakings.*

As the crises in the Empire multiplied, so did the appeals to the force of will to overcome greater odds. The self-perpetuating cycle of disintegration ran from stubborness in opposing the force of history, to defeat, to loss of confidence, back to a renewed stubborness. Nowhere is this better expressed, perhaps, than in the words of the great old Governor General of Algeria Viollette speaking late in 1953 of the possibility of negotiations with Ho Chi Minh:

> *I protest with all my energy against actions so humiliating—I was going to say so shameful. . . . I am afraid, and I begin to ask myself—and this would be serious—if perhaps what France needs is not the dynamism of the French (l'élan des Français).*

All the French had learned from eight years of warfare in Indochina was a destructive self-doubt. Afterwards there was the premonition that Algeria too would be lost, just as Indochina had been, not because of the objective obstacles to French rule stemming from the development of the colonial societies but because "this disqualified form of government, this impotent Republic" would lay France low once again.

The postwar decision by the political leaders of France to base their country's return to international greatness on the preservation of the Empire followed an established logic in French thinking. At least since the defeat of 1870, the impending decline of the nation's international rank had troubled its leaders. Under the auspices of Jules Ferry, France had conducted a vigorous imperial policy to compensate both symbolically and materially for the burning loss of Alsace and Lorraine. The persistence of French Malthusianism through the first decades of the twentieth century combined with the demonstrated value of the Empire during World War I to silence most anti-colonial sentiment. After 1919, most critics sought to reform, not to end, French imperial rule. The young French Communist Party was virtually the only exception to this trend. Thus long before the leaders of the Fourth Republic began to elaborate a policy for the Empire, the Third Republic had established what would come to be two of its most important features. First, the Third Republic witnessed the gradual demobilization of leftist colonial criticism, thereby paving the way for the later collaboration of the French Socialist Party with the forces of imperial reaction. Second, and more importantly, domestic vitality came to be identified with international greatness which in turn was indissociable from imperial rule. The competition with other powers for the possession of territory, the celebration of bold explorers and military heroes, the evocation of French colonial greatness in classroom texts, parades and fairs became part of the collective conscience of the nation, putting a damper on the fires of class and cultural conflict at the same time as they were a stimulus to national pride and solidarity. In France as in other countries of Europe, nationalism and imperialism were twins.

It was no coincidence, therefore, that de Gaulle embarked on a policy of imperial preservation after World War II. On the one hand, as the General frequently noted, the strategic and material contribution of the Empire to the forces of Free France had been decisive.

On the other hand, however, de Gaulle did not see French strength as an end in itself but as a means in the service of the spiritual needs of his nation. As he told President Roosevelt:

> *I know that you are preparing to aid France materially, and that aid will be invaluable to her. But it is in the political realm that she must recover her vigor, her self-reliance and, consequently, her role. How can she do this if she is excluded from the organization of the great world powers and their decisions, if she loses her African and Asian territories—in short, if the settlement of the war definitely imposes upon her the psychology of the vanquished?*

"France cannot be France without greatness" wrote de Gaulle in the most celebrated phrase of his *War Memoirs*. France, in other words, could only recover her self-confidence through standing up to the challenges which the world was sure to throw at her. In the process of affirming her greatness, she would recover herself. This is the spirit of what Stanley Hoffmann has called the General's *"jacobinisme dressé contre la décadence,"* de Gaulle's

> *will to exorcize the demons of doubt and dispersion, of disorder and decline that made him repeat that a great international undertaking was indispensable as much to "what all the universe expects of us" as to "what the self-esteem and hope of our people demands."*

In this sense, the General's emphasis on the unity of France above factional disputes and his constant concern that this unity be both achieved and expressed through an ambitious foreign policy grew from a well-established Jacobin tradition and would lead him naturally to an ambitious colonial policy in the aftermath of World War II.

With the fatality of a Greek drama, his stirring crusade for national regeneration showed its tragic flaw in its excess of virtue. De Gaulle's fateful words sum up the disaster:

> *In Europe, in Africa, in Asia where France had suffered an unprecedented abasement, an astonishing recovery and an extraordinary combination of circumstances already offered her the opportunity to play a role in accord with her genius.*

In the years immediately following his departure from power in January 1946, the General urged a firm hand in regard both to Indo-

china and to Algeria, reiterating that the loss of these French possessions would be an unpardonable failing on the part of the Fourth
Republic. Unfortunately, his successors clung to this vision of the
world. Henceforth, try as they would to free themselves from the
humiliation of the disaster of 1940 and give birth to the renewed
sentiment of Jacobin mission which the Resistance had inspired,
the leaders of the country would only bring more disaster upon the
land through the pursuit of an ambitious imperial policy.

Public opinion polls reflect the character of the colonialist mind
as well. While the number of Frenchmen favoring the full integration
of Algeria into France fell between October 1955 and September
1957 from 47 percent to 36 percent, only 18 percent of those inter-
viewed called for granting Algeria independence while 34 percent
called for a solution giving Algeria "internal autonomy . . . within the
French Republic" (the remaining 12 percent expressing no opinion).
Most significant in marking the breadth of the colonial consensus
three years after the Revolution's outbreak—and the place of the
Communists outside it—were the answers to a number of questions
where respondants identified the political party of their allegiance
(see Table 1).

France in the postwar period was a nation whose leaders were
morbidly preoccupied with power. Socialist concerns in this respect
were little different from those of the majority of their fellow countrymen. German power had conquered them, American or Soviet
power now threatened to overwhelm them, but it was especially
their own power—or more precisely, lack thereof—which tormented
them. They had determined on a rebirth of national power as a
means to assuage the pain of a humiliating impotence. This sensitive point was not forgotten by the enemies of the regime—de
Gaulle and the military-colonialist alliance—who exploited it on every
possible occasion. Reversals, when they came in the Empire then,
were not seen so much in terms of the internal development of the
colonial societies, the character of the new international order, and
the corresponding power of local nationalist groups, but as reflec-
tions of French inadequacy. In this sense, Algeria was, as it was
often said, the "last chance" upon which France would found her
salvation or her eternal fall. Algeria's loss or preservation was not,
therefore, an end to be weighed against the means to be used or

TABLE I
Party Affiliation and Position on Algeria (in percent)

	PCF	SFIO	Rad.	MRP	Indep. Moderates	Rep.-Soc. URAS ARS	Others
The majority of Muslims:							
—supports the rebels.	75%	20%	21%	14%	17%	18%	21%
—does not support them.	11	49	49	56	50	57	25
The call for independence:							
—is justified.	88	34	30	27	21	23	31
—is not justified.	7	51	54	60	61	60	42
In the overseas territories France has done:							
—very good work.	5	28	28	22	37	32	—
—rather good work.	23	48	51	52	43	46	—
Between two extremes I would choose:							
—to give Algeria independence.	89	31	43	35	19	—	39
—to use all possible military means to crush the rebellion.	2	48	41	41	58	—	28

against other ends. It was a stake of unique and complete importance, closed to bargaining. To submit to "defeat" would solve nothing; indeed it would only aggravate the very causes of failure. The
moral was clear: French defeats were largely self-inflicted; to reverse the course of events, France must pull herself together and
win. "The victory is more than half won," declared Socialist Resident Minister Lacoste on May 8, 1958. "It will be certain the day
when those who lead France understand that there is no longer any
room for the pessimists—the 'willful pessimists'—and show a determination without hesitation and fully expressed, despite the incomprehension of our allies." Here was a potentially fatal pattern of
interpreting events since the perceived lessons of history only confirmed French misconceptions of its logic. Colonial confrontations
in general—but Algeria in particular—became a testing ground
where the French felt called upon to prove themselves and where
they risked to confirm their own bad image of themselves by failing
once again. The entire process had a self-aggravating momentum
with one setback preparing the scene for another. It was like fighting quicksand—each effort to right the course of history only made
it all the more difficult to control.

In a library in Paris there is a forgotten journal of an officer who
fought with Bugeaud in the first French campaigns in Algeria against
the warrior chieftain Abd el-Kader. After the description of a total
rout of Arab tribesmen in circumstances which sounded like a massacre, the writer concluded: "We had beaten the British." Over the
100 years separating the final surrender of el-Kader and the beginning of the Algerian Revolution in 1954, this scene was to replay itself in various ways time and again. What Algeria represented to
most Frenchmen of all political persuasions had far less to do with
the actual situation in North Africa than with other concerns, domestic or international, which had developed for the most part quite
independently of what the Third Republic had come to call its "three
North African departments." France had always used the Empire as
the powerful do the weak, reckoning it a counter in interests Paris
had elsewhere, able first to neglect then to mythologize about the
native populations. In the case of Algeria especially, one wonders
whether the Revolution of 1954, such as it was in leadership, mass
following, justification and promise ever escaped serious distortion

in the eyes of most of the political leaders of the Fourth Republic, whose hopes and fears made the reality of this land as distant as it was for that officer who in killing some poor Berbers thought he was revenging the defeat at Waterloo.

Prime Minister Ramadier
THE FRENCH STAND IN INDOCHINA, MARCH 18, 1947

The Ramadier Government, formed in January 1947, was the first ministry operating under the terms of the Fourth Republic's newly ratified Constitution. It was the obligation of this government and its Socialist Prime Minister, therefore, officially to define the Republic's policy toward the first major uprising to threaten the integrity of the Empire—the Indochinese Revolution. The question was not a new one before the French parliamentarians, however. In his Declaration of March 24, 1945, General de Gaulle, then head of the Provisional French Government, made it clear that whatever formal changes might occur in the relations between France and Vietnam, Paris would remain firmly in control. In September 1945 French soldiers returning to Saigon after the Japanese surrender there confirmed de Gaulle's intentions by launching a coup against the Vietminh regime in control of the city. But then on March 6, 1946, two months after de Gaulle's departure from power, the French concluded a significantly more liberal accord with Ho Chi Minh in Hanoi "recognizing the Republic of Vietnam as a free State, having its Government, its parliament, its army and its finances belonging to the Indochinese Federation and the French Union." At the Fontainebleau Conference during the summer of 1946, however, the French reversed themselves once again, exploiting the obvious ambiguity of the accord (since in the phrase cited, the first part conceded sovereignty while the latter seemed to limit it), and sought to impose on Ho Chi Minh virtually the same conditions as those laid out in the Declaration of March 1945. In November 1946, the French fleet shelled Haiphong, causing several thousand civilian casualties. In December, the Vietnamese attempted a coup against the French in Hanoi and the most momentous of the wars of decolonization was underway.

Reprinted from the *Journal Officiel de la République française,* Débats Parlementaires, March 18, 1947, pp. 904–905. Translated by Tony Smith.

Ramadier's speech of March 18, 1947, is important in two respects. First, it climaxed eight days of debate in the National Assembly and constituted the first considered public decisions made by the Fourth Republic's political elite that concerned not intentions but actions toward the empire: France would fight challengers to her sovereignty. Secondly, for a Socialist Prime Minister and a Socialist Minister for the Colonies (Moutet) to take the lead in striking a belligerent stance demonstrates the popularity of the policy with all but the Communists. A comparison of this speech with those made by Attlee in 1946 and 1947, reprinted earlier in this volume, suggests the great difference in national mood between France and Great Britain.

(To understand parts of this speech, the reader should know that in the French National Assembly deputies sit with their parties in a semicircle from right to left according to their ideological patents. Thus "applause from the extreme left," for example, means it comes from the Communists.)

The Prime Minister (Ramadier): Ladies and gentlemen, two things are certain, affirmed by all and should be considered as unanimous conclusions of this debate.

The first is that France must stay in Indochina, that her succession there is not in question and that she must carry out there her civilizing work. *(Applause from the left, center and right.)*

The second is that the old ways are over. They have been criticized, they have been praised. There have assuredly been excesses. There have also been glorious pages written. A work has been accomplished which no one can deny, least of all probably those in the ranks of our opponents who came to gain their culture from our hands. *(Applause from the same benches.)* These are two certain facts, two established principles. Faced with the situation in Indochina we have wanted to have a policy of understanding. . . . Perhaps we have been carried away too quickly by the events; we have treated, we have negotiated. For almost a year, from March 6 until the morning of December 19, we have not ceased to negotiate.

The Overseas Minister (Moutet): Very good!

The Prime Minister: And then, on the 19th of December, we were obliged to recognize that the negotiations, even the accords, did not settle everything and that certain acts of violence, of savagery, tore up all the accords and ruined any thought of conciliation.

I have here, ladies and gentlemen, photographs of the mutilated bodies found in the burned-out houses of Hanoi. But perhaps more than any other act of savagery, the total destruction of the Pasteur

Institute is the symbol of a wild, destructive will which is not, I am sure, that of the Vietnamese people, but of certain men.

We were then obliged to fight.

Everyone has accepted this struggle, from the time of Leon Blum's Government just as at the moment, on January 21, when I made my declaration [of investiture] before the National Assembly. *(Applause from the left, center and right.)*

At that time I said: "We cannot accept that the peace be disturbed. We must protect the life and the goods of those Frenchmen, foreigners and our Indochinese friends who put their confidence in French liberty. We must assure the security of our forts, reestablish essential communications and insure the security of the people who seek refuge with us."

This we have done.

The Government has sent the necessary reinforcements. We have sent them in force and as fast as we could. Not all have yet left. The departures continue. But already we can confirm the results.

And it is here that I want to render homage to our Far East Expeditionary Forces, to those soldiers who fight in a climate they are not used to, with a French faith which allows them to hold and to advance under the most difficult circumstances.

They have shown their heroism. France should express her gratitude. *(Prolonged applause from the left, center and right. The deputies seated on these benches rise.)*

(Numerous voices from the right and center call to the extreme left [i.e., to the Communists] "Get up!" From the center: "It is a disgrace to remain seated!")

René Pleven: I see that the Minister of Defense [Billoux, a Communist] has not risen. *(Exclamations from the extreme left.)*

Florimond Bonte [Communist]: It is we who defend the lives of our soldiers. We are not at your command! *(Exclamations from the right.)*

The President: The Prime Minister has the floor. It is to him alone at this time to express the sentiment of the Assembly and the country.

The Prime Minister: France should render homage to those who have fallen. France should render homage to those who fight and who continue to fight. *(Applause from the left, center and right. The deputies seated on these benches rise again.)*

Fernand Bouxom: France rises!

The Prime Minister: She can proudly recognize the results obtained. We were speaking of forts it was necessary to open, of communication lines to reestablish along the Chinese border between Langson and the sea. Communications have been reestablished. From Hanoi to Haiphong, the road is open. A clever and audacious operation launched by troops from Tourane and a detachment from Savanaket have permitted us to rejoin the Mekong to the sea. Recently, on Government orders, Nam-Dinh has been cleared of the enemy. *(Applause to the left, center and right.)* . . .

There is no solution but a political solution. Now we must build. And we know what it is we must build. We know because the Constitution says it. . . . Within the framework of the French Union we are going to create and organize an association of nations and peoples who will put or coordinate in common their resources and their efforts in order to develop their respective civilizations, increase their well-being, and insure their security. Not domination, not subjugation: association. We are not masters who have just spoken as masters. We want to be instructors and counsellors. We are associates. This implies that we respect the independence of peoples. The preamble of the Constitution prescribes it: "Faithful to her traditional mission, France intends to guide the peoples for whom she has responsibility into freedom to administer themselves and conduct their own affairs democratically."

That is why, last January 21, I stated before you: independence within the framework of the French Union, that is the right to conduct and administer democratically their own affairs, to choose their government, to fix the framework in which the Vietnamese people want to live. We expressed no preference. We were not going to impose our views. We recognize, we proclaim, we assure liberty—entirely and completely.

I also said: union of the three Vietnamese countries if the Vietnamese people wish, and I should have added, in the manner they wish.* We know without any question that the Vietnamese peoples have a feeling of their common culture and history, as well as of

---

* France conquered Indochina over more than a 30-year period and so could claim that not only were Cambodia and Laos distinct from Vietnam, but that this latter country, in turn, was composed of three distinct parts: Cochin China (capital, Saigon); Annam (capital, Hue); and Tonkin (capital, Hanoi).—Ed.

their differences, and that they want at once a certain unity and a certain flexibility within this unity. We want to respect their will just as we want to have respected the will of those other peoples, the Cambodians, the Laotians and the Montagnards. Here we are the servants of liberty, and the cause of the French Union and of French influence is tied to this cause of liberty. . . .

From xenophobia, that mindless hatred of the foreigner, we have everything to fear because it is negative and rests upon hatred. But from patriotism we have nothing to fear so long as we remember to respect the liberty of others. In Vietnam we will see new republics built with new liberties knowing, after all, that if the word liberty can be spoken in the Far East it is because France spoke it there first. *(Applause from the left, center and right.)* But this cannot be realized except within the framework of the French Union which, in addition to such broad freedom, implies mutual obligations as well. The 62nd article of the French Constitution states that "the members of the French Union will pool all their resources in order to guarantee the defense of the entire Union. The Government of the Republic shall see to the coordination of these resources and to the direction of the policy appropriate to prepare and assure this defense."

That is to say that all these countries share a common foreign policy and military defense and that the French Republic is charged in the interest of all to direct them.*

Most probably this was not clearly indicated in the Treaty of March 6. The Constitution had not then been approved; it had not even been written. Today there is no longer any question of the framework of the Treaty of March 6. We can only be bound by the framework of the new Constitution which offers the possibility of a constructive effort. . . .

In order for this work to be accomplished, it is first of all necessary that France—that all of France—wants it and that it not be the

---

* The structure of the French Union was spelled out in articles 60 through 82 of the Constitution. The 62nd article, which Ramadier quotes here, was the most important. In addition, article 66 provided for half the deputies to the Assembly of the Union to be from metropolitan France; article 71 made it impossible for the Assembly of the Union to initiate any legislation, restricting it to a review of legislation concerning the member states and territories, although without any power of revision or veto. In short, the 23 articles of the French Union insured the continued sovereignty of Paris over the former Empire. Legalistic studies that weigh the "assimilationist" against the "federalistic" features of the document commonly obscure this basic point.—Ed.

policy of a majority against a minority, but the policy of France, wanted by her Assembly, wanted by her Parliament. . . . I address [the Communists]: this is our policy. It is the policy of freedom. It is the policy of the French Union. You accept this policy or you refuse it: here is the issue. *(Sharp applause from the left, center and right.)* . . .

Prime Minister Mollet
THE FRENCH STAND IN ALGERIA, MARCH 27, 1957

How ironic that Mollet, who had opposed Ramadier's Indochina policy a decade earlier because it was so repressive, should adopt the same policy himself once in office and faced by an insurrection in Algeria. The irony is compounded when one considers that Mollet came to power in January 1956, after 15 months of fighting in North Africa, on a platform promising to bring peace to Algeria. The Mollet Government—the longest-lived in the history of the Fourth Republic, lasting nearly 18 months—committed France wholeheartedly to the preservation of French Algeria and so marked the decisive period of this Republic's involvement there. The continued resistance of the Algerian nationalists prompted a civilian uprising among the North African settler population, which was abetted by the French military. Less than a year after Mollet's departure from power, the Fourth Republic fell.

The themes of Mollet's speech are characteristic of the period—as this selection demonstrates—as much among the men who believed themselves to be on the political Left, like the Prime Minister himself, as from the more vociferous proponents of Algérie française. Here, then, Mollet expresses concerns common to most Frenchmen: that the Republic show itself decided to prosecute the war and be firm against "abandon"; that the nation's worst enemy might be its own lack of confidence; that programs obviously designed to continue Paris's control over Algeria be called "emancipation" for the Muslim population; and that (in sections not reproduced) the army be defended from charges (later proved to be true) of wholesale torture of Algerian nationalists. Five years after his term in office, Mollet, still head of the French Socialist Party, continued to confirm the correctness of his

Reprinted from the *Journal Officiel de la République française*, Débats Parlementaires, March 27, 1957, pp. 1907 ff. Translated by Tony Smith.

earlier policy in two short books: Bilan et perspective socialistes *and* 13 mai 1958–13 mai 1962.

Guy Mollet, Prime Minister: ... France intends to maintain indissoluble ties with Algeria and to assure the coexistence in justice and equality of the collectivities which people Algeria. France proposes to guide the overseas peoples which are linked to her to the democratic administration of their own affairs while assisting their economic and social development. She intends, in particular, to assure the development of the Sahara's ample resources for the common benefit of Africa and the metropole. France also intends to continue her own national development in all its aspects—be it intellectual, industrial, agricultural or housing investments—and particularly atomic development. France intends to prepare her economy for its entrance into the European Common Market. She wants social legislation and a more just distribution of national income. Finally, France intends to give her full support to European and Atlantic defense.

Who among you would permit France to abandon the responsibilities she has assumed in all domains, in Algeria, overseas, in Europe and in the world? Not a single republican deputy, I am sure. ...

The Government has never ceased to give an absolute priority to the necessities of Algeria. It has never hesitated before measures which might have appeared nonetheless very unpopular. The Resident Minister in Algeria, Robert Lacoste, to whose courage and tenacity I would like once again to render homage, has always found in the Prime Minister and the entire Government the unreserved support which he has the right to expect. ... Corroborating information has led me to the conviction that a wait-and-see attitude on the part of our adversaries in Algeria—an attitude which manifests itself in a maddening refusal of propositions which all democratic nations have recognized as equitable—comes from their hope in a change of French policy. Last Friday, their spokesman confirmed, with some cynicism, that "in order to obtain victory" the FLN was counting especially on the "pressure" which "French opinion"—I cite—could exert on the Government. Our adversaries are not the only ones to wait-and-see. For different motives it is also the attitude of the great mass of Algerian Muslims, not because they hope for a modification of French policy, but because they keep fearing that once more promises made will not be kept and that a change in government will be accompanied by putting into question all the commitments made. It is as important to quiet this fear as to dissipate the presumptuous hopes of our opponents. . . .

Those who, in Parliament or outside, encourage such sentiments by imprudent declarations assume a heavy responsibility before the country. *(Applause from the left, center and right.)*

To discharge and dissipate this wait-and-see attitude, actions speak louder than words. On the military level, the Government intends to leave no doubt as to its decision to continue regularly to send the conscript troops to spend a part of their time in Algeria even, and I should say especially, when calm is reestablished. Their presence is for the good of Algeria and the entire nation and, in the long run, it will contribute to strengthening the ties and improving the understanding between the Algerian and metropolitan populations. . . .

Let us then reaffirm the essential and first of all this important position: the demonstration of a unanimous will that France remain present in Algeria. Then how can our adversaries continue to do Parliament the injury of believing that other leaders coming to power would practice some policy of abandonment? *(Applause from the left, center and several benches to the right.)* . . .

Oh, I know, some reproach us for not granting Algeria her independence pure and simple, "national independence." An independence which would have for certain the consequence of social and economic regression, political regression toward dictatorship or the quasi-feudal regime of certain Arab states—would this then be progress? *(Applause from the left, center and right.)* Would it be progress if Algeria became a Muslim state in which the inhabitants of European origin would be, as a spokesman of the FLN has just confirmed again, strangers in their own homeland if not hostages in any discussions with France? . . .

Alfred Grosser
DE GAULLE AND DECOLONIZATION

Alfred Grosser, one of France's leading political scientists, places de Gaulle's policy toward Algeria and French Africa squarely in the context of the General's overall foreign-policy design and his style of statesmanship. De Gaulle's own account of his policy, appearing five years after Grosser's book (and in part reprinted next in this volume), confirms the following analysis. Grosser is also the author of Germany in Our Times: A Political History of the Postwar Years *and* La IVè République et sa politique extérieure.

On September 28, 1958, approximately 80 percent of those casting ballots voted "Yes" in the referendum to approve the new constitution (but the real meaning of the referendum was the approval of de Gaulle's return to power). At the time, there was much discussion over whether this was a "Defferre-Yes" or a "Bidault-Yes." That meant, then, a liberal "Yes" on Algeria or an *"Algérie française-Yes."* I believe that even then the discussion made little sense, for what most characterized the Algerian affair was that it divided each Frenchman within himself. I will concede that certain French people were 99 percent in favor of Algerian autonomy and 1 percent in favor of French Algeria, while others were 99 percent sympathetic to French Algeria and 1 percent sympathetic to the political ideal of self-determination. But I believe that by far the majority of French people simultaneously held contradictory desires: that Algeria should remain French, and that a liberal solution—in the style of the right of peoples to self-determination—should be applied in Algeria.

To a lesser degree, the American situation in 1952 was not fundamentally different: people desired at once an end to the Korean War—"Bring the boys home"—and victory in Korea. In theory, this was contradictory. So Eisenhower was elected as the reasonable warrior who would resolve the contradiction. We might also see in the massive pro-Adenauer vote of 1957 in Germany the contradictory desires for European unification and German reunification. The two are incompatible. It was for one man to resolve the contradic-

Alfred Grosser, *French Foreign Policy Under de Gaulle* (Boston: Little, Brown and Co., 1967), pp. 30–50. Translated by L. A. Pattison from a revised version of *La politique extérieure de la Cinquième République* (Paris: Editions du Seuil, 1965). Reprinted by permission. Footnotes omitted.

tion. I believe that the "Yes" vote in 1958 was primarily a vote of hope in the miracle, surrendering to one man the problem of reconciling contradictory desires.

Having completed these introductory remarks, I now come to the question: What was General de Gaulle's position on Algeria in 1958? To begin with, we must recall the mystery of 1955–1958: General de Gaulle not only accepted the existence of rival political groups, each claiming to be faithful to him, but also encouraged from Colombey both liberals and antiliberals on decolonization issues. There were likewise the faithful Gaullists—some like Mr. Fouchet in one camp, others like Mr. Triboulet in the other. In the special case of Mr. Soustelle, when was he most fully Gaullist? As Mendès-France's envoy in Algiers or as the destroyer of the successive *Lois-cadres* in 1957?

Did General de Gaulle have precise ideas on how to deal with Algeria in 1958? To begin with, he would assess the situation empirically—"If I am there, it will be better by definition than without me, and I shall see what can be done concretely." This idea—"With me, there will be a state; and with a state, one can do the same things, but well, that others wanted to do, but would have done poorly because there was no state"—this argument was resorted to continually by General de Gaulle and Michel Debré, when they adopted the very same policies as the Fourth Republic on overseas territories or Europe. It is not the same thing, since it is being pursued by a France that has a state, whereas then it was being pursued by a France that had no state. . . .

Nonetheless, it is difficult to ascertain what General de Gaulle truly desired in 1958, because of his great talent for dissimulation. From 1958 on, General de Gaulle developed very highly the art of the deliberately ambiguous statement. Let us consider the meaning of the opening words of his speech in the Forum of Algiers on June 4, 1958: "I have understood you." *("Je vous ai compris.")* In the mind of the crowd, that meant: "I agree with you." Now, this "I have understood you" *never* meant "I agree with you." It could have meant that, it could have been understood that way, but it could also have meant: "I understand you; but, this being said, I am going to lead you elsewhere." In the Algiers speech, one finds indications that point to a vision of the Algerian war and of the goal that must be sought, even through the dissimulation.

An incidental remark, but for me an important one: Was the dissimulation necessary? I have no certain reply. This is a moral and political question which is difficult to resolve, and which I cannot resolve. Would a straightforward statement of certain ineluctable truths earlier in the game have provoked the explosion and civil war? Would it, on the contrary, have appeased in advance resentments which grew all the more violent in that de Gaulle's dissimulation passed—and not without reason—for deceit? But how much dissimulation was involved?

In my opinion, General de Gaulle did not, from the beginning, desire the policy that he adopted in the end. There is nothing like having enemies for dramatizing your intentions! In my opinion, the vision of de Gaulle in Algeria developed by Maître Tixier-Vignancour in his pleading at the Salan trial does not in the least conform to reality, because it portrays a General de Gaulle knowing from the beginning, on May 13, 1958, where he wanted to go, how he wanted to get there, and proceeding precisely and methodically, almost without trial and error. Two points, however, appear certain to me. To begin with, as early as May–June, 1958, he had an idea of what the future of Algeria should be like: domination must disappear in order to arrive at a sort of internal autonomy. I refer you to the 1958 version of the Community: an Algeria occupying, as General de Gaulle was to say later, a particular place within the Community— that Community conceived as leaving defense, foreign relations, and other questions within the hands of the President of the Republic. A second certainty: in 1958, General de Gaulle was indeed French concerning overseas affairs—that is, as I pointed out apropos the Fourth Republic, *he did not succeed in distinguishing clearly between individual freedoms and equalities, and freedom and equality for a political community.* In other words, when he said in the Forum of Algiers: "There are only French citizens with full and equal rights," and when almost a year after his speech on self-determination, he assessed the record of what had been accomplished at his press conference on September 5, 1960, pointing to the fact that "complete equality of civil rights has been established in Algeria," we again encounter one of the two notions in the Preamble of 1946. Decolonization signifies the equality of individuals having the same rights as all French citizens—a notion continually confused with the right of peoples to self-determination. But, at the same time, there is a commitment to equality, in contrast to past policy in Algeria. As early as the Forum speech, de Gaulle was the first head of a French government since 1954 to speak of the causes of rebellion as other than a plot of a few irresponsible leaders or the influence of Moscow, to speak of the humiliations suffered by the Moslems for over a hundred years, to speak of dignity and the desire to erase inequalities. When he spoke of the "Peace of the Brave" to the FLN, on October 23, 1958, it was received as a call for surrender, but the very label "Peace of the Brave" runs counter to what the leaders of the Fourth Republic had called the Algerian rebels. Similarly, there was a desire to overcome trickeries resorted to in the past. The instructions to General Salan prior to the referendum of 1958 stated: "The worst danger would be the drawing up of single lists favored by the official authorities." His illusion was probably then—and later, too—that elections in Algeria could at any time resemble normal Metropolitan elections.

Let us now attempt to consider the relationship of the Algerian question to other areas of French foreign policy between 1958–1962. *The United Nations.* The Fourth Republic's policy was continued. On the one hand, there was disdain and resistance to the UN because it involved itself in matters that did not concern it; but on the other hand, there was an effort to influence the positions of friendly countries so that the UN would not be too hostile. Partisans of French Algeria were reassured that certain statements and decisions were made not for themselves, but in order to satisfy the UN. In the "stew" following the self-determination speech of September 16, 1959, the comment "Leave all that to the UN" contributed to maintaining the ambiguity. The high point in hostile relations with the UN, however, concerned not Algeria, but Tunisia. That was to come at the time of the Bizerta crisis, in July 1961. Partially because the President of the General Assembly, Mr. Mongi Slim, happened to be a Tunisian, the French Government and its representatives in Bizerta displayed great discourtesy toward Dag Hammarskjöld.

Morocco and Tunisia. The Algerian question continued to affect relations with Tunisia and Morocco, but less directly than under the Fourth Republic. At the outset, in 1958, relations between Paris and Rabat and Paris and Tunis were not bad—quite the opposite. During the summer of 1958, the transitional government of General de Gaulle accepted all the clauses of the Franco–Tunisian agreements (notably those concerning air bases) which had led to the fall of the Gaillard government. We encounter here a technique dear to the Fourth Republic: the new government immediately adopted the policy over which the previous government fell. The idea which emerged in 1958, or more exactly, which was taken up again, involved a North African solution to the Algerian problem. It seems that in exchanges with both Tunis and Rabat, the question was raised as to whether one day a North African ensemble might be created, within which Algeria would have a place. Unfortunately, there is a striking lack of documentation on this issue. As under the Fourth Republic, however, there was one major obstacle from the start: the Algerian Army of National Liberation had become a much more important military force than the Tunisian or Moroccan armies (or at least, such was the opinion at the time), and the Moroccans and Tunisians were not particularly enthusiastic about joining with their Algerian brothers in creating a united Maghreb.

Relations with Tunisia reached a sort of apogee on February 27, 1961, with the visit of Habib Bourguiba to Rambouillet. General de Gaulle listened at length, then made several oblique comments to the Tunisian President, who came away believing that he had convinced de Gaulle of the necessity that the Algerian affair be settled quickly. A few months later, however, between July 5 and 20, 1961, the Bizerta crisis broke out: shots were fired in Bizerta, blood was spilled. The responsibility of Tunisia was indeed involved, but the French retaliated with surprising violence. Tunisia referred the matter to the UN Security Council on July 20.

On the French side, it is difficult to ascertain what this "firmness" was intended to accomplish, since there was certainly no desire to remain permanently in Bizerta. On October 15, 1963, slightly more than two years after the bloody incidents of July 1961, there was no longer a French soldier or sailor left in Bizerta. But in 1961, it was essential to fight in Bizerta because Bizerta was indispensable. Here we run into an aspect of Fifth Republic policy very reminiscent of the Fourth Republic style—an aspect that we will encounter again and again in Algerian policy. Why talk of "never," "inevitable," or "indispensable," when a short time later policy will reveal that such categorical statements were false.

Bizerta represents a particularly revealing precedent or example. Indeed, during the discussion of the budget for Algerian affairs in the National Assembly in December 1963, when the Government declared that France would remain for a very long time at Mers-el-Kébir, the wave of skepticism swept even through the UNR benches!

The Community. The Community was at once the model for and the consequence of the Algerian affair. It is probably true that General de Gaulle saw in the constitution of the Community, 1958-style, a potential model for Algeria. Inversely, the acceleration of independence within the Community would have been inconceivable without the Algerian war. When the people of the Ivory Coast congratulate themselves in their national anthem for having achieved independence without violence, Algerians reply: "True enough, but because the Algerians resorted to violence, it eliminated the need for the people of the Ivory Coast to do so." There was a very tight interdependence between the acceleration of the political situation in Black Africa and developments in Algeria. African leaders tried on several occasions to serve as mediators in the Algerian affair. They never succeeded. One could make a long list of the trips to Paris, of the interviews with President Houphouët-Boigny and others. I do not believe that this ever, at any point, appreciably influenced the evolution of the Algerian situation.

Algeria and the Atlantic Alliance. We encounter here, as in policy toward Germany from 1947–1950, a twofold and contradictory policy pursued simultaneously, or, at any rate, a new policy undertaken alongside the old. In October 1960, more than a year after the self-determination speech, Mr. Paul Reynaud declared in a speech before the National Assembly: "It is not normal that we do not fulfill our commitments toward NATO under the guise that we are obliged to send our divisions to Algeria." Prime Minister Michel Debré replied: "It is not possible to compare the state of our divisions in Germany and that of the allied divisions, and to pretend that we are betraying our European engagements. It is the state of our divisions in Algeria that must be compared with the forces of our allies. To submit that we are not defending the West in Algeria is to support the argument of our adversaries." This statement is

based on the old argument: "It is through the Algerian war that we
are faithful to the spirit of NATO, and it is up to the other Atlantic
nations to support us in Algeria."

Now, parallel to this, another policy was outlined: tend toward
self-determination and autonomy. This policy was in keeping with
the nearly unanimous opinion within the Alliance, excluding Portugal: the Communist threat did not lie, as the General Staff of Mr.
Debré maintained, in reaching Europe through the South, whence
the necessity of maintaining the Paris-Algiers-Brazzaville military
axis. The danger was that the prolongation of the war threatened
to throw the FLN more and more into the arms of the Soviet bloc
and to contaminate the rest of North Africa, if not the rest of Africa.
It is nearly certain that a few days before making his speech on self-
determination on September 16, 1959, General de Gaulle had informed President Eisenhower of the major points of his self-determination policy, during Eisenhower's trip to Paris, September 2–4,
1959. That briefing must have satisfied Eisenhower as the major
leader of the Atlantic Alliance. For him, Algerian policy, as it had
been conducted from 1954–1959, represented an element of breach,
an element of danger for the Atlantic Alliance.

This is very likely what General Challe had not understood during the putsch of the generals that took place in Algiers in April,
1961, in defiance of official policy. At about the same time as the
putsch occurred, the *Revue de Défense Nationale* published an article by General Challe that is extremely interesting in that he criticized rather severely the Atlantic and European policies of General
de Gaulle. His reasoning appeared to run: "Since I am more European and more in favor of Atlantic integration than General de
Gaulle, there is some chance that the Americans will support me."

Now, there was no doubt that, for the Americans, the policy of
"Algérie Française" represented a much graver threat to the unity
of NATO and to NATO policy than all the difficulties that General
de Gaulle might create over the policy of Atlantic military integration and European integration. Anything was preferable to a
defender of *Algérie Française.*

This is precisely why the solution of the Algerian impasse and
the evolution towards independence brought about a sort of reestablishment of unity within the Atlantic Alliance until 1962. It is

also, indeed, for this reason that American criticisms of General de Gaulle only really became violent after the independence of Algeria.

Let us now turn to the stages and the method of the evolution. *Chronology.* The point of departure in 1958 was the idea expressed in de Gaulle's speech in Algiers and in the October 23 speech on the "Peace of the Brave"—that if the FLN really could see what was in its interest, it would end hostilities and then all Algerians could participate in forming some vaguely unspecified kind of new Algeria. On September 19, 1958, however, at the same time as the Fifth Republic was proclaimed, the "Provisional Government of the Republic of Algeria" (GPRA) was established. Immediately, and in part because of the referendum scheduled for September 28, the FLN was transformed into the GPRA.

The hesitations of 1958–1959 were in part eliminated by the speech of September 16, 1959, which envisioned two solutions: integration, which was labeled *"francisation":* and independence, which was labeled secession. Finally, there was a proposal which had no label in the speech. and which was subsequently referred to in commentaries as "association"—". . . the government of Algerians by Algerians, backed up by French help and in close relationship with her, as regards the economy, education, defense, and foreign relations." What are the implications of the words "in close relationship with"? A reading of the Charter of the Community in 1958 reveals the meaning behind the maintenance of French domination regarding the economy, defense, and foreign relations. There was a vision of limited internal autonomy, but interpretations remained very free and open.

January 1960: the week of the "barricades" and General de Gaulle's two speeches to end the insurrection. On January 25 he made a statement which to my mind, even more than the *"Je vous ai compris,"* represents the epitome of equivocation. In his radio speech, General de Gaulle declared: "Our task, in uniting all the communities of strife-torn Algeria, is to assure the triumph of a solution that is French." This statement could mean either *"Algérie française"* or "It is unworthy of France not to give independence to a dominated country." Both interpretations are perfectly feasible. For many of those manning the "barricades," a "solution that is French" very much resembled *"Algérie française."*

On January 29, they were confirmed in that interpretation by another statement in a speech by General de Gaulle: "To lose Algeria... would be a disaster for us and for the West." It is difficult not to interpret this in the same way as Debrè's reply to Paul Reynaud, quoted earlier. In the same speech on January 29, General de Gaulle likewise announced categorically that there would be no negotiations with the FLN. "That, I will not do."

Then the final call: "Frenchmen of Algeria, how can you listen to the liars and conspirators who tell you that in granting a free choice to the Algerians, France and de Gaulle want to abandon you, to pull out of Algeria and hand it over to the rebellion!" This was in January 1960. Here again, it is difficult to interpret this statement in the light of what finally took place. It remains a moot question whether what finally happened was a willful policy, or whether General de Gaulle to some extent applied the celebrated principle: "Since events have taken things out of our hands, let us pretend to have planned on the events ourselves."

"No negotiations with the FLN," but as early as June 25–29, 1960, negotiations indeed took place in Melun—they produced no results and were not true negotiations.

On November 4, 1960, a speech was broadcast over radio and television, extremely interesting in that for the first time Algeria was presented as in the natural line of evolution of Tunisia, Morocco, and Black Africa—a speech in which General de Gaulle first spoke of the independence granted to Tunisia, Morocco, and Black Africa. Algeria remained; and at that point it was obvious to all that Algeria was an issue like Tunisia, Morocco, and Black Africa, and especially, that this was the case in the mind of General de Gaulle.

December 20—a speech: the Algerians will take charge of their own affairs, and it is up to them to "found a State with its own Government, its own institutions, and its own laws."

The first French referendum on Algeria took place on January 8, 1961: abstentions totaled 23 percent, which was more or less average; 75.2 percent voted "Yes," and 24.8 percent voted "No." This was the decisive moment—the turning point paving the way for the mechanisms of the years 1961–1962. Still, there were ups and downs in the negotiations: the negotiations at Evian were announced, then postponed for the first time on March 31 because the French Government did not want to negotiate with the FLN alone, and attempted to include in the negotiations the Algerian Nationalist Movement (MNA) of Messali Hadj.

From April 22–26, the so-called "putsch of the generals" took place, and it might well be asked (one of the most interesting questions that future historians might raise) why, following the failure of the putsch, there was not a speed-up in events concerning Algeria. There was, on the contrary, a slowdown. Personally, I am inclined to believe that this was due to General de Gaulle's determination to avoid drastic action, and to take care not to "break" the army's spirit. If any one policy was pursued from beginning to end, I believe it was the determination to *diminish* as much as possible the margin of opposition on both sides—those in favor of *Algérie française* and those in favor of unconditional independence —to bring both wings together around a solution of "independence within interdependence," as Edgar Faure had said about France and Morocco in 1955. This desire to convince the great majority perhaps made it impossible, following the putsch of the generals, to take steps that would have avoided the development of the OAS ("Organisation de l'Armée Secrète"—the French terrorist organization) in 1961 and 1962.

The first negotiation took place in Evian: May 20–June 13, 1961. Failure.

There was another negotiation in Lugrin: July 20–28. Failure, because of the Sahara: Should it be a part of the independent Algeria?

On July 12 came a radio and television speech: "France agrees without any reservation that the Algerian populations [a more multiform phrase than the Algerian "people"] shall constitute a completely independent State."

However, "we must negotiate, and notably with the FLN in particular." Finally, there were no negotiations with the FLN "in particular," but with the FLN *alone,* and these were the last negotiations in Evian in March 1962.

There followed an interim period from March 19–31. In the referendum that took place on April 8, there were 24.4 percent abstentions, and 90.6 percent of those voting said "Yes." Until June 27, the OAS had its day; after that it was virtually finished in Algeria. The referendum on Algerian independence took place July 1. On October 8, 1962, Algeria entered the United Nations.

This brief chronology is intended simply to review the essential events. *The Method and the Factions Involved.* We now return to consider the method and the various factions involved. The most faithful Gaullists were certainly those put to the most severe test. When the UNR formed its first parliamentary group, the political declaration that the entire group was supposed to file before the National Assembly contained in one of its provisions the stated goal of "maintaining Algeria under French sovereignty." Then too, General de Gaulle made it rather difficult for his faithful followers to reinterpret his thinking. I say "reinterpret" because in 1961–1962, we were spectators at the *a posteriori* reconstruction of General de Gaulle's policies since 1944. Hence, at the press conference on April 11, 1961, he declared: "Since Brazzaville, I have not ceased to affirm that the populations dependent on us should have the right to self-determination." Now, the final text of the Brazzaville conference in 1944 stated that "any idea of autonomy, any possibility of evolution outside the French bloc, as well as the eventual, even far-off, constitution of self-government in the colonies, must be set aside." The myth of Brazzaville was followed by a new myth: "In 1947," General de Gaulle declared at the same press conference: "I approved of the Statute of Algeria." Now, the violence of General de Gaulle's opposition to the Statute of Algeria (passed by Parliament in 1961 and making some progress toward giving the Moslems equality) was particularly noteworthy.

There was another characteristic: General de Gaulle's reluctance to receive the support of the nonfaithful. The successive attitudes of General de Gaulle on Algeria more and more came to resemble that of those who voted "No" in the referendum of 1958, and of a small fraction of those who voted "Yes." But General de Gaulle steadfastly refused their support, which was not forthcoming in any case. Thus, we arrive at the paradoxical situation of 1961–1962, when the forces of order struck out against demonstrators (even killing some of them) for protesting against the enemies of the Government. This was due both to General de Gaulle's refusal to accept the support of those who opposed him on other grounds and also to a more general confusion.

I should like to insist on the last point for a moment. On the whole the clairvoyants so far as the Algerian situation was concerned were not numerous. Blindness took several forms, the most widespread in France being not to see the Algerian question as including decolonization, the rights of the Algerians, etc.—not to realize what was involved in the Algerian question. This blindness was powerfully developed and maintained by our scholarly books and by our major newspapers and periodicals. In an excellent article, the *Canard Enchaîne* reproached Pierre Lazareff, editor-in-chief of *France-Soir,* for his article in that paper expressing astonishment at the French people's ignorance of what was going on in Algeria. The *Canard* suggested that it was perhaps because *France-Soir* had never reported many events. The silence of the major press organs, for the reasons that I have already explained, combined with what we learned in textbooks on Algeria—or more precisely, what we did *not* learn in the textbooks on Algeria—contributed amply to this blindness.

The other blindness (but a rather minor one) was the idealization of the FLN. It considered France a decadent country, whose salvation could only come through the purity of the FLN, incarnation of wholesome force; and thus, to aid the FLN was to aid France. This was the attitude, for instance, of Simone de Beauvoir. But it must not be forgotten that the extremists of Algerian independence were amply encouraged over the years by the horrors that took place in Algeria. Of course, some of them reacted only to the horrors on one side. But for many of the French, the striking issue was the acts committed in the name of France, which were always denied (or more precisely, long denied) but later discovered with certitude to have taken place. . . .

Before the Court of Justice, at the time of the trial of the pro-*Algérie française* generals, a captain filed a deposition that confirmed in August 1962 what certain people had written regarding Algeria since 1954: "I declare," stated Captain Estoup, "under oath, that Godot [one of the accused officers], along with about a hundred other officers, received the order, at that time, to use torture to gather information. Do not ask me the details. I do not know the torments of the man who gave the order, but I do know the anguish of the man who executed it. For a young graduate of Saint-Cyr, all myths and illusions collapsed at that moment. Why wouldn't he have executed the order, since the goal was supposedly of unquestionable ultimate importance, and was represented as a sort of crusade? It was said that the end justifies the means, and that the victory of France depended on it, but this justification vanishes when the end is not attained."

(I note in passing that this is a curious interpretation of the justification of the means. One has the impression of a blot on one's honor because of failure.)

The Jeanson network of young Frenchmen helping the FLN, and the "121," intellectuals stating their approval of disobedience, cannot be explained without this kind of fact, not so much to sanction as to demonstrate that, ultimately, the most guilty, in my opinion, are neither the people in the Jeanson network, nor the future officers of the OAS, nor even those who practiced torture, but the majority of the French people who tranquilly set off on vacation. The tendency to place all blame *a posteriori* either on the Jeanson network, or on the officers who applied methods that were disapproved of—and perhaps not that much, moreover—is a facile solution, in that most of the French population continued to hope that it could duck all participation in solving a problem that it sought to avoid.

The Moral Record. When independence came, these different factions reacted in different ways. To begin with, a number of officers considered that since they had been deceived, and knowing full well that nothing could be saved (all the statements of the OAS that I have read seem to demonstrate that none of its leaders entertained the slightest illusion), the policy to pursue was to burn the ground behind them, to prevent any middle-range solution in order to prove that the catastrophe was inevitable. This was the reaction of those who felt that they had been deceived, or that they themselves had let down the Algerians who had placed confidence in them.

The pro-independence "ultras" grew disenchanted. The FLN, which had become the Algerian government, was not composed of saints and heroes possessed of all the virtues of Socrates and Themistocles. Curiously, one part of those who had fought hard for Algerian independence lost all interest in independent Algeria, because, obviously, the latter necessitated a different kind of effort. For instance, approval of a policy of aid to independent Algeria on the part of a government that one had despised would, if one were consistent, require protesting against events in independent Algeria just as one had protested against what had taken place in the name of France in Algeria prior to independence. Therefore, some of the former "ultras" avoided the Algerian issue completely—they no longer went there, nor were they even tempted to do so. But others, among the more farsighted, departed for Algeria in order to aid the young Algerian state.

What was the attitude of the bulk of the French population at the time of the Evian agreements? I believe that at that time, it was necessary to speak out in a way that only a minority did. The cause of the French populations in Algeria should have been pleaded well before Evian; this was extremely difficult during the period of the OAS. When Pierre Nora published *Les Français d'Algérie*, I wrote a critique of his book, and my principal criticism concerned its date of publication. Most of what he wrote about the French in Algeria was probably true, but it should have been written at a time when a small amount of pressure could have brought about some change. To write such things about the vanquished was to grant a clear conscience too easily to the French people, who were prepared to consider the defeated French Algerians as of no importance.

It is for this reason that the task of the year 1961–1962, for a number of those who had fought against the successive Algerian policies of successive governments, should have been to bring out the fact that all French political organizations and unions on the other side of the Mediterranean had supported the French populations in Algeria, and that, therefore, we had no right to consider the latter as the black sheep of the French community. . . .

Let us begin by examining what was decided at Evian, and the substance of the texts.

The Texts.   Who negotiated with whom?

This poses a first question. On the one hand, there was France, a sovereign state. When the text refers to "the two parties" (Article 2 of the cease-fire agreement), the other party named in the agreement was the FLN, which appeared this time as a party to a treaty, to an agreement signed with France. The FLN finally obtained the monopoly of representation that it had claimed for long years. The major text, the General Declaration, notes that discussions took place in Evian from March 7–18, 1962 between the government of the Republic and the FLN. One also finds the following: "The founding, following self-determination, of an independent and sovereign State appearing in conformity with the facts in Algeria. . . ." In other words, this time self-determination can only result in an independent state. "The cooperation of France and Algeria corresponding to the interests of both countries, the French government, together with the FLN, considers that the solution of the independence of Algeria in cooperation with France is that which corresponds to this situation." In other words, self-determination will be the ratification of an agreement between France and the FLN, accepting both independence—a major concession in comparison with the policy of September 16, 1959—and cooperation—a minor concession on the part of the FLN, since it had never expressly stated that it did not desire it, but a more basic concession if it were intended to engage the future Algerian state.

Now we come to a point that seems important to me. The FLN assumed responsibility for the future Algerian state. That is to say, more or less, that self-determination would bring to power, in independent Algeria, the signatories of the Evian agreements, or their successors accepting their signatures. To obtain the guarantees given in the Evian agreement, it was in France's best interest to see the leaders of the FLN become the government of Algeria—which constituted the second aspect by virtue of which self-determination became simply ratification.

The Algerian state was to be totally independent: "The Algerian state will freely choose its own institutions, and the political and social regime that it judges most in conformity with its interests. On the international plane, it will define and apply the policy of its choice in full sovereignty."

Two comments on this important paragraph: on the one hand, the social regime would imply (if the state were to become socialist) a number of measures that would be incompatible with the guarantees given to owners of real property in Algeria. A subsequent paragraph, Article 12, stated: "Algeria will ensure, without any discrimination, the free and peaceful enjoyment of patrimonial rights acquired on its territory prior to self-determination. . . ." Either this paragraph makes no sense, or else the provision for the free determination of social regime makes no sense. Consequently, right from the start, there was a contradiction between the "social regime of its choice" and the guarantees given to industrialists and landowners.

On the international plane, there was scant provision for coordination; there was no provision at all for harmonizing foreign policies, and independent Algeria was empowered, from the very beginning, to pursue whatever policies it desired.

In the general declaration, there was also, of course, a definition of the future cooperation, founded on the presence of the French community in Algeria: "Algeria guarantees the interests of France, the rights acquired by individuals and legal persons under conditions established in the preceding declarations. In counterpart, France will grant Algeria cultural and technical assistance, and will contribute a privileged financial aid to its economic and social development." In other words, from the beginning, in the Evian agreements, cooperation was the counterpart of the status of the French populations in Algeria.

Cooperation and Socialism. When, mostly through the fault of the OAS, the French populations of Algeria departed, and again when, following the land nationalization decrees of the Algerian government in March 1963, new departures took place, the reciprocity of the guarantees of cooperation no longer existed, and on this point, the Evian agreements were voided of all substance. Another justification for cooperation had to be found. The question of the social regime was one of the most difficult for the Algerian government itself, in the first place because, there as elsewhere, domestic and foreign policies were inextricably bound togther.

In order to launch a program of economic development, and to initiate the changes that would lead the population out of its state of misery, the organization of the economy had to be transformed. In order to obtain foreign aid, particularly French aid, it was necessary not to make a complete break with the liberal economic system. The choice for the Algerian leaders was approximately as follows: without capital, no economic development; but to achieve the economic development that they considered indispensable to the establishment of a socialist system—the only system that they considered ultimately favorable to the whole population—structures would have to be transformed so radically that foreign capital would no longer have any interest in making investments. In other words, for the Algerian leaders, the choice lay between socialism with, as a possible consequence, a prolonged economic failure; or remaining under an economic regime that they considered neo-colonialist, or at least little likely to give Algerians equal economic opportunities.

What was expected of France, with its largely liberal economy, was that it would aid, in spite of everything, a socialist experiment. It seemed that France alone could understand this situation. General de Gaulle stated it at the beginning in fairly harsh words. While the war was still being fought, on at least two occasions, he brought up the idea that the Algerians had every interest in remaining on good terms with France, for no other country would willingly provide them with such massive and disinterested assistance.

At his press conference on September 5, 1960 he said: "Is it necessary or is it not for Algeria to change into a modern and prosperous country? If the answer is yes, which power can lend itself to this task, can cooperate to the degree and on the terms desired? Only one: France."

Much ink was spilled over the phrase addressed to the United States and the Soviet Union at the press conference of April 11, 1961: "Some people say also, 'Either the Soviet Union or the United States—or both at once—would try to take France's place in the territories from which she withdrew.' My answer is: I wish both of them a lot of fun." On the basis of this comment, it might be asked what was the goal of the aid provided? What was the purpose behind cooperation, once some tens of thousands of Frenchmen living in Algeria had departed? Naturally, there was a question of economic interest: there was the question of oil.

A second element must not be underestimated: one continues in order to continue. This explanation may appear to be little enlightening or logical, but it appears to me to be the essential explanation behind the continuing of aid both to Algeria and to Africa. Once begun, there is no reason to stop. Things are in place, the structures, the forms of financial aid, of technical assistance. One is there; there is no reason to stop.

In Algeria, another consideration certainly intervened: that was Cuba. I am convinced, without being able to prove it, that in the eyes of General de Gaulle the aid provided to Algeria serves as an example. Even if Ben Bella had not come to the Château de Champs to meet the head of state on March 13, 1964; even if more

Frenchmen had been dispossessed in Algeria, aid would have been maintained to show the Americans how a country can be prevented from shifting into the Soviet camp by not compelling it to declare itself to be nonsocialist and "occidentophile" in its foreign policy. It was to some extent a demonstration to the United States of what it should have done in Cuba in order to prevent Castro from becoming Communist.

Charles de Gaulle
MEMOIRS OF HOPE

De Gaulle's own account of the decolonization process he designed and directed is remarkable not only for its exact sense of history but also for the flavor of the man which pervades it. Historian and statesman—no one can better present de Gaulle with his concepts and his methods than the General himself. True, de Gaulle had been in good part responsible for the disastrous decisions taken in the forties to preserve the Empire at all costs, but at the same time he alone was capable of correcting this course while saving republican government in France. Only de Gaulle had the ability both to make the break with Algeria and to do so in a manner that would not poison the political atmosphere in France for more than a generation with humiliation and mutual recrimination. Once again, as he had done during the blackest days of World War II, Charles de Gaulle had found a reason to declare victory where before his coming the defeat seemed total. The very title of his last volume of memoirs conveys this new feeling of confidence.

On resuming the leadership of France, I was determined to extricate her from the constraints imposed upon her by her empire and no longer offset by any compensating advantages. As can be imagined, I did not undertake it lightly. For a man of my age and upbringing, it was bitterly cruel to become through my own choice

Charles de Gaulle, *Memoirs of Hope: Renewal and Endeavor* (New York and London, 1971). Translated by Terence Kilmartin from *Mémoires d'Espoir: le Renouveau, 1958–1962* (Plon, 1970), pp. 37–48; 53; 57–58; 64–67; 75–82. Copyright © 1970, 1971 by Librarie Plon. English translation copyright © 1971 by George Weidenfeld and Nicholson Ltd. Reprinted by permission of Simon and Schuster and Weidenfeld and Nicholson Ltd.

the overseer of such a transformation. Not so long ago our country had put forth an immense and glorious effort in order to conquer, administer and develop her overseas dependencies. The colonial epic had been an attempt to compensate for the loss of her distant possessions in the seventeenth and eighteenth centuries and then for her European defeats in 1815 and 1870. She appreciated the worldwide prestige won for her by proconsuls of the stature of Bugeaud, Faidherbe, Archinard, Brazza, Doumer, Gallieni, Ponty, Sarraut, Lyautey. She was conscious of the services rendered in the ranks of her army by several generations of valiant African, Malagasy and Asian contingents, their contribution to our victory in the First World War, and the part played during the Second by our overseas territories, their troops, workers and resources, in the epic of Fighting France. She took pride in the human achievement represented by the basis of modern development laid down in these rough lands as a result of the activities of countless soldiers, administrators, settlers, teachers, missionaries and engineers. What an agonizing ordeal it was to be then for me to hand over our power, furl our flags and close a great chapter of History!

Nevertheless, I could see a gleam of hope piercing the sadness. It was true that in the past the advantages we were able to reap from our colonies had seemed on balance to outweigh the sum total of their cost to us. Having obtained the submission of the native populations in one way or another, what we had to spend to maintain and administer their slow-moving, backward existence was not beyond our means, whereas the fields of opportunity and the extension of power which these possessions offered us were far from negligible. But all this had visibly changed. While progress, there as elsewhere, multiplied needs, we were obliged to bear the increasing costs of administration, public works, education, social services, health and security over vast areas while at the same time we witnessed a growing desire for emancipation which made our yoke seem heavy if not intolerable to our subjects. The more so since, in bringing them our civilization, we had established in each of these territories a centralized system prefiguring the nation-State in place of their former anarchic divisions, and trained native elites imbued with our principles of liberty and human rights and eager to replace us from top to bottom of the hierarchy. It should be added that this movement was hastened on by the ostentatious solidarity of the Third World with its unemancipated brethren, and by the propaganda and promises of America, Russia and China, who, though rivals, were all three in search of political and ideological clientships. In short, however much one might regret the fact, the maintenance of our authority over countries no longer willing to accept it was becoming a hazard from which we had everything to lose and nothing to gain.

But did this mean that, in allowing them henceforth to govern themselves, we should "sell out," leave them in the lurch, dismiss them from our sight and from our hearts? Clearly not. Because of their long connection with us and the magnetic attraction exercised by the angels and demons of France upon them as upon all who come into contact with her, they were disposed to maintain close links with us. Conversely, what we had already contributed towards their progress, the friendships, habits and interests resulting therefrom, and our immemorial vocation for influence and expansion, committed us to seeing them as privileged partners. If they were to speak our language and share our culture, we must help them to do so. If their raw administrations, their nascent economies, their unorganized finances, their tentative diplomacies, their rudimentary defenses, required our help to put them on their feet, we must supply it. In short, to lead the peoples of "Overseas France" to self-determination and at the same time to organize direct cooperation between them and us—these were my simple and straightforward aims.

But the realities of the situation in the territories concerned were nothing if not diverse. Some, having for long—sometimes for centuries—been merged with France, would doubtless wish to remain so, either as *départements*—Martinique, Guadeloupe, Guiana, Réunion—or with a status of internal autonomy—Saint-Pierre-et-Miquelon, French Somaliland, the Comoro Archipelago, New Caledonia, Polynesia, Wallis and Futuna. For them it was simply a question of providing an opportunity of making a choice under the terms of the new Constitution. In Black Africa, which was characterized by an extreme variety of regions, tribes and dialects, the administrative entities which we ourselves had created—Senegal, Sudan, Guinea, Mauritania, Dahomey, the Ivory Coast, Upper Volta, Niger, Congo, Chad, Ubangi and Gabon—would provide a natural framework for future States. Here, there was no doubt that, prompted by their elites, the people would opt for independence. The question was whether they would do so in agreement with us, or without us, or even against us. A considerable proportion of the more advanced elements, indoctrinated to a greater or lesser extent by totalitarian blandishments, visualized emancipation not as the final stage in an evolutionary process but as a defeat inflicted on the colonizers by the colonized. That was the only sort of independence they cared about. Nevertheless, there was reason to believe that, when it came to the point, reason and sentiment would persuade most of the leaders to maintain firm links with France. It was for this, at the outset, that the Community would provide, although later it was to evolve into a series of contractual agreements.

On the other hand, Madagascar, in former times a State with its people, its language, its traditions, would certainly prefer to deal with us. Two more territories, Togoland and Cameroon placed under our tutelage by the United Nations, would wish to be released from it but would almost certainly ask for our continued aid. As for our Protectorates, whose independence had been recognized in principle—Morocco under its king and Tunisia as a republic—it was simply a question of restoring complete sovereignty to them. This I was determined to do, assuming incidentally that they would wish to remain linked with us in spirit and in practice. This was already the case with the kingdoms of Laos and Cambodia, over which we no longer held suzerainty but where I intended to maintain France's special position. And it would perhaps be the case—I proposed to work towards this end—with North and South Vietnam, whenever that country, already sorely tried and about to be terribly decimated and ravaged, emerged from its misfortunes.

Provided that we respected their emergent or reconstituted nationhoods, that we were careful not to exploit the troubles which could not fail to beset them, that we furnished them with all the reasonable support which they required, there was a chance that a vast complex, based on friendship and cooperation, might form itself round us. I wanted to seize this opportunity for France, putting aside all regrets for the past, overcoming all prejudices, remolding our relationships with our former subjects who would now become our partners.

But what of Algeria? There we were faced, not with a situation to be settled by amicable agreement, but with full-scale tragedy; a

French tragedy as much as a local one. Algeria assumed an importance in our national life beyond comparison with that of any other of our dependencies. We had conquered it, after the long and somber episodes of the Berber era, at the cost of an enormous military effort in which both sides had fought bravely and suffered heavy losses. Even then we had had to suppress many subsequent revolts. Thus we were all the more gratified to have become the masters of a land which had cost us so dear. Moreover, thanks to Algeria, our position in Africa and the Mediterranean was powerfully reinforced. It had served as a base from which to launch our penetration of Tunisia, Morocco and the Sahara. More recently, in addition to recruiting once again a number of excellent *tirailleurs* from its inhabitants, we had formed our Liberation Government there and, with our allies, mustered a considerable proportion of the means of our victory. The million Frenchmen who had settled there had achieved a remarkable economic development of the country thanks to their own abilities, the help of capital from metropolitan France, and the support of the administration, while a magnificent infrastructure had been created by French money, French technology and local labor. And now we had found deposits of oil and natural gas which could make good our grave deficiency in sources of energy. For a variety of reasons, therefore, the French people were inclined to regard the possession of Algeria as valuable and, moreover, well-earned. True, it was not without uneasiness and some impatience that they endured the costly struggle that was being waged there, and if they had condemned the Fourth Republic, it was above all because it had failed to extricate them from it. But they thought that de Gaulle, now that he was at the helm, would find some means of ending it at the minimum cost.

For the settlers, the maintenance of the status quo seemed vital, whatever the cost to France. Living in the midst of an Arab and Kabyle population which outnumbered them by ten to one and was increasing at a faster rate, they were haunted by the fear that if France ceased to govern, to administer, to repress, they themselves would be ineluctably submerged, dispossessed, driven out. Moreover, their own society and that of the Moslems, though juxtaposed, remained in practice totally estranged from one another. Those who called themselves *pieds-noirs,* born or brought up in a conquered land, proud of what they had achieved—not without risk and by dint of their own efforts; secure in their privileges of status, education, employment and wealth; in possession of all the most important agricultural, industrial and commercial enterprises, monopolizing almost entirely the higher echelons in every field, including the liberal professions, naturally supported by the civil service; and confident that in any case the Army would once again restore order for their benefit, had always held themselves above and apart from the more or less submissive masses who surrounded them. Any reform tending towards equality between the two categories of citizen seemed to them a grave threat. In their eyes, the only conceivable outcome of the tragedy for which Algeria had now been the stage for several years was the crushing of the insurrection and the maintenance of what they called "French Algeria," that is, the confirmation of our direct authority and their own supremacy. It was for fear of being abandoned that they had supported the May 13 movement against the previous regime. It was in order to alter the semblance of French domination without modifying it in reality that they now affected to favor integration. In fact they saw it as a means of warding off the evolution towards equality of rights and Algerian autonomy, of not only avoiding being engulfed by ten million Moslems but of submerging them instead among fifty million Frenchmen. In this way, encouraged by long experience, they thought that with a firm Governor-General, reliable prefects and above all the presence of powerful police and security forces, their situation would remain unchanged. This was what they expected and would if necessary demand from General de Gaulle, believing him to be a strong man but incapable of conceiving that he could be strong in a cause other than their own.

Their intransigence was matched by that of the determined and in some cases armed Moslems. After long years of resignation, punctuated by periodic outbreaks of rebellion, years during which notables concerned about their property or hankering after jobs and honors, ex-servicemen loyal to the brotherhood of arms, and a few people with careers in the public service or politics had given the French their more-or-less sincere support; years during which they had cherished and then lost one illusion after another as regards their acquisition of full civil rights and an autonomous status for Algeria, the Moslems as a whole were now sympathic to the National Liberation Front and the insurrection, even if they did not take

part in it. Moreover they were well aware that if the plight of their
fathers had left the world indifferent, there was now a vast wave of
sympathy and sometimes active support for their cause abroad.
This was the case with their neighbors in North Africa and the other
Arab countries. But elsewhere, too, there was a considerable body
of opinion in their favor which was regularly expressed in the United
Nations Assembly. Furthermore, since the French Republic had renounced its sovereignty in Indochina in 1954, since parliament had
passed an outline law in 1956 grating wide autonomy including au-
tochthonous councils of government and elected assemblies to
every territory in Black Africa as well as to Madagascar, and since
Tunisia and Morocco had finally been emancipated from Paris in
1957, the Algerians were confident that in the long run, provided
they themselves opened the breach, their independence was a fore-
gone conclusion. . . .

The Army, for its part, and especially the generals and senior
officers, expected much from my return. For, at grips with the rebellion, their constant preoccupation had been to avoid a political
stab in the back. They dreaded the collapse of governmental authority, pressure from foreign powers, a mood of abdication on the
part of a public weary of the military and financial commitment and
shocked by deplorable incidents during the repression which were
exploited in certain circles—all of which threatened to undermine
military operations in the field and ultimately to cause some grave
reverse. The restoration of national authority, they felt, would give
them the time and the means to win the war and would discourage
the enemy. As for the political solution which was to crown their
victory, broadly speaking they conceived it as a new winning-over
of Algeria to France, with a vast program of economic, social and
educational development on the part of the mother country by way
of compensation. What it saw for itself on the spot inspired the
Army with sympathy for the sufferings and miseries of the people
and a fierce resentment against a colonial regime which left them
so destitute. But above all, whatever the personal calculations of
certain of its leaders and the mischief fomented in its midst by a
small batch of fantasy-spinning and ambitious officers, the army
was conscious of the need to be commanded by the State. Hence,
for the moment, it was thankful to see me govern France and to en-
trust me with the Algerian question.

From the moment I took the helm, I was up to the eyes in the problem. Needless to say, I approached it with no strictly predetermined plan. The facts I had to go on were too varied, too complex, too shifting for me to be able to decide in advance on the precise details, the phasing and the timing of the solution. In particular, how was one to discover at that time which Algerians could or would fall in with it when it came to the point? But the main outlines were clear in my mind. Indeed, as early as June 30, 1955, when the insurrection was at its height, I had said at a press conference in reply to questions on the subject: "No other policy but one which aims at replacing domination by association in French North Africa can be valid or worthy of France."

In the first place, I excluded from the realm of possibility all idea of the assimilation of the Moslems into the French population. Perhaps this might have been conceivable a hundred years earlier, provided it had then been possible to transplant several million Frenchmen to Algeria and an equal number of Algerian immigrants to France; all the inhabitants of the combined nation thus enjoying the same laws and the same rights. Perhaps it might still have been attempted after the First World War, in the proud flush of victory. Perhaps, after the Second, in the spirit of the Liberation, the gradual establishment of an autonomous Algeria evolving of its own accord into a State attached to France by federal ties, a solution adumbrated by the still-born Statute of 1947, might have been feasible. Now it was too late for any form of subjection. The Moslem community, by reason of its ethnic origins, its religion, its way of life, and because it had for so long been treated as inferior, held at a distance, fought against, had developed too powerful and too prickly a personality to allow itself to be dispersed or dominated, especially at a time when, all over the world, people were taking their destiny into their own hands. Integration, then, was in my view no more than an ingenious and empty formula. But could I, on the other hand, contemplate prolonging the status quo? No! For that would be to keep France politically, financially and militarily bogged down in a bottomless quagmire when, in fact, she needed her hands free to bring about the domestic transformation necessitated by the twentieth century and to exercise her influence abroad unencumbered. At the same time, it would condemn our forces to a futile and interminable task of colonial repression, when the future of the country demanded an Army geared to the exigencies of modern power. On the essential point, therefore, my mind was made up. Whatever the dreams of the past or the regrets of today, whatever I myself had undoubtedly hoped for at other times, there was in my view no longer any alternative for Algeria but self-determination.

But having decided to accord her this right, I would do so only on certain conditions. First of all it must be France, eternal France, who alone, from the height of her power, in the name of her principles and in accordance with her interests, granted it to the Algerians. There could be no question of her being compelled to do so by military setbacks, or prevailed upon to do so by foreign intervention, or induced to do so by partisan and parliamentary agitation. We would, therefore, put forth the effort required to make ourselves masters of the battlefield. We would pay no attention to any overtures from any capital, to any offer of "good offices," to any threat of "agonizing reappraisal" in our foreign relations, to any debate in the United Nations. When the moment came, it would not be some fortuitous assembly of deputies but all our people who would vote the necessary changes. Furthermore, should it prove desirable, particularly for Algeria itself, that some Frenchmen should remain there, it would be for each of them to decide individually, our army guaranteeing their freedom and security until they had chosen one way or the other where they would settle. Finally, for the mutual advantage of France and Algeria, treaties would have to be drawn up between them providing for preferential relations, notably as regards civic status, trade, cultural agreements, and the exploitation of Saharan oil and gas. Believing as I did that the "French Algeria" for which I heard people clamoring in the early days of my administration was a ruinous Utopia, I nevertheless hoped to ensure that, in the sense in which France had always remained in some degree Roman ever since the days of Gaul, the Algeria of the future, by virtue of the impress which she had received and would wish to preserve, would in many respects remain French.

Such was my strategy for the realization of this policy. As for my tactics, I should have to proceed cautiously from one stage to the next. Only gradually, using each crisis as a springboard for further advance, could I hope to create a current of consent powerful enough to carry all before it. Were I to announce my intentions point-blank, there was no doubt that the sea of ignorant fear, of shocked surprise, of concerted malevolence through which I was navigating would cause such a tidal wave of alarms and passions in every walk of life that the ship would capsize. I must, therefore, maneuver without ever changing course until such time as, unmistakably, common sense broke through the mists.

On June 4 [1958], almost as soon as I had come to power, I flew to Algiers. . . . When I appeared on the balcony of the *Gouvernement-Général* an unbelievable surge of cheering rose up from the vast crowd gathered in the square. Then in a short speech I tossed them the words, seemingly spontaneous but in reality carefully calculated, which I hoped would fire their enthusiasm without committing me further than I was willing to go. Having shouted "I have understood you!" in order to establish emotional contact, I evoked the May 13 movement, to which I attributed two of the noblest motives: renovation and fraternity. I took cognizance thereof, and declared that France would accordingly grant equality of rights to all Algerians irrespective of their community. Thus, the differences in civic status and the separate electoral colleges were swept away at a single blow, so that within a stated period the Moslem majority would at any rate be able to make itself felt as such. Thus the necessity was affirmed to "open doors which have hitherto been closed to many . . . to give the means of livelihood to those who have lacked them . . . to recognize the dignity of those who have been deprived of it . . . to guarantee a motherland to those who may have doubted that they had one." In the reconciliation between the two communities, of which Algiers that evening was setting the example, I called for the participation of "all the inhabitants of the towns, the *douars,* the plains and the *djebels,* and even those who, through despair, have felt it their duty to wage upon this soil a struggle which is undoubtedly cruel and fratricidal but whose courage I recognize. Yes! I, de Gaulle, open the doors of reconciliation to them too!" Meanwhile I did not neglect to confer upon the Army, "which is carrying out a magnificent task of understanding and pacification," a public token of my confidence.

A frenzied ovation greeted my words. Yet the prospect which they opened up by no means gratified the desires of the mass— three-quarters French—of my listeners in the Forum. But a wind had stirred to which, momentarily, no one offered any resistance. All realized that this time it was France herself who spoke, with all her authority and generosity. All saw that, after the great convulsion we had just come through, the State had risen to assert itself. All felt that, whatever happened, de Gaulle had the duty and the right to solve the problem. In Constantine, where the audience was principally Moslem, in Oran, where the French were largely predominant, in Mostaganem, where the two communities were evenly balanced, my message was the same: no more discrimination between Algerians no matter who they were! This was tantamount to saying that the day would come when the majority among them could decide the destiny of all. It was by this means that Algeria would remain in her own way French, and not by virtue of a law imposed upon her by force. . . .

I returned to Paris on June 7. The following week saw the implementation of the agreements with Tunisia and Morocco which I had proposed to their Heads of State on the 3rd and under which our troops were withdrawn from their territories, with the exception of Bizerta in the former and Meknes, Port-Lyautey,. Marrakesh and Agadir in the latter. At the beginning of July I returned to Algeria accompanied by Pierre Guillaumat and also Guy Mollet. The latter had gone there as Prime Minister in 1956 and his presence had raised such a storm of threats from the *pieds-noirs* that he had been forced to recall his Minister for Algeria, General Catroux, appointed only a week before. Now, in spite of some booing in Algiers which he stood up to gallantly, he took part in my tour, which was mainly devoted to military outposts, without mishap. After these two visits I was to return to Algeria on six further occasions up to December 1960, traversing the entire country several times. What Head of State or Government had done as much since 1830, although few of them had been septuagenarians? But in order to reach a decision, there too, there above all, I had to see and hear, be seen and heard.

It was for this reason that, in August, I betook myself to Black Africa. Pierre Pflimlin, Minister of State, Bernard Cornut-Gentille, Minister for Overseas France, and Jacques Foccart, my special adviser for African and Malagasy affairs, flew with me. My purpose was to explain to our territories the significance of the forthcoming referendum; to emphasize that to vote "Yes" meant sovereignty combined with continued association with metropolitan France, and to vote "No" meant to break off all ties. It was inevitable that the impression my visit made and the speeches I delivered would have a powerful influence on the attitude of the educated minority and the reaction of the masses, and consequently on the result. . . .

Returning to Paris on August 29 after another visit to Algiers, I concluded from my journey that with the sole exception—would it be permanent?—of Guinea, all our colonies in Black Africa, together with Madagascar, were determined to remain linked to France while at the same time becoming their own masters. But I could also see that it was high time we set them upon the road; that to refuse or even to postpone this step would be to invite serious clashes; that, on the other hand, in taking it we would be inaugurating a fruitful and exemplary undertaking.

The constitutional referendum, a triumph in metropolitan France, was even more so overseas. Guinea apart, all the Black African territories and Madagascar voted "Yes" with majorities in excess of 95 percent. In December, the same figures were recorded for my own election as President of the Community. . . .

. . . Throughout the years 1959 and 1960, the African territories and Madagascar were forming themselves into states. All of them chose to do so on the basis of democracy save totalitarian Guinea who, once outside our orbit and deprived of our support, did not hesitate to have recourse to the aid proffered by foreign States— the Soviet Union, the United States, Germany, Great Britain, Ghana —all of whom, for various reasons, were equally gratified to see her estranged from France. Our former colonies in the dark continent, together with the great island in the Indian Ocean, thus became republics, each voting itself a Constitution, electing a President and a parliament, forming an administration. This assumption of sovereignty took place everywhere without undue incident, in the habitual euphoria of new departures. It must be said that we helped considerably to get things under way, the Community playing its supporting and transitional role in this respect. The "Executive Council" composed of Heads of State, which was to settle the many questions raised by the transfer of power, met in Paris under my presidency in February, March, May and September of 1959. In July, I convened a meeting of the Council in Tananarive. The demonstrations in the capital proved to me how grateful Madagascar was to France for restoring her former independence while at the same time helping her to make her way in the future. On the occasion of this journey, I revisited French Somaliland and the Comoro Archipelago, overseas territories of the Republic which gave enthusiastic expression to their joy at having chosen to remain so. I also went back to Réunion, our ancient île Bourbon, still passionately French in the depths of the Indian Ocean and prepared to demonstrate it yet again in unforgettable fashion.

The "Senate of the Community," composed of delegates from our Parliament and of elected African and Madagascan representatives, which opened in my presence in the Luxembourg Palace in July, gave certain political elements in France and the overseas countries the opportunity of debating subjects of common interest. On July 14 in the Place de la Concorde, thirteen Heads of State received from my hands the "flag of the Community" and attended a march-past of our troops and theirs. Gradually, then, without hesitating to ask for and to follow our advice, the young governments assumed their responsibilities. Indeed, at their request, we continued to maintain a number of officials, technicians, teachers, doctors and officers in the ranks of their administrations.

The emergence of these nations, almost all new-fledged, each containing elements of very different ethnic groups within frontiers which had been drawn up during the colonial period simply for purposes of partition between European States or for administrative convenience, could, with the disappearance of our old "Federations" of West Africa and Equatorial Africa, have led to a haphazard balkanization. But regional groupings were formed among neighbors which we ourselves helped to create and foster. For instance the Equatorial Customs Union between Congo-Brazzaville, the Central African Republic, Chad and Gabon, soon to be joined by Cameroon, was signed in Paris in January 1959, and in April the "Council of the Entente," comprising the Ivory Coast, Dahomey, Niger and Upper Volta, and later Togo, established technical and economic cooperation between countries stretching from the Sahara to the Bight of Benin. It is true that the attempt to merge Senegal and the Sudan into a federation known as Mali was to fail because the liberal and democratic leaders in Dakar were afraid of being stifled by the Marxists of Bamako; Senghor, the President of the Federal Assembly, broke with Modibo Keita, the Head of Government, and Senegal resumed its former name while the Sudan kept that of Mali. But subsequently the "Organization of the Senegal River States" was set up, in which Senegal, Mali, Mauritania and even Guinea were to cooperate. In addition to this, in many other African regions, river navigation, access to the sea, the building of roads and railways, were the subject of multilateral agreements negotiated with our help. Throughout our former territories, the airlines were operated by a single company, *Air-Afrique*. Later, the *Organisation commune africaine et malgache* was created, which all the French-speaking countries except Guinea were to join, including even Rwanda and the former Belgian Congo.

But, not unexpectedly, as the new States established themselves de facto and de jure, they were more and more inclined to assert their individual personalities. Wisely, in defining their relations with us, our Constitution had provided not only at the outset for the "Community" formula, which placed foreign affairs, currency, defense, the Court of Cassation and higher education in the common domain, but also, with an eye to the future, the "association" formula, whereby cooperative agreements in every sphere, notably those above, would be enshrined in special treaties. By the end of 1959, it was "association" that the new Republics, one after another, came to propose to us.

The first to do so were Madagascar and Mali, the latter at the time still a union of Senegal and Sudan. As this transformation was legally valid and in no way undermined our interests, merely altering the form without affecting the basis of Franco-African solidarity, we willingly accepted it. On December 11, after calling at Nouakchott, I arrived at Saint-Louis to preside over the Executive Council of the Community on the following day. There, warmly supported by the Prime Minister, Michel Debré, who was at my side, I made it known publicly that France was ready to accede to these requests. But I said to the assembled Heads of State, as the pilgrims of Emmaus said to the traveller: "Abide with us. The day is far spent. Night is falling upon the world." On December 13, speaking to the Mali General Assembly in Dakar, I announced officially that we, the French nation, sanctioned the change from Community to Association, and this was the signal for moves in the same direction on the part of the other States. Meanwhile, although the United Nations had, with our consent, rescinded our trusteeship over Togoland and Cameroon, recognized their complete international sovereignty and admitted them as members, both countries had decided to maintain the closest possible links with us by means of special agreements.

The year 1960 was thus to be devoted to the signing of treaties of cooperation in the fields of economic affairs, education, culture, defense, communications, civic status and property rights, etc., with fourteen different States of which six, Madagascar, Senegal, Congo-Brazzaville, Chad, Central African Republic and Gabon, nevertheless wished to remain titular members of the Community. The text of the constitution embodying these various changes of status was submitted to parliament in May.

Thus, between France on the one hand and a sizeable part of Africa and Madagascar on the other, an assemblage of men, territories and resources was built up, whose common language was French, which in terms of currency constituted a "franc area," in which goods of every kind were exchanged on a preferential basis; in which there was regular consultation on political and diplomatic matters; in which each was pledged to help the others in case of danger; in which sea and air transport and the telegraph, telephone and radio networks were coordinated; in which every citizen, wherever he came from and wherever he went, knew and felt himself, far from being a stranger, to be welcome, esteemed, and to a large extent at home. . . .

On September 16, 1959, France, through me, announced her intention to place Algeria's destiny in the hands of the Algerians. In my view, this destiny could consist either of complete secession from France, who would then "cease to provide Algeria with so many benefits and so many millions," would henceforth do nothing to help her to avoid "poverty and chaos," and would "take the necessary measures to regroup and resettle those Algerians who wished to remain French"; or else "Francization," by which "the Algerians would become an integral part of the French people," enjoying complete equality of political, social and economic rights, "residing wherever they pleased in any of our territories"; or else, "the government of Algeria by the Algerians," a government supported by French aid, based on universal suffrage, by all means including "the present political organization of the insurrection" but without allowing it "the right to impose itself with knife and submachine-gun." I pointed out that Algeria would not be in a position to govern itself until pacification had made further progress, no doubt stretching over a number of years, and that, in the meantime,

France would continue her efforts to bring about the economic transformation of the country.

The decisive step had been taken. Undoubtedly, before everything was settled, there would be more delays, more fighting, more crises, more bargaining. But France had proclaimed that it was for the Algerians, that is to say the Moslems, to choose what their future should be; she had no intention of deciding for them under the cloak of "French Algeria"; she foresaw and accepted the fact that Algeria would become a State and, once this had been achieved, she was equally prepared to dissociate herself completely from it or to offer it her cooperation. At a press conference on November 10, I confirmed the position I had adopted. I reiterated the offer already made to the leaders of the insurrection to discuss with the French government, in complete security, "the political and military conditions for an end to the fighting." At the same time, I cited a few statistics relating, first of all, to pacification: half as many monthly exactions and half as many civilian victims as there had been two years earlier; secondly, to investments directly financed by the French Treasury: two hundred billion old francs over the year, three hundred billion in the following year; thirdly, to the development of the country by comparison with the situation before the rebellion: agricultural production increased by 50 percent, electricity consumption, foreign trade and schooling doubled, four times the number of houses built, five times the number of roads, and ten times the number of factories; and fourthly, to the bringing of the oil pipe-line from the Sahara to the port of loading at Bougie which would henceforth secure for Algeria the basic financial resources she had always lacked.

As a catalyst thrown into boiling liquid precipitates crystallization, so the position I had taken over self-determination provoked a radical division of opinion among the public. In metropolitan France there was overwhelming approval. I received proof of this in the course of a visit I made to the Nord and the Pas de Calais at the end of September. Wherever I referred to my decision, the crowds went wild with enthusiasm. Ministers, to whom I had outlined it in Cabinet on August 26 on the eve of my military inspection tour in Algeria, and explained it in detail on September 16 before making my public pronouncement, had proved, in the main, extremely favorable. On October 16, the National Assembly, in which the Prime Minister had opened a debate on the subject which he himself had asked to be put to the vote, expressed its confidence by a huge majority. At the same time, however, all those bent upon wrecking my plans redoubled their virulent opposition.

The activists in Algeria, inciting and exploiting the feelings of the local population of French stock, were already talking of revolt in the public palavers they held and the tracts they distributed. A "French National Front" was organized semi-clandestinely, under the leadership of Ortiz. "We need a Charlotte Corday!" an orator shouted at one meeting, and was loudly applauded. The principal organ of the *pieds-noirs,* the *Echo d'Alger,* which in the articles of its editor, Alain de Sérigny, had hitherto displayed a moderate attitude towards me, now adopted a tone of the utmost hostility. A fair number of Algerian deputies poured out bitter diatribes. In the melting-pot of Algiers life, both officers and civil servants indulged in contacts which were detrimental to their loyalty. "There are ways," the whisper in offices and messes went, "of forcing the General to see the error of his ways." In France itself, Georges Bidault and a few members of parliament founded the Committee for French Algeria, which forthwith provided a platform for the usual agitators of the so-called "extreme Right." In December, the ex-Premier undertook a lecture tour of Algeria which further stirred up passions. In Paris, the speeches and articles in which Marshal Juin—born in Bône, married in Constantine and a veteran of the African army—expressed his sorrow and General Weygand took the opportunity to give vent to old Vichy resentments, nourished the animosity of certain social, political, journalistic and military circles. In short, by the beginning of 1960, as national support grew more pronounced, the storm clouds were gathering on the Algerian horizon.

The storm did indeed break. The incident which caused the thunderbolt to strike was an interview which a German journalist had obtained in January with General Massu, army corps commander in Algiers, where he was very popular. In the course of the interview this valiant soldier, my old comrade, caught off guard, had been foolish enough to rail against my policy. Although I understood the distress it must cause a man of his kind (was I, its begetter, any happier about it?), although I made every allowance for the influence of his immediate circle, although I took into account his partial disclaimer and above all the protestation of loyalty he had taken it upon himself to publish, I felt that his outburst could not go unpunished. He was recalled to Paris, never to return to Algiers. Meanwhile, at a conference on Algeria which Challe attended at the Elysée on January 22, I informed him of Massu's transfer. In spite of the objurgations of the Commander-in-Chief, who warned of the risks of an explosion and talked of resignation, I stood by my decision.

The civilian and military activists in Algeria did in fact seize upon this pretext to put their prearranged plans into action. On [January] 23rd [1960], Pierre Lagaillarde, the young firebrand deputy and leader of the students' union, occupied the university at the head of a large group of demonstrators many of whom belonged to the Territorial Defense Units, a sort of *pied-noir* militia created in 1954, and were armed and in uniform. Lagaillarde himself wore the uniform of a reserve officer. There they established a stronghold, digging themselves into the faculty buildings and cellars, throwing up barricades, observing military discipline and swearing to turn the campus into a "French Algeria" redoubt. Meanwhile the word went out to the population to assemble the following afternoon, a Sunday, on the "Plateau des Glières" in the center of the city to demonstrate solidarity with the "defenders" of the university and put pressure on the authorities.

The latter, however, took steps to clear the "Plateau," where a considerable crowd, almost entirely French, had gathered. Two columns, one of *gardes mobiles,* the other of paratroops, were to converge on the square and disperse the demonstrators. The first column discharged its mission, but as it debouched into the square it came under fire from armed groups, suffering heavy casualties, both dead and wounded, and replied with a burst of machine-gun fire which wounded several civilians. The paratroops had meanwhile failed to intervene, and this at once created the impression that the loyalty of at least one section of the security forces was now in doubt. Thereupon, with the Algiers cauldron boiling over, the agitation and unrest spread to France and even into the government itself. Believing as I did that the immediate objective of the rioters was simply to force me to renege on self-determination, I was determined to lance the abscess, make no concessions whatever and obtain complete obedience from the Army.

I indicated as much briefly over the radio on January 25, describing the previous day's events as "a stab in the back for France," expressing my confidence in Delouvrier and Challe, and declaring that "I shall do my duty." The next few days were heavy with suspense. General Challe, who had at first reacted as a leader should, publicly condemning the disorder, declaring his intention to quell it, calling up powerful reinforcements, throwing a cordon of troops around the university to isolate it from the population, later modified his attitude, became engrossed in consultations with Army and civilians, did nothing to subdue Lagaillarde and his companions, and allowed them to communicate with the town as much as they pleased. He also gave Paris to understand that it was going to be necessary to compromise. He said as much to Michel Debré, who arrived in Algiers together with Pierre Guillaumat during the night of the 25–26th, and had it repeated by a bevy of colonels assembled for the purpose. He sent two or three of them to me at the Elysée the following day so that I too should hear it. In the end, after Paul Delouvrier, for fear of being swept away in the general uproar, had decided to leave Algiers on January 28 for Reghaia whence he addressed a moving appeal to the city, the Commander-in-Chief left his command post and followed the Delegate-General. That same day he gave General Ely, who went to see him on my instructions to lay down his course of action, every indication of irresolution. Meanwhile the security forces wavered; a sort of saturnalia developed on the barricades surrounding the university, with insurgents, civilians and soldiers all intermingling; and Algiers, strike-bound, without transport, shops closed, seemed to be sliding into anarchy. However, without discounting the possibility that the worst might happen, I had the impression that in all this there was more of an attempt to intimidate me than any real eagerness to cross swords. Having let the agitation "stew in its own juice" for a few days, I sensed that the moment had come to bring the affair to an end and dispel all illusions.

So on January 29 I once more appeared at the microphone and on the television screen. I had donned my uniform. I first of all confirmed that "the Algerians will have the right to decide their own destiny" and that "self-determination, as defined by the Head of State, decided on by the government, approved by parliament, adopted by the French nation, is the only possible outcome." I then

addressed myself to "the Algerian community of French stock" in
order to calm its fears, to the Army in order to call upon it to observe discipline and to give it strict orders to see that "force remains in the hands of the law," and finally "to my old and beloved
country," France, in order to "ask her to give her support whatever
happens." I ended by saying: "Since the guilty men who dream of
usurping power are using as a pretext the decision I have taken
concerning Algeria, let it be understood everywhere, let it be understood clearly, that I shall never go back on it!"

The effect was instantaneous. In France, there was every indication of general approval. In Algiers, where my speech had been
heard during a thunderstorm which seemed symbolic, every Frenchman realized that the adventurers must either surrender or go to
such extremes that few would be ready to follow them. Without
more ado, the men in command made up their minds. On Saturday
January 30, General Gracieux, appointed to the command of the
Algiers sector by Challe, was given strict orders by General Crépin,
Massu's successor, to clear the precincts of the university, and thus
blockaded the rebels; seeing which, a number of them came out
and gave themselves up. The remainder, summoned to do likewise,
laid down their arms and asked to be allowed to enlist in regular
units. With the exception of their leaders, they were permitted to do
so. By February 1 it was all over. Lagaillarde was arrested and sent
to Paris for trial. Similar action was taken in the case of several
ring-leaders, including Alain de Sérigny and the ex-deputy Demar-
quet. Ortiz escaped to Spain. Algiers calmed down and the Army
resumed its task of pacification.

The proclamation of self-determination, the revolt of the Barricades and the demonstration of the authority of the State marked a
decisive turning-point in the painful saga of the Algerian settlement.
Thenceforward, however severe and dramatic the obstacles that
still lay ahead, there was no longer any doubt that a solution could
be found, that it must inevitably lead to the emancipation of Algeria
by France and some form of association between the two countries,
and that it would not result in the rupture of our national unity. Bearing in mind the free choice made by the overseas territories which
remained within the Republic, what had been achieved in Black
Africa and Madagascar, what was happening in relation to Morocco
and Tunisia, what was still going on in Laos and Cambodia, and

the glimpse of what might one day be possible in Vietnam, it was clear that the evolution from colonization to modern cooperation now had every chance of being accomplished in such a way that France would not only be relieved of what had become an unjustifiable burden but offered the promise of fruitful cooperation in the future.

Destiny had entrusted me with this momentous task. As happened to those men who likewise in the course of our history were called upon to enforce the supreme interest of the nation, as had already happened to me in other circumstances, I was obliged, in order to achieve my aim, to coerce and sometimes punish other Frenchmen who opposed it but whose first impulse may have been well-intentioned. I was obliged to overcome the anguish which gripped me as I deliberately put an end to a colonial domination which was once glorious but would henceforth be ruinous. I was obliged, against great odds, to carry the national ambition into other fields. I knew that France called upon me to perform this task. I believed I had the ear of the people. When the time came, I would ask them whether they thought me right or wrong. And their voice would then for me be the voice of God.

IV THE END OF THE DUTCH AND BELGIAN EMPIRES

Rudolf von Albertini
THE DECOLONIZATION OF THE DUTCH EAST INDIES

Around 1700, climaxing a century of international predominance, Holland begau extending protectorates over various parts of the area known today as Indonesia. This, their major colony, the Dutch were able to hold for nearly two and a half centuries until the Japanese occupied the islands during World War II. This occupation substantially accelerated the rise of Indonesian nationalism.

The size discrepancy between the tiny Netherlands and the Indonesian archipelago, whose population had reached seventy million in 1940, explains why special forms of indirect rule were provided for in the Dutch administration and formed a part of the colonial concept from the start. It was only natural to try to economize on administrative staff and to utilize existing institutions and authorities. In the eighteenth century the East India Company had signed protectorate agreements with Indonesian princes and forced them to supply certain products. In the nineteenth, Van den Bosch's infamous "culture system" employed local regents and the village aristocracy as organs of repression. In the "ethical policy" after 1900, by contrast, the village structure was to be maintained and encouraged, while on the other hand the former loose control over island life was to be tightened. Like Great Britain with its protectorate in Malaya, the Netherlands operated on a "short contract" in the Outer Provinces. . . .

We should recall here that Ceylon had had semi-responsible government since 1931 and Burma since 1935–1937, each with its own government responsible to an elected legislative council. In 1934 the Philippines obtained a deadline for independence. But the Netherlands would not contemplate dissociation. Indonésia "belonged" to the mother country, was a part of the national territory and a source of Dutch wealth. The Dutch colonial concept stood between that of England and that of France, with the exception that there was no provision made for future decolonization. Vague references were made to an association between two autonomous areas under the Dutch Crown, but in effect the Dutch simply defended the status quo and tried to evade the question of the future. The paternalistic policy had some positive achievements to boast, but the nationalists naturally saw it as a form of ruthless colonialism which offered no hope of reform and therefore provoked radical attitudes.

Even after the outbreak of the Second World War and the Japanese invasion the government did not feel impelled to adopt a more flexible attitude. A new Indonesian proposal in the *volksraad* (the Wihowo resolution of February 1940) asked for an imperial conference to prepare for a responsible parliamentary system; it was rejected, after the invasion, on the grounds that the responsibility for such a conference lay with the Dutch parliament which, however, could not take action at the moment. Even the modest proposal of replacing the official description "Inlander" by "Indonesian" and "Dutch Indies" by "Indonesia" was rejected. It is understandable that the Indonesians reacted sharply to this tactical error! A commission was set up in September 1940 under the chairmanship of Visman but it only submitted its report in December 1941. It said Indonesians and Europeans should have full equal rights but the archipelago should obtain autonomy, with an imperial council as superordinate body. But these proposals were too vague and came too late to have any affect. Many Indonesians welcomed the Japanese as liberators and a large part of the nationalist opposition proved willing to collaborate with the occupying forces.

At first the Dutch government-in-exile in London continued to pursue its former policy. After the war, it said, a conference with representatives from the mother country, Indonesia and Surinam would meet to discuss the future—no decision could be made until then. In October 1942 in an article in *Foreign Affairs* the foreign minister, Van Kleffens, sharply attacked American anti-colonialism and the Americans' phrases about democracy, independence and self-determination, "as if these were constant values for all times and for all circumstances . . . we still are blind to what the world really needs." In Southeast Asia the requirements for independence were nonexistent, and in any case the *volksraad* had legislative power "for practically all Indian affairs." Dutch colonial policy adhered to the Atlantic Charter, asserted the foreign minister, although he also stressed that the Indonesian archipelago would remain "part of the Kingdom of the Netherlands" and that only the constitution of Indonesia and its position within the Dutch kingdom were open to discussion. Shortly afterwards, on 6 December, the Dutch government-in-exile found itself obliged, probably under American pressure, to take a stand on postwar policy. A declaration by Queen Wilhelmina stated:

I am convinced, and history as well as reports from the occupied territories confirm me in this, that after the war it will be possible to reconstruct the Kingdom on the solid foundation of complete partnership, which will mean the consummation of all that has been developed in the past. I know that no political unity nor national cohesion can continue to exist which is not supported by the voluntary acceptance and the faith of the great majority of the citizens. I know that the Netherlands more than ever feels its responsibility for the vigorous growth of the Overseas Territories and the Indonesians recognize in the ever-increasing collaboration the best guarantee for the recovery of their peace and happiness. The war years have proved that both peoples possess the will and the ability for harmonious and voluntary cooperation. . . . I visualize, without anticipating the recommendations of the future conference, that they will be directed towards a Commonwealth in which the Netherlands, Indonesia, Surinam and Curaçao will participate, with complete self-reliance and freedom of conduct for each part regarding its internal affairs, but with the readiness to render mutual assistance. . . .

It is my opinion that such a combination of independence and collaboration can give the Kingdom and its parts the strength to carry fully their responsibility, both internally and externally. This would leave no room for discrimination according to race or nationality; only the ability of the individual citizens and the needs of the various groups of the population will determine the policy of the government.

This declaration, which followed on the heels of a number of proposals between the wars and then became the basis of the Indonesia policy after 1945, stated the Dutch concept of decolonization. It shows how the terminology had changed during the war. Anti-imperialist statements now seemed necessary and the declaration spoke of partnership; the term "Commonwealth" was used to express the association of independence and collaboration. It did not imply the British system, however, but a form of federation in which the individual parts of the Empire would have internal autonomy while foreign policy, defense, and also tariff and currency questions were decided by superordinate imperial bodies. The Dutch concept is actually more comparable to the French Union with its associated states. The December 1942 declaration did not describe the federal structure in detail but left this to later conferences, raising the question of whether the Dutch were really prepared to transfer external sovereignty to federal bodies. What kind of autonomy was Indonesia to have? Did the Dutch intend to accept an Indonesian Government, or did they believe they would be able to guarantee their influence by means of a veto right and special powers for the governor?

It would be wrong to judge the queen's declaration and similar pronouncements only by their lack of success in implementation. In contrast to the rigidly conservative prewar attitude, they at least proclaimed the principle and guidelines of a generous reform policy which complied with the demands of the moderate nationalists and seemed to promise better relations. And we must not forget that Van Mook, who had a part in formulating the declaration of 6 December and played a very important role in the following years, was a member of the Stuw movement and a proponent of a liberal policy. Under "normal" circumstances and if Indonesia had remained under Dutch rule during the war, there would surely have been some chance of gradually pursuing emancipation and improving relations with the former colonial power by negotiation.

The Japanese occupation created an entirely new situation whose effects were either not recognized or not taken sufficiently into account by the Dutch government-in-exile. As in Indochina, Japan not only removed the colonial administration and dealt a severe blow to the European power, but also disseminated systematic anti-Dutch propaganda and managed to enlist the Indonesian nationalists in its own purposes. The Japanese released nationalist leaders from prison, formed a representative council under Sukarno, set up an Indonesian army and created youth associations. In October 1944, Japan promised independence and set up a constitutional commission which prepared the Republic of Indonesia, which was proclaimed on 17 August 1945, a few days before the Japanese capitulation, by Sukarno and Hatta. A constitution was approved on short notice and a cabinet set up. Japanese weapons were used to arm at least rudimentary forces. Much like the French in Indochina, the Dutch now found themselves, at the moment when they wanted to resume their prewar position, faced with the fait accompli of a proclaimed republic controlled by the young and radical generation of nationalists who had refused to collaborate with the colonial power before the war and had spent several years In exile.

Van Mook had counted on a strong national movement but not on finding an already established republic. Like the French Government, the Dutch now asked itself whether it should recognize this republic and in what form. The returning colonial power had few troops at its disposal and was dependent on Allied help. But Lord Mountbatten, the high commander on this front, was, as Dutch historians all too willingly overlook, the representative of a distinctly liberal policy and he showed much goodwill to the nationalists in Burma. So it is understandable that he would not install strong military forces in Indonesia or engage in open battle with the Republic. The English even recognized the Republic de facto and called on the Dutch to begin negotiations. But the Dutch saw the Republic as a regime set up by Japan, and wanted to arrest the members of the government as collaborators and traitors rather than consider them legitimate partners. In November 1945 Van Mook made a declaration to this effect: the Netherlands recognized Indonesian aspirations to nationhood and was prepared for friendly cooperation within the "Commonwealth"; Indonesians would obtain a considerable majority in the *volksraad* and could form a ministerial council under the governor-general. This declaration reaffirmed that of 6 December and indicated a decisive step forward by comparison with prewar times; but by 1945 it was overtaken by events. For there was no talk of accepting a Republic of Indonesia, and the Dutch officially ignored its existence. Van Mook, who represented the mother country in Indonesia, was still under pressure from his own conservative government.

We have no space here to outline the subsequent laborious negotiations, the numerous proposals and counterproposals, the ineffectual arguments, the intervention of the United Nations and two Dutch "police actions." We shall confine ourselves to a few comments on Dutch policy.

The Netherlands had to start negotiating with the Republic and accept Indonesia's right to decide its destiny, i.e., to agree to the

planned association with the mother country or to choose independence. The Dutch claimed that for the time being they still held the
only sovereign power in the achipelago while the Republic pointed
out that it existed de facto and demanded bilateral negotiations.
Only after France, on 6 March 1946, had accepted Ho Chi Minh's
republic as part of the federation of Indochina did the Dutch accept
the Indonesian Republic. Indonesia for its part agreed to this and,
for the time being at least, gave up its claim to represent the entire
archipelago as a sovereign republic.

At the conference of Manilo in Celebes, the Dutch tried to gain
control of the Outer Provinces that were not in the Republic and to
install autonomous governments which were to have equal rights
within the federation. For this maneuver the Dutch exploited the
traditional distrust of Java and the local sense of patriotism in order
to exaggerate the opposition to the Republic and to deny its claim
to leadership. In this way they hoped to assume a decisive role in
the federation of Indonesia and the proposed Union. This is a striking parallel to the situation in Indochina and the attempts of the
French Government to neutralize the republic of Ho Chi Minh! But
the agreement of Linggadjali (27 March 1947) forced the Dutch to
recognize the de facto authority of the Republic over Java and
Sumatra, who for their part declared themselves willing to enter
into a federation with two other republics, which would then associate itself with the mother country. However, the Dutch did not
manage to create a basis of trust and each of the two "partners"
tried to build up positions of power in the territory of the other. The
Dutch began an economic blockade and after the Catholic party
came to power it embarked on its first "police action," which
started on 21 July 1947 and ended with the armistice on 17 January
1948. On 9 March 1948 an interim federal government was unilaterally
announced, consisting of the governor-general and a majority of
Dutch department heads; the Republic had to accept the conditions
laid down by the colonial power before the real government of the
"United States of Indonesia" was formed. In addition the Dutch
wanted to incorporate the Republic with the other autonomous territories on a parity basis only and wanted, as far as possible, to
totally "liquidate" it in the transitional period.

The Republic saw through this maneuver and stressed that the complete preponderance this would give Java utterly excluded parity representation; it dismissed the other territories as products of Dutch "neo-colonialism." A short-term ultimatum was finally followed, on 19 December 1948, by the second Dutch "police action." But although the police occupied the most important towns of Java and Sumatra it did not manage to put an end to the guerrilla warfare. At this point the United Nations intervened and the United States, which had hitherto tried to mediate, openly attacked Dutch actions. On 1 August 1949 a cease-fire was agreed and on 2 November, after a round-table conference, an agreement was signed in The Hague by which the Netherlands pledged itself to transfer its entire Indonesian Empire, with the exception of West New Guinea, to the United States of Indonesia, which was to consist of the Republic together with fifteen other autonomous states and would be a partner in a Dutch-Indonesia Union. The "partners" were independent sovereign states, although they recognized the Dutch queen as head of the union. So, instead of the federation proclaimed on 6 December 1942 a kind of Commonwealth had now come into being. But this non-British Commonwealth did not prove viable and was terminated by Indonesia in 1954. After the withdrawal of the Dutch, the Republic had, as expected, very quickly managed to assert its claim to leadership.

Arend Lijphart
THE DUTCH AND WEST NEW GUINEA

Professor Lijphart's study of the Dutch withdrawal from West New Guinea is interesting in its own right as a document on the Dutch political mind and, also as a case study of the sentimental factors involved in European decolonization. Here was an area devoid of strategic or economic significance, yet terribly important to the Dutch. This work serves to substantiate,

Arend Lijphart, *The Trauma of Decolonization: The Dutch and West New Guinea,* Chapter 12. Copyright © Yale University Press, New Haven, 1966. Reprinted by permission of Yale University Press.

then, the type of argument made earlier in the Thornton and Smith essays that the "collective mind" of the political elite must be understood as an important factor in foreign-policy decision-making. Professor Lijphart is the author of several books on international and European politics.

The agonies of the decolonization process are well exemplified by the painful and reluctant withdrawal of the Netherlands from its colonies. It did not grant independence to Indonesia until after more than four years of bitter conflict. Then another twelve and a half years were spent in a vain attempt to hang on to West New Guinea, the last remnant of its colonial empire. These experiences were extremely traumatic. Holland acted with an intense emotional commitment, manifested in pathological feelings of self-righteousness, resentment, and pseudo-moral convictions. These emotions started to decrease in intensity in the late 1950s, but protracted and ultimately unsuccessful resistance to decolonization still left the country internally divided, frustrated, and humiliated. In addition to these psychological wounds, Holland was physically hurt. Investment and trade opportunities in Indonesia, the livelihood of thousands of Dutchmen in Indonesia, and the lives of Dutch soldiers who died in the defense of New Guinea were sacrificed in the useless and futile struggle to resist colonial disengagement. This last colonialist effort damaged Holland's well-being even more seriously by dominating its foreign policy and diverting its energies away from more vital pursuits.

Undoubtedly the psychological and physical wounds account for Dutch feelings on the New Guinea issue since Holland's departure from the territory in 1962. Almost immediately after decolonization the New Guinea issue disappeared from the Dutch scene. Concern for the future of New Guinea and the Papuans, which ostensibly motivated the Dutch before 1962, are hardly voiced any longer. This is not merely indifference; rather, the deep trauma attending the fruitless struggle for New Guinea has caused a compulsive urge to forget. The Dutch now anxiously and guiltily want to banish New Guinea from their range of attention. In fact this reorientation has been of metamorphic proportions: diplomatic relations with Indonesia have been restored, and exchanges of amicable and cordial visits by high government officials took place less than two years after the two countries were at war in New Guinea.

What were the causes of the passionate attachment of the Dutch to their colonial empire, and especially to West New Guinea? The Dutch themselves justified their continued presence in New Guinea with a whole series of historical, geographical, ethnological, legal, and ethical arguments. They were far from convincing. Holland assumed the "white man's burden to promote the economic welfare and political development of the Papuans, but its paternalistic guardianship was not in the best interests of the native population, especially because Holland was too weak to execute its designs in the long run. Furthermore, Holland's insistence on keeping *exclusive* responsibility for the Papuans revealed how the Dutch concern for New Guinea was overlaid with selfish motives. Holland's altruism was strongly egocentric. The Dutch themselves were not entirely unaware of their ambivalence toward the Papuans. For instance, the important Call to Reflection issued by the General Synod of the Dutch Reformed Church forcefully called attention to the "selfishness which is not focused on material gain, but on the pursuit of high ideals." The ultimate shallowness of Dutch altruism is also demonstrated by its sudden disappearance after the departure from New Guinea.

Many observers, both Communist and non-Communist interpreted the New Guinea issue in economic terms and asserted that Holland wanted to keep possession of the territory because of its material wealth, especially its rich natural resources and immigration possibilities. This image of West New Guinea played a very important role on the Dutch domestic political scene, too. In particular, the Eurasian minority and its interest groups regarded New Guinea as an area suitable for settlement and assumed that it had the economic potential to sustain a large population. West New Guinea was often compared with the rich Belgian Congo and with the prosperous former Dutch colony in the Gold Coast. These attractive images of New Guinea were prevalent among some Cabinet members, many legislators, right-wing politicians, high bureaucrats in the Ministry of Overseas Territories, and various nationalistic and colonialistic groups.

The view of New Guinea as an economically advantageous area was completely false. New Guinea was a liability rather than an asset to the Dutch treasury: it offered no rich source of raw materials, no trade advantages, no investment opportunities, and no possibilities for immigration either by Eurasians or by white Dutchmen. On balance, Holland's national economic interests suffered as a result of the New Guinea issue, for it contributed to the loss of Holland's economic interests in Indonesia. The same can be said of Dutch special interests in New Guinea. Some Dutch firms made profits there, but these were offset by greater losses in Indonesia. Therefore Holland's refusal to decolonize can certainly not be explained on the basis of economics.

Another explanation of Holland's motivation emphasizes the strategic significance of New Guinea. It was argued that Holland served the cause of the Western alliances by refusing to hand the territory over to the Indonesians. Outside Holland only Communist spokesmen and commentators used this argument. Few of Holland's allies were sufficiently impressed by it to give meaningful support to the Dutch. On the Dutch domestic political scene this image of Holland's role as the guardian of the free world's military interests was widespread. Various right-wing, nationalistic, veterans', and militaristic groups were insistent advocates of Holland's retention of New Guinea for military-strategic reasons, but in the 1950s it also struck a responsive chord among more moderate groups and even among the Socialists. Again, this view was utterly false. Holland had neither a direct nor an indirect strategic interest in New Guinea. Similarly, the idea that Holland's prestige in world politics could be maintained by remaining a colonial power was incorrect. New Guinea only contributed to a misplaced self-esteem for the Dutch.

Objective interests cannot explain Holland's reluctance to decolonize. Holland was, in fact, hurt rather than helped by its last efforts to remain a colonial power. When objective interests did begin to play a major role in the New Guinea issue, their influence was exerted in the direction of disengagement rather than continued colonialism. In the late 1950s and early 1960s the Dutch were shocked into realizing the futility of their policies by outside military and diplomatic pressures, as well as domestic pressures of the Dutch Reformed Church, the increasingly oppositional Labor Party, business groups with interests in Indonesia, and the press. The actions of the Dutch Reformed Church were prompted at least partly by its missionary interests, and the business lobby to restore cordial economic relations with Indonesia. The growing Socialist opposition and the radical change in press opinion occurred primarily in response to very real military dangers to which Holland was exposing itself. In short, analysis of the reasons behind Holland's policies toward New Guinea does reveal the presence of certain objective interests, but these played a role in the process of decolonization only, *not* in the policies of retaining colonial control.

The real motives behind Holland's reluctance to decolonize were entirely subjective and psychological: the search for national self-esteem, feelings of moral superiority, egocentric altruism, and deep resentment against Indonesia. The common denominator was the sense of frustrated nationalism. To the Dutch, New Guinea became the symbol of Holland's continued national grandeur, power, and moral worth. The attachment to New Guinea was definitely pathological: it was a symptom of a serious and protracted inferiority complex, which healed only very slowly. The symbolic value of New Guinea overshadowed all other considerations. This accounts for the totally unrealistic appraisals of the objective economic, strategic, and political importance of the territory. Because New Guinea symbolized Holland's political and moral strength, it *had* to be rich and potentially prosperous and a vital strategic bastion, with a population yearning for benevolent Dutch tutelage. In other words, the expectations of economic and other benefits from New Guinea were mere appendages and subjective conditions of the psychological symbolism of New Guinea.

The sense of frustrated nationalism that was the fundamental causative factor in Dutch policies toward New Guinea was felt with particular intensity by a number of special groups, such as the Eurasians, veterans' groups, and the whole array of right-wing extremist and superpatriotic associations. They played an important role in Dutch politics and were able to exert considerable influence. Nevertheless, it would be wrong to blame the New Guinea problem exclusively on these relatively small and weak groups. The Dutch people and their political leaders could easily have ignored their pleas. These groups were extreme and vocal, but they represented ideas that permeated the entire nation. It should be remembered that the responsibility for retaining Dutch control over New Guinea in 1949 lay with the center groups and in particular the Liberal Party.

By the middle of the 1950s the Dutch were virtually unanimous in their opposition to colonial disengagement, and dissenting voices were almost completely stifled.

The conclusion that Holland's stubborn refusal to abandon New Guinea was motivated exclusively by subjective and irrational factors gives the New Guinea problem a special significance in the context of theories of imperialism and colonialism.... Many of these theories attribute some importance to subjective forces but generally emphasize the role of objective factors. The case of New Guinea clearly disproves the contention that colonialism is solely motivated by objective interests. But this is only a negative conclusion. Unfortunately, the study of one case cannot lead to the formulation of a positive general proposition; no case study can ever prove anything. A case study can, however, exemplify, indicate significant problems for further analysis, or suggest the need for reappraisal of well-established and accepted theories.

The case of New Guinea cannot and does not prove that colonialism is caused by subjective forces to the exclusion of all objective forces. It merely shows that, in one instance, subjective forces alone were sufficiently powerful to keep colonialism alive. This strongly suggests that subjective forces should not be underestimated, even in cases where objective interests also play a major role. A brief glance at the history of colonialism and decolonization since the Second World War reveals the prominent role of nationalistic pride and self-righteousness in the refusal to decolonize, not only in the case of the Netherlands, but also in many other instances, especially French and Portuguese colonialism. Another aspect of the New Guinea case that suggests a conclusion of wider applicability is the influence exerted by white settler groups identified with the colonial ruler and motivated by totally unrealistic expectations of continued supremacy: the Eurasians in the case of New Guinea; the *colons* of Algeria; the white settlers of the Congo, Kenya, and Southern Rhodesia; the American "Zonians" of the Panama Canal Zone. Other parallels between New Guinea and other cases of colonialism suggest themselves when the roles of various right-wing groups, the military, the bureaucracy, etc., are investigated.

This thesis is stated in hyperbolic form in the preamble to the UNESCO Constitution: "wars begin in the minds of men..." As a monistic thesis it has obvious limitations, because it overlooks the effect of the political framework of international action and because the proposed remedy that "it is in the minds of men that the defenses of peace must be constructed" is difficult to apply. Moreover, the "minds of men" thesis is clearly insufficient: conflicts can often be traced to competition for real, objective advantages rather than imaginary interests and may even be aggravated rather than ameliorated by improved international communication and mutual understanding. Yet even where conflicts appear to be clashes of objective interests, subjective elements may be more basic. In the case of West New Guinea, the subjective attachment of the Dutch to this worthless area was often camouflaged by assertions of the objective advantages of the territory. This finding contradicts the view of the cynical realist that subjective considerations merely hide the true motives of nations, namely the pursuit of objective self-interest. Analysis of Dutch actions in the New Guinea issue demonstrates that subjective, often irrational factors—nationalistic feelings, stereotyped thinking, and moralistic slogans—can be important forces leading to international conflict. Holland's involvement in the bitter struggle with Indonesia over New Guinea was not prompted by Dutch objective interests at all, but wholly and exclusively by its emotional commitment.

Crawford Young
THE END OF THE BELGIAN CONGO

Leopold, King of the Belgians, decided to carve out of central Africa an area known as the Congo—nearly 80 times the size of Belgium—in the late 1870s. After a period of terrible exploitation of the Africans, the colony passed to the Belgian state to which it continued to provide a sizable revenue. Crawford Young recounts here the postwar policy of the Belgian government.

Selections from "Decolonization: The Belgian Division," in Crawford Young, *Politics in the Congo: Decolonization and Independence*, pp. 36–58. Copyright © 1965 by Princeton University Press; Princeton Paperback, 1967. Footnotes omitted. Reprinted by permission of Princeton University Press.

The fundamental assumption in the decolonization process was that there was still plenty of time. Before World War II, there is no evidence that any real thought was given to a future outside the colonial framework; Ryckmans in his 1937 address referred to the Congo as a "tenth province." In 1946, G. Caprasse, in the *Courrier d'Afrique,* Catholic daily in Leopoldville, suggested that the centennial of the establishment of the Congo Free State in 1985 might be an appropriate target for termination of colonial status; but this had little echo. In 1952, Petillon, in his first speech as Governor-General, declared that the time had come to begin preparing for eventual "emancipation"; and, in 1954, the newly installed Liberal-Socialist coalition government used the word "independence" in a vague way, but with no indication as to how far off this might be. Few in 1956 found Van Bilsen's thirty-year plan anything other than the naive dream of a soft-headed *"indigèniste."* Beginning in 1957, however, there was a gradual realization that the sands were running out, and, by 1958, responsible officials were thinking in terms of ten years. But until virtually the last minute, the colonial system approached the problem of adaptation with the assumption that several decades would be available to carry it out. Ironically, the Achilles' heel of the Belgian rule in Africa was always felt to be Ruanda-Urundi, where, through the embarrassing entanglement of trusteeship obligation, growing pressure from the UN was being felt for the establishment of a deadline for independence.

Linked with the belief that there was no urgency to begin the process was the assumption that decolonization would remain under full Belgian control. Hodgkin's philosopher-king in his wisdom, after seeking what advice he felt appropriate to solicit, would create by decree the Congolese state. This premise permeates official declarations from the moment that Petillon announced the emancipation goal in 1952. It appears in both the Royal Message and Government Declaration of January 13, 1959; Baudouin declared, "We are today resolved to lead without fatal delays, but also without precipitate haste, the Congolese populations to independence in prosperity and peace." The Colonial Minister added, "Belgium intends to organize in the Congo a democracy capable of exercising the prerogatives of sovereignty and of deciding on its independence." Another revealing symptom was the designation of an all-European *Groupe de Travail* in August 1958 to undertake a fact-find-

ing inquiry on the basis of which to announce a new government
policy for the Congo. The technical explanation for this was that
it was to be a "national" mission reporting to the Belgian government. The mission made certain colossal misjudgments of the tem-
per of Congolese opinion; an example of this is the following
observation: "A large number of Congolese interlocutors asked immediate independence.... [On the basis of their explanations], the
Groupe de Travail concluded that its interlocutors meant by immediate independence the immediate liberation of the individual."

This approach, in addition, made the conclusions and the resulting new policy suspect to large sectors of Congolese opinion. The
first act of the group of Congolese in Leopoldville who, in October
1958, formed the *Mouvement National Congolais* (MNC)) was to submit a letter to Minister (and ex-Governor-General) Petillon, declaring: "The undersigned ... deeply regret that the Minister did not
include any Congolese members in the *Groupe de Travail;* ... fear
that, without the participation of the latter, the conclusions which
will emerge ... will reflect too unilateral a viewpoint, inspired by a
certain conservatism attached to the colonialist spirit ... and formu-
late as of now reservations concerning the final decisions which
Parliament will be led to take, following on these conclusions."

The related assumption of the pliable mass, remarked in Hodgkin's Platonian metaphor, can be uncovered on both sides of the
protracted debate on indirect versus direct rule. Franck, the archi-
tect of indirect rule, stated, "We are not obstinately trying to train
an imitation European, a black Belgian, but rather a better Congolese, *c'est-à-dire un nègre robuste, bien portant et travailleur.*"
The Commission for the Protection of Natives, an adversary of indirect rule, retorted, "Colonization consists in the final analysis in
causing to participate in European civilization a backward population ... that this participation must be pushed as far as possible, so
that assimilation should be the final end of all colonization ... [and]
that the more backward the population and the more radical the
reforms which its accession to our civilization necessitates, the
stronger, more general, and more constant our intervention in native life must be." During World War II, one of the young Catholic
intellectuals grouped around the progressive Elisabethville lawyer
Antoine Rubbens added in the same vein: "The issue is, during the
coming years, to show that we are capable of transforming this

country and grouping these fragments of clans, of groups, of races in a living unit. . . . We have made this country, we have conquered it and we have grouped it, we have liberated it from the slave trade and from its internal struggles."

This motif can be found, implicitly or explicitly, in most of the colonial literature and official pronouncements. Its longevity is reflected in the efforts of the three major Belgian parties, beginning especially in 1956 with congresses to define their respective approaches to the challenge of decolonization, to extend their activities to the Congo—each hoping to insure that the future Congolese state would be erected upon the basis of its particular precepts of social and political organization.

An important corollary of controlled gradualism is the pervasive legalism which characterizes much of Belgian political thought. The study of government still takes place within the walls of the faculties of law. The basic texts in political science are written in the form and spirit of a handbook in constitutional law. Many of the senior policy-making officials had been trained as magistrates. One cannot help being struck by how much of the scholarly and official discourse on political adaptation took place in the idiom of the jurist, and how little was informed by any apparent sociological perceptions. The deeply ingrained respect for law in Belgium is no doubt a national virtue; the arid legalism of much of the debate on colonial policy, however, partially explains its frequent lack of reality.

In retrospect, the assumptions of abundant time, controlled development, and pliable subjects seem to betray a *naïveté* unusual to a normally practical and hard-headed nation such as Belgium. It is true that the Belgians failed as prophets and that they insufficiently extrapolated from trends elsewhere in Africa and Asia the implications for the Congo. But it is vital to recall that the colonial establishment was not subjected to serious African challenge until after the Leopoldville riots in 1959. Until about 1954, articulated African grievances related almost entirely to African status within the colonial society. In the following years, the harbingers of a nationalist awakening appeared with growing frequency, but African impact on colonial decision-making processes was minuscule.

There was simply no comparison with most British and French

territories, especially those in West Africa, where the colonial establishment was under constant African pressure and a broad range of
policy was formulated in reaction to (although not always affording
satisfaction to) nationalist demands. Until about 1957, the policy of
subordinating political development to economic and social advances had the appearance of success from the Belgian point of
view. Critics such as Van Bilsen had little Congolese evidence to
prove that this success was more apparent than real; their arguments were based on the inevitability of emergent trends visible
elsewhere in the Congo. Accurate as this reasoning was, it lacked
compelling urgency to the colonial trinity.

A universally shared belief was that political construction should
take place from the ground up. The mystical value attached to local
institutions has deep roots in Belgian history. The British also gave
considerable emphasis to the question of workable and effective
local governmental institutions, but never with such single-minded
devotion to a "build-from-the-ground-up" theory. The centralized
French political tradition placed very little value on local government. In neither case was the mystique of the communes as reposi-
tories of the civic virtues of the people so embedded as it is was
in Belgian political culture. Belgian medieval history is dominated
by the rise of the commune, not the rise of a centralizing monarchy.
The great Belgian national heroes were the communal leaders, who
defended the people against the exactions of the succession of
alien rulers who laid claim to Belgium. . . .

When the debate began over means of political training and the
nature of the new institutions to be created, all agree that the grass-
roots approach was the only feasible solution. Petillon in his 1952
annual declaration as Governor-General declared that the Congolese would be more closely associated with the administration
of the Congo through beginning with the base. Responsibility could
only be learned, it was felt, by immersion in the problems of building sewers and paving roads which are the warp and woof of urban
administration. "The only effective training," wrote one authority
in 1953, "is that achieved through contact with the immediate and
daily needs of the population." The only level of political institutions in the independent Congo which was really the product of
careful study and even loving nurture was that of the urban and
rural *circonscription,* each reformed in 1957 by the important de-

crees of March 26 (urban) and May 10 (rural). A CEPSI study in 1951, urging that priority be given to these reforms, declared: "As it happened in Belgium, the commune, progressively becoming aware of its interests and those of its inhabitants, will furnish to all an effective protection. It will be the natural framework in which the rules of a new life will be forged, in order and liberty."

Another persistent theme with evident origins in Belgian political and social values was the interest in creating an African middle class. This object was not in fact consistently pursued in policy, because its premises were clearly open to question and because, though many would join in willing the end, few were prepared to will the means. But it is logical that to the European the Congo would seem to be a stage for the reenactment of Belgian history, whose fulfillment called for the creation of a strong middle class which would be motivated by the same impulses to stability and material progress as the artisan-merchant group who are the Belgian social heroes. An outstanding spokesman for this view was Henri Depage, who argued that building universities and granting political rights without first making it possible for Africans to attain the same economic level as Europeans "was to favor the formation of malcontents and agitators." The influential *Centre d'Etudes des Problèmes Sociaux Indigènes* (CEPSI) in Elisabethville declared in 1951:

> The colonial experience of European nations must incite us to avoid creating hastily a class of highly privileged natives from whom would spring probably the elements seeking to win over the ignorant mass to accede to power and deprive it of the still indispensable assistance of the colonizer. It is, on the contrary, appropriate to favor above all and by all means the creation of middle classes. The middle classes will be finally composed of blacks and whites and will constitute the foundation upon which future elites can solidly base themselves.

. . . Shortly after Buisseret took office in 1954, the *Association des Classes Moyennes Africaines* (ACMAF) was launched, with considerable assistance from European settler groups in many places. Buisseret as a Liberal was particularly susceptible to this line of reasoning and gave substantial encouragement through facilitating study trips to Belgium, participation in seminars, and the like. A key to applying such a policy would have been a willingness to allow Africans to own land. Although a theoretical legal right to own land existed from the Congo Free State days, it was not applied, even after more specific permissive legislation was adopted in 1953. In 1960, a bare handful of landowners could be found among the Africans. For the most part, they were recipients of land from the *Comité Spécial du Katanga* rather than the domain lands of the government

Another important assumption in Belgian policy which sharply distinguishes the Congo from West Africa was that the European community was destined to play an important role not only as technicians but as participants jointly with the Congolese in the political institutions of the new state. Impossible contradictions arose between this goal and the requirement that Belgium as a constitutional democracy based on universal suffrage should bequeath to the Congo a similar set of institutions. The conundrums growing from this dilemma were a crucial factor in understanding the *immobilisme* in Belgian postwar policy.

A Eurafrican state was assumed by both European and Congolese in the early postwar years. Belgium had always resisted settler demands for the exercise of political rights on the grounds that these could only be extended when the African population was in a position to share in them. European agitation for political rights date back, especially in the Katanga, almost to the first arrival of permanent settlers about 1911. Close contact with the Rhodesias and South Africa whetted their appetites; as early as 1920, a group of leading clerics, businessmen, and settlers in Elisabethville published a plan for reorganizing the Congo, which included a demand for elected European urban councils. These European demands became more insistent after World War II, and at the same time the emerging Congolese elite began for the first time to ask that African leadership be consulted before decisions affecting them were taken. As a leading missionary remarked in 1951: "Powerful forces seem to be at work, propagating feverishly new ideas: the Congolese nation is formed by the settlers and the natives; legislative power belongs to that nation; and especially to the elite of that nation which will for a long time be composed chiefly of whites."

The difficulty came to a head between 1948 and 1957, in the effort to define a new regime for governing urban areas. For a time, parity institutions seemed to offer a solution, but writing this into the statutes implied making a clear distinction between the European and African communities, and offered the latter a second-class form of representation. A temporary solution was found by adding enough interest-group representation, so defined as to be largely European, to achieve a de facto parity, without making it a formal legislative principle. The *Groupe de Travail* in 1958 found that the Europeans were still strongly attached to the parity notion as the only way in which they could be guaranteed a permanent role in Congo political institutions. They justified this on the grounds that the two races were at different stages of evolution and that a role out of proportion to that nose-counting would have provided was necessary for the European community. In its report, the *Groupe de Travail* assumed European participation at all levels; the only question really raised was whether Europeans should be integrated into the rural *circonscriptions* at the lowest level, or only at the level of the territorial council.

Until 1959, the notion of a Congo state in which Europeans played a large role was generally accepted by African opinion as well. The 1956 Manifesto of *Conscience Africaine* talks of a community built together by Europeans and Africans, although it warns that many Belgians will have to alter their attitudes. Lumumba, in 1956, wrote:

> *The new Eurafrican society which we are building today must be administered and directed jointly by Belgians and Congolese. Neither of the two fractions of the Belgo-Congolese community should dominate or oppress the other. One will find in each service or department, African and European civil servants working side by side in the direction of their country.*

Five years earlier, Joseph Okito, *Mouvement National Congolais-Lumumba* (MNC/L) leader who was assassinated with Lumumba in the Katanga in early 1961, had written in terms that would have warmed a Mississippian heart: "We must collaborate modestly with our civilizers in the evolution and well-being of our country, but in realizing that only the Belgians have been able to create the impulsion and maintain the direction. . . . We must remain in our place."

African statements at this stage must be placed in the context of the severe restraints on free expression of political opinion and the exigencies of "tactical action." On the other hand, political perspectives for change have as their starting point the existing situation.

A Congo as radically Africanized as that of 1960 would have been literally unimaginable in 1956, and it seems fair to conclude that at that time most of the Congolese leadership was prepared, or resigned, to accept substantial European participation. A final significant assumption was that the King of the Belgians would remain as the personal and institutional link binding Belgium to the Congo. Again there is no real parallel in colonial history for the vital role the royal family has played in the Congo. Leopold II became convinced in his youthful travels that Belgium absolutely needed a colony to expand the narrow horizons of the country, to capture its imagination and embark it upon a grandiose adventure. Without the extraordinary tenacity of Leopold, the Congo Free State would never have been created. Leopold then "bequeathed" the Congo to Belgium, which took over administration of the giant royal domain with enthusiasm limited to a very narrow circle of missionaries, adventurers, and students of the reports of the geological missions to Katanga. But the royal family always retained a special interest in the Congo and a powerful conviction that tradition called for the King to take an active part in the formulation of Congo policy.

King Albert and King Leopold each visited the Congo as Crown Prince; the latter in 1933, shortly before succeeding to the throne, made a dramatic speech proposing important innovations in the field of African agriculture. It was here that the *paysannat indigène* was first formally suggested, and some grumblings were caused by the clear option expressed in favor of African agriculture instead of large-scale European settlement. As part of the campaign to gain psychological acceptance for the Belgo-Congolese community idea, Baudouin paid a royal visit to the Congo in 1955, which proved to be a spectacular success. . . .

It has sometimes been alleged, without much supporting evidence, that the dynasty's concern with Congo affairs has been related to financial interests in colonial companies. There is strong reason to suppose that the royal family has significant holdings in the *Société Générale*. This enormous financial empire was founded in 1822 on the initiative of King William of the Netherlands (under the influence of Saint-Simon). When the company was reorganized after Belgium broke away from the Netherlands in 1830, Leopold I apparently obtained a substantial participation. Three of the twelve current members of the Board of Directors bear the title of "Grand Marshal of the Court," and are generally recognized to represent the dynasty. However, there is no evidence that they play an important role in the management of *"La Générale."*

Rather, the role of the dynasty should be related to the complex of historic myths which have grown out of Leopold II's foundation of the Congo Free State. The behavior of the monarchy is most comprehensible in recent years as a conscious effort to fulfill a role believed to be historically prescribed. This brief recapitulation does not fully capture the important network of influence radiating from the Palace. The royal family and its entourage sought to remain closely informed on Congo developments; they were in touch with all important milieux of colonial society. Most Belgian academic specialists concerned with the problem of political adaptation in the Congo have been invited to visit the royal residence at Laeken. The annals of Belgian political gossip and *petite histoire* are replete with tales relating the current Palace standing of the various well-known colonial authorities.

Since Ryckmans first called for an end to classic-patterns of colonial rule in 1946, Belgium moved slowly, at first imperceptibly, toward a definition of its terminal objectives. The first moves were in the direction of giving body to the traditional doctrine of paternalism. Judgment day was to be postponed and the new exigencies of international accountability satisfied by redoubling efforts in the economic and social realm. Coupled with this were efforts to head off nationalist aspirations among the emerging modern elite by insuring that special status satisfaction was accorded through the badge of "civilization" of an immatriculation decree and a campaign against racial discrimination. The illusion that the crux of the difficulties lay in race relations was particularly resilient. After the royal visit in 1955, Baudouin pointed to "human relations" as the basic problem confronting the Congo. The *Groupe de Travail* could conclude that by "immediate independence" their Congolese interlocutors merely were asking to end racial discrimination. The parliamentary commission dispatched to inquire into the causes of the Leopoldville riots in 1959 placed frustration over continued racial disabilities as the central factor.

Beginning with Petillon's speech in 1952, the idea of the Belgo-Congolese community served as a transitional goal between the intolerable prospect of total rupture and the impossibility of maintaining colonial domination as an end unto itself. Like the Commonwealth and the French Community, it was a vague and somewhat formless idea, capable of a variety of interpretations. In itself, it was a hopelessly inadequate program; Van Bilsen accurately points out, "It expressed beyond any doubt the desire to find new forms of hegemony or a prolonged Belgian tutelage." But it did at least give formal recognition to the need for a concrete goal. To an extent, it provided the liberal with a framework within which to urge change and adaptation, and the conservative a way of accepting it. Not even progressive Belgians could be expected to desire an independence which involved a sharp break in Belgium's special relationship with the Congo; as Van Bilsen observed, all secretly hoped for some form of Belgo-Congolese union.

The content of the Belgo-Congolese community idea gradually was transformed, even while the slogan continued to be employed. In 1955, Baudouin declared that Belgium and the Congo formed a single nation. Former Colonial Minister Wigny held that the objective was "permanent maintenance of an enlarged Belgium." Although never fully articulated as government policy, the accent seemed to be placed upon some sort of integration of the Congo with Belgium. Thereafter, the Belgo-Congolese community hypothesis was altered to assume that the Congo would possess full internal autonomy, and that the community would be a parity association between the two states, linked by the Crown, with the unspoken assumption that, as the older partner, Belgium would enjoy seniority rights in the partnership. It will be recalled that at this point it was also assumed that the Congo would have its internal institutions built upon the parity principle.

The premise of internal autonomy and a community linking two separate states had a major shortcoming: logic and the postulates of democracy required that this community could not be imposed by one of the partners, but rather had to be freely negotiated by both. Its creation therefore supposed the erection of a Congolese state whose structures were legitimated by some organization of the consent of the population compatible with Belgian democratic precepts. It was on this assumption that Lumumba wrote in favor of the Belgo-Congolese community in 1956; the authors of the *Conscience Africaine* Manifesto set forth this idea explicitly:

> *To speak clearly, the Congolese who reflect on these problems fear that certain persons may deform the idea of a Belgo-Congolese Community, to make it a brake on the total emancipation of the Congolese people, a means also for indefinitely perpetuating the domination of at least the preponderate influence of the Europeans, forming a privileged caste. In the sense which we give the idea, such a Community, far from being an obstacle, must be the means for realizing our total emancipation.*

In 1957, publicist Jean Labrique, a press attaché of the Governor-General who had extensive Congolese contacts, found in a series of interviews with Congolese leaders a belief that the construction of a democratic Congolese polity was a prerequisite to the definition of any Eurafrican formulas. Cynicism about this formula grew as the years passed without any clear definition of its content. The influential Katanga editor Jean Sépulchre denounced it as *"fantomale"* and a pretext for *immobilisme*. And the brilliant son of the Congo's ablest Governor-General, André Ryckmans, wrote in a letter in early 1957: "As for the Belgo-Congolese Community, I sincerely wonder if there is a single African who believes in it; the Africans are psychologists enough to recognize the enormous ingredient of hypocrisy there is in the present declarations. . . . There again I agree with Van Bilsen that we were wrong to trumpet this theme at every turn, rendering it thus suspect; there is nothing so ridiculous as an all-purpose slogan."

As Belgian rule in the Congo neared its close, however, the community slogan gradually faded away. The *Groupe de Travail* affirmed that the great majority of persons testifying expressed the desire to see Belgium lead the Congo to full internal autonomy, and that at this time the two parties would freely negotiate the new links of association; the two aspects were said to be indissolubly interrelated. Count d'Aspremont-Lynden, in a memorandum on the special fact-finding mission to the Congo to which he was assigned, still maintained, in August 1959, "It goes without saying that the authorities of the Congo have never envisaged any other final objective than the creation of a community between Belgium and the Congo." Belgian expectations in this regard then rapidly dwindled to a meager Treaty of Friendship and Technical Assistance, signed on June 29, 1960, but not ratified by either Parliament.

Finally, when the time came to give a political superstructure to the bureaucratic colonial system, the norms of representative democracy in Belgium necessarily came into play. All agreed in principle that institutions should be "adapted," but in the final analysis the only familiar standard of reference for Belgians and Congolese was the Belgian constitution. "Far from imposing purely European solutions, we intend to favor original adaptations, based upon African characteristics and cherished traditions," stated the royal message. Yet, when work was completed on the provisional constitution, the *Loi Fondamentale,* it was virtually a replica of the Belgian constitution, even down to the maverick features, such as coopted Senators. The self-respect of both departing Belgian rulers and succeeding Congolese elite required that the regime they defined pass scrutiny as "democratic." The *Groupe de Travail* suggested that one criterion was universal suffrage, "which alone gives to the representation of the people an unquestioned legitimacy," and another the application of the UN Universal Declaration of Human Rights. In virtually improvising from scratch a political system, the metropolitan model became even more important than in most former British and French territories, where a certain amount of experience in the functioning of representative political institutions before transfer of power was permitted.

Although Belgian postwar colonial perspective slowly changed beneath a façade of policy immobility, the stubborn attachment to outworn shibboleths has proved costly. A number of the key assumptions underlying the first approaches to the decolonization problem were increasingly out of joint with the times. It became clear that time was not going to be limitless, that the "empire of silence" would dissolve under the gradual coagulation of latent nationalist forces, that African society was ceasing to be malleable clay in the hands of the colonizer, that a handful of African barkeepers could not be a black bourgeoisie vigilant to defend the colonial order. The tides of nationalism would not be reversed simply by building more schools and hospitals, issuing a few immatriculation cards to the prominent members of the modern elite, or admitting a few well-groomed Congolese to European restaurants. However vague and unrealistic it was, the Belgo-Congolese community slogan had some value as a transitional idea, which by its very existence forced some debate on adaptation. This, in turn, clearly revealed a number of the contradictions in the Belgian view of the future. Parity institutions in the Congo could not be reconciled with democracy; a Belgo-Congolese community which was in fact initially thought of as an association between a horse and a rider could hardly be viable if both were to be given a chance to consent freely to the relationship.

In the long run, the very posing of these problems provided the answer. It was inevitable that the democratic values of metropolitan Belgium would triumph over the desires of Europeans in the Congo to build a paritary wall around their privileges. And subordinating the construction of the Belgo-Congolese community to the free consent of both parties meant necessarily abandoning the kind of relationship implied in the first formulations.

Until 1959, the debate on terminal objectives took place virtually in a vacuum, within the walls of the European community. After the Leopoldville riots, there was for the first time a real effort to negotiate the future with African leadership; this profoundly transformed the nature of the dialogue. The pattern of events elsewhere in Afro-Asia and the increasingly apparent inconsistency and impracticality of schemes which sought attenuated hegemony under the guise of autonomy and a Belgo-Congolese community had invisibly transformed Belgian perspectives. In 1955–1956, Van Bilsen's proposals were indignantly repudiated by nearly all sectors of metropolitan and colonial opinion. Only three years later, the promise of independence "without fatal delays" from Baudouin found unanimous acceptance.

V THE QUESTION OF NEO-COLONIALISM

Kwame Nkrumah

NEO-COLONIALISM: THE LAST STAGE OF IMPERIALISM

Graduated from an American university in 1935, Nkrumah subsequently spent time in London working with the Pan-African movement before returning to his native Gold Coast in 1947 to become the leader of the nationalist liberation movement. In 1952, Nkrumah became Prime Minister of his country, and in 1957, Ghana obtained its independence. Nkrumah soon became one of the most outspoken opponents of neo-colonialism and advocates of African unity. In 1966 he was forced from power and died several years later in exile. His many books have found an audience in the United States as well as throughout Africa.

The neo-colonialism of today represents imperialism in its final and perhaps its most dangerous stage. In the past it was possible to convert a country upon which a neo-colonial regime had been imposed—Egypt in the nineteenth century is an example—into a colonial territory. Today this process is no longer feasible. Old-fashioned colonialism is by no means entirely abolished. It still constitutes an African problem, but it is everywhere on the retreat. Once a territory has become nominally independent it is no longer possible, as it was in the last century, to reverse the process. Existing colonies may linger on, but no new colonies will be created. In place of colonialism as the main instrument of imperialism we have today neo-colonialism.

The essence of neo-colonialism is that the State which is subject to it is, in theory, independent and has all the outward trappings of international sovereignty. In reality its economic system and thus its political policy is directed from outside.

The methods and form of this direction can take various shapes. For example, in an extreme case the troops of the imperial power may garrison the territory of the neo-colonial State and control the government of it. More often, however, neo-colonialist control is exercised through economic or monetary means. The neo-colonial State may be obliged to take the manufactured products of the imperialist power to the exclusion of competing products from else-where. Control over government policy in the neo-colonial State may be secured by payments towards the cost of running the State, by the provision of civil servants in positions where they can dictate policy, and by monetary control over foreign exchange through the imposition of a banking system controlled by the imperial power.

Where neo-colonialism exists the power exercising control is often the State which formerly ruled the territory in question, but this is not necessarily so. For example, in the case of South Vietnam the former imperial power was France, but neo-colonial control of the State has now gone to the United States. It is possible that neo-colonial control may be exercised by a consortium of financial in-terests which are not specifically identifiable with any particular State. The control of the Congo by great international financial con-cerns is a case in point.

The result of neo-colonialism is that foreign capital is used for the exploitation rather than for the development of the less devel-oped parts of the world. Investment under neo-colonialism increases rather than decreases the gap between the rich and the poor coun-tries of the world.

The struggle against neo-colonialism is not aimed at excluding the capital of the developed world from operating in less-developed countries. It is aimed at preventing the financial power of the de-veloped countries being used in such a way as to impoverish the less developed.

Nonalignment, as practiced by Ghana and many other countries, is based on cooperation with all States whether they be capitalist, socialist or have a mixed economy. Such a policy, therefore, in-volves foreign investment from capitalist countries, but it must be invested in accordance with a national plan drawn up by the gov-ernment of the nonaligned State with its own interests in mind. The issue is not what return the foreign investor receives on his invest-ments. He may, in fact, do better for himself if he invests in a non-aligned country than if he invests in a neo-colonial one. The ques-tion is one of power. A State in the grip of neo-colonialism is not master of its own destiny. It is this factor which makes neo-coloni-alism such a serious threat to world peace. The growth of nuclear weapons has made out-of-date the old-fashioned balance of power which rested upon the ultimate sanction of a major war. Certainty of mutual mass destruction effectively prevents either of the great power blocs from threatening the other with the possibility of a worldwide war, and military conflict has thus become confined to "limited war." For these neo-colonialism is the breeding ground. Such wars can, of course, take place in countries which are not neo-colonialist controlled. Indeed their object may be to establish in a small but independent country a neo-colonialist regime. The evil of neo-colonialism is that it prevents the formation of those large units which would make impossible "limited war." To give one example: if Africa was united, no major power bloc would attempt to subdue it by limited war because from the very nature of limited war, what can be achieved by it is itself limited. It is only where small States exist that it is possible, by landing a few thousand marines or by financing a mercenary force, to secure a decisive result.

The restriction of military action of "limited wars" is, however, no guarantee of world peace and is likely to be the factor which will ultimately involve the great power blocs in a world war, however much both are determined to avoid it.

Limited war, once embarked upon, achieves a momentum of its own. Of this, the war in South Vietnam is only one example. It escalates despite the desire of the great power blocs to keep it limited. While this particular war may be prevented from leading to a world conflict, the multiplication of similar limited wars can only have one end—world war and the terrible consequences of nuclear conflict.

Neo-colonialism is also the worst form of imperialism. For those who practice it, it means power without responsibility and for those who suffer from it, it means exploitation without redress. In the days of old-fashioned colonialism, the imperial power had at least to explain and justify at home the actions it was taking abroad. In the colony those who served the ruling imperial power could at least look to its protection against any violent move by their opponents. With neo-colonialism neither is the case.

Above all, neo-colonialism, like colonialism before it, postpones the facing of the social issues which will have to be faced by the fully developed sector of the world before the danger of world war can be eliminated or the problem of world poverty resolved.

Neo-colonialism, like colonialism, is an attempt to export the social conflicts of the capitalist countries. The temporary success of this policy can be seen in the ever-widening gap between the richer and the poorer nations of the world. But the internal contradictions and conflicts of neo-colonialism make it certain that it cannot endure as a permanent world policy. How it should be brought to an end is a problem that should be studied, above all, by the developed nations of the world, because it is they who will feel the full impact of the ultimate failure. The longer it continues the more certain it is that its inevitable collapse will destroy the social system of which they have made it a foundation.

The reason for its development in the postwar period can be briefly summarized. The problem which faced the wealthy nations of the world at the end of the Second World War was the impossibility of returning to the prewar situation in which there was a great gulf between the few rich and the many poor. Irrespective of what particular political party was in power, the internal pressures in the rich countries of the world were such that no postwar capitalist country could survive unless it became a "Welfare State." There might be differences in degree in the extent of the social benefits given to the industrial and agricultural workers, but what was everywhere impossible was a return to the mass unemployment and to the low level of living of the prewar years.

From the end of the nineteenth century onwards, colonies had been regarded as a source of wealth which could be used to mitigate the class conflicts in the capitalist States and, as will be explained later, this policy had some success. But it failed in its ultimate object because the prewar capitalist States were so organized internally that the bulk of the profit made from colonial possessions found its way into the pockets of the capitalist class and not into those of the workers. Far from achieving the object intended, the working-class parties at times tended to identify their interests with those of the colonial peoples and the imperialist powers found themselves engaged upon a conflict on two fronts, at home with their own workers and abroad against the growing forces of colonial liberation.

The postwar period inaugurated a very different colonial policy. A deliberate attempt was made to divert colonial earnings from the wealthy class and use them instead generally to finance the "Welfare State." As will be seen from the examples given later, this was the method consciously adopted even by those working-class leaders who had before the war regarded the colonial peoples as their natural allies against their capitalist enemies at home.

At first it was presumed that this object could be achieved by maintaining the prewar colonial system. Experience soon proved that attempts to do so would be disastrous and would only provoke colonial wars, thus dissipating the anticipated gains from the continuance of the colonial regime. Britain, in particular, realized this at an early stage and the correctness of the British judgment at the time has subsequently been demonstrated by the defeat of French colonialism in the Far East and Algeria and the failure of the Dutch to retain any of their former colonial empire.

The system of neo-colonialism was therefore instituted and in the short run it has served the developed powers admirably. It is in the long run that its consequences are likely to be catastrophic for them.

Neo-colonialism is based upon the principle of breaking up former large united colonial territories into a number of small nonviable States which are incapable of independent development and must rely upon the former imperial power for defense and even internal security. Their economic and financial systems are linked, as in colonial days, with those of the former colonial ruler.

At first sight the scheme would appear to have many advantages for the developed countries of the world. All the profits of neo-colonialism can be secured if, in any given area, a reasonable proportion of the States have a neo-colonialist system. It is not necessary that they *all* should have one. Unless small States can combine they must be compelled to sell their primary products at prices dictated by the developed nations and buy their manufactured goods at the prices fixed by them. So long as neo-colonialism can prevent political and economic conditions for optimum development, the developing countries, whether they are under neo-colonialist control or not, will be unable to create a large enough market to support industrialization. In the same way they will lack the financial strength to force the developed countries to accept their primary products at a fair price.

In the neo-colonialist territories, since the former colonial power has in theory relinquished political control, if the social conditions occasioned by neo-colonialism cause a revolt the local neo-colonialist government can be sacrificed and another equally subservient one substituted in its place. On the other hand, in any continent where neo-colonialism exists on a wide scale the same social pressures which can produce revolts in neo-colonial territories will also affect those States which have refused to accept the system and therefore neo-colonialist nations have a ready-made weapon with which they can threaten their opponents if they appear successfully to be challenging the system.

These advantages, which seem at first sight so obvious are, however, on examination, illusory because they fail to take into consideration the facts of the world today.

The introduction of neo-colonialism increases the rivalry between the great powers which was provoked by the old-style colonialism. However little real power the government of a neo-colonialist State may possess, it must have, from the very fact of its nominal independence, a certain area of maneuver. It may not be able to exist without a neo-colonialist master but it may still have the ability to change masters.

The ideal neo-colonialist State would be one which was wholly subservient to neo-colonialist interests but the existence of the socialist nations makes it impossible to enforce the full rigor of the neo-colonialist system. The existence of an alternative system is itself a challenge to the neo-colonialist regime. Warnings about "the dangers of Communist subversion" are likely to be two-edged since they bring to the notice of those living under a neo-colonialist system the possibility of a change of regime. In fact neo-colonialism is the victim of its own contradictions. In order to make it attractive to those upon whom it is practiced it must be shown as capable of raising their living standards, but the economic object of neo-colonialism is to keep those standards depressed in the interest of the developed countries. It is only when this contradiction is understood that the failure of innumerable "aid" programs, many of them well-intentioned, can be explained.

In the first place, the rulers of neo-colonial States derive their authority to govern, not from the will of the people, but from the support which they obtain from their neo-colonialist masters. They have therefore little interest in developing education, strengthening the bargaining power of their workers employed by expatriate firms, or indeed of taking any step which would challenge the colonial pattern of commerce and industry, which it is the object of neo-colonialism to preserve. "Aid," therefore, to a neo-colonial State is merely a revolving credit, paid by the neo-colonial master, passing through the neo-colonial State and returning to the neo-colonial master in the form of increased profits.

Secondly, it is in the field of "aid" that the rivalry of individual developed States first manifests itself. So long as neo-colonialism persists so long will spheres of interest persist, and this makes multilateral aid—which is in fact the only effective form of aid—impossible.

Once multilateral aid begins the neo-colonialist masters are faced by the hostility of the vested interests in their own country. Their manufacturers naturally object to any attempt to raise the price of the raw materials which they obtain from the neo-colonialist territory in question, or to the establishment there of manufacturing industries which might compete directly or indirectly with their own exports to the territory. Even education is suspect as likely to produce a student movement and it is, of course, true that in many less-developed countries the students have been in the vanguard of the fight against neo-colonialism.

In the end the situation arises that the only type of aid which the neo-colonialist masters consider as safe is "military aid."

Once a neo-colonialist territory is brought to such a state of economic chaos and misery that revolt actually breaks out, then, and only then, is there no limit to the generosity of the neo-colonial overlord, provided, of course, that the funds supplied are utilized exclusively for military purposes.

Military aid in fact marks the last stage of neo-colonialism and its effect is self-destructive. Sooner or later the weapons supplied pass into the hands of the opponents of the neo-colonialist regime and the war itself increases the social misery which originally provoked it.

Neo-colonialism is a millstone around the necks of the developed countries which practice it. Unless they can rid themselves of it, it will drown them. Previously the developed powers could escape from the contradictions of neo-colonialism by substituting for it direct colonialism. Such a solution is no longer possible and the reasons for it have been well explained by Mr. Owen Lattimore, the United States Far Eastern expert and adviser to Chiang Kai-shek in the immediate postwar period. He wrote:

Asia, which was so easily and swiftly subjugated by conquerors in the eighteenth and nineteenth centuries, displayed an amazing ability stubbornly to resist modern armies equipped with airplanes, tanks, motor vehicles and mobile artillery.

Formerly big territories were conquered in Asia with small forces. Income, first of all from plunder, then from direct taxes and lastly from trade, capital investments and long-term exploitation, covered with incredible speed the expenditure for military operations. This arithmetic represented a great temptation to strong countries. Now they have run up against another arithmetic, and it discourages them.

The same arithmetic is likely to apply throughout the less-developed world.

This book is therefore an attempt to examine neo-colonialism not only in its African context and its relation to African unity, but in world perspective. Neo-colonialism is by no means exclusively an African question. Long before it was practiced on any large scale in Africa it was an established system in other parts of the world. Nowhere has it proved successful, either in raising living standards or in ultimately benefiting the countries which have indulged in it.

Marx predicted that the growing gap between the wealth of the possessing classes and the workers it employs would ultimately produce a conflict fatal to capitalism in each individual capitalist State.

This conflict between the rich and the poor has now been transferred on to the international scene, but for proof of what is acknowledged to be happening it is no longer necessary to consult the classical Marxist writers. The situation is set out with the utmost clarity in the leading organs of capitalist opinion. Take for example the following extracts from *The Wall Street Journal,* the newspaper which perhaps best reflects United States capitalist thinking.

In its issue of 12 May 1965, under the headline of "Poor Nations' Plight," the paper first analyzes "which countries are considered industrial and which backward." There is, it explains, "no rigid method of classification." Nevertheless, it points out:

A generally used breakdown, however, has recently been maintained by the International Monetary Fund because, in the words of an IMF official, "the economic demarcation in the world is getting increasingly apparent." The breakdown, the official says, "is based on simple common sense."
In the IMF's view, the industrial countries are the United States, the

United Kingdom, most West European nations, Canada and Japan. A special category called "other developed areas" includes such other European lands as Finland, Greece and Ireland, plus Australia, New Zealand and South Africa. The IMF's "less-developed" category embraces all of Latin America and nearly all of the Middle East, non-Communist Asia and Africa.

In other words the "backward" countries are those situated in the neo-colonial areas.

After quoting figures to support its argument, *The Wall Street Journal* comments on this situation:

The industrial nations have added nearly $2 billion to their reserves, which now approximate $52 billion. At the same time, the reserves of the less-developed group not only have stopped rising, but have declined some $200 million. To analysts such as Britain's Miss Ward, the significance of such statistics is clear: the economic gap is rapidly widening "between a white, complacent, highly bourgeois, very wealthy, very small North Atlantic élite and everybody else, and this is not a very comfortable heritage to leave to one's children."

"Everybody else" includes approximately two-thirds of the population of the earth, spread through about 100 nations.

This is no new problem. In the opening paragraph of his book, *The War on World Poverty*, written in 1953, the present British Labour leader, Mr. Harold Wilson, summarized the major problem of the world as he then saw it:

For the vast majority of mankind the most urgent problem is not war, or Communism, or the cost of living, or taxation. It is hunger. Over 1,500,-000,000 people, something like two-thirds of the world's population, are living in conditions of acute hunger, defined in terms of identifiable nutritional disease. This hunger is at the same time the effect and the cause of the poverty, squalor and misery in which they live.

Its consequences are likewise understood. The correspondent of *The Wall Street Journal,* previously quoted, underlines them:

. . . Many diplomats and economists view the implications as overwhelmingly—and dangerously—political. Unless the present decline can be reversed, these analysts fear, the United States and other wealthy industrial powers of the West face the distinct possibility, in the words of British economist Barbara Ward, "of a sort of international class war."

What is lacking are any positive proposals for dealing with the situation. All that *The Wall Street Journal's* correspondent can do is to point out that the traditional methods recommended for curing the evils are only likely to make the situation worse.

It has been argued that the developed nations should effectively assist the poorer parts of the world, and that the whole world should be turned into a Welfare State. However, there seems little prospect that anything of this sort could be achieved. The so-called "aid" programs to help backward economies represent, according to a rough U.N. estimate, only 0.5 percent of the total income of industrial countries. But when it comes to the prospect of increasing such aid the mood is one of pessimism:

> A large school of thought holds that expanded share-the-wealth schemes are idealistic and impractical. This school contends climate, undeveloped human skills, lack of natural resources and other factors—not just lack of money—retard economic progress in many of these lands, and that the countries lack personnel with the training or will to use vastly expanded aid effectively. Share-the-wealth schemes, according to this view, would be like pouring money down a bottomless well, weakening the donor nations without effectively curing the ills of the recipients.

The absurdity of this argument is demonstrated by the fact that every one of the reasons quoted to prove why the less-developed parts of the world cannot be developed applied equally strongly to the present developed countries in the period prior to their development. The argument is only true in this sense. The less-developed world will not become developed through the goodwill or generosity of the developed powers. It can only become developed through a struggle against the external forces which have a vested interest in keeping it undeveloped.

Of these forces, neo-colonialism is, at this stage of history, the principal.

Frantz Fanon
THE COLLABORATING CLASS IN NEO-COLONIALISM

Born in Guadeloupe in the French West Indies, Frantz Fanon was educated
as a psychiatrist in France and was working in Algeria when revolution
broke out there in late 1954. Fanon subsequently became the best-known
of the Revolution's proponents and remains one of the significant ide-
ologues of people's war. Of his four works (one being a collection of short
essays) The Wretched of the Earth, *published just before his death in 1961,*
is his most important.

History teaches us clearly that the battle against colonialism does
not run straight away along the lines of nationalism. For a very long
time the native devotes his energies to ending certain definite
abuses: forced labor, corporal punishment, inequality of salaries,
limitation of political rights, etc. This fight for democracy against
the oppression of mankind will slowly leave the confusion of neo-
liberal universalism to emerge, sometimes laboriously, as a claim to
nationhood. It so happens that the unpreparedness of the educated
classes, the lack of practical links between them and the mass of
the people, their laziness, and, let it be said, their cowardice at the
decisive moment of the struggle will give rise to tragic mishaps. . . .

This traditional weakness, which is almost congenital to the national consciousness of underdeveloped countries, is not solely the
result of the mutilation of the colonized people by the colonial
regime. It is also the result of the intellectual laziness of the national middle class, of its spiritual penury, and of the profoundly
cosmopolitan mold that its mind is set in.

The national middle class which takes over power at the end of
the colonial regime is an underdeveloped middle class. It has practically no economic power, and in any case it is in no way com-
mensurate with the bourgeoisie of the mother country which it hopes
to replace. In its willful narcissism, the national middle class is easily
convinced that it can advantageously replace the middle class of

the mother country. But that same independence which literally
drives it into a corner will give rise within its ranks to catastrophic
reactions, and will oblige it to send out frenzied appeals for help to
the former mother country. The university and merchant classes
which make up the most enlightened section of the new state are
in fact characterized by the smallness of their number and their
being concentrated in the capital, and the type of activities in
which they are engaged: business, agriculture and the liberal professions. Neither financiers nor industrial magnates are to be found
within this national middle class. The national bourgeoisie of underdeveloped countries is not engaged in production, nor in invention,
nor building, nor labor; it is completely canalized into activities of
the intermediary type. Its innermost vocation seems to be to keep
in the running and to be part of the racket. The psychology of the
national bourgeoisie is that of the businessman, not that of a captain of industry; and it is only too true that the greed of the settlers
and the system of embargoes set up by colonialism has hardly left
them any other choice.

Under the colonial system, a middle class which accumulates
capital is an impossible phenomenon. Now, precisely, it would seem
that the historical vocation of an authentic national middle class
in an underdeveloped country is to repudiate its own nature insofar
it as it is bourgeois, that is to say insofar as it is the tool of capitalism, and to make itself the willing slave of that revolutionary
capital which is the people.

In an underdeveloped country an authentic national middle class
ought to consider as its bounden duty to betray the calling fate has
marked out for it, and to put itself to school with the people; in
other words to put at the people's disposal the intellectual and
technical capital that it has snatched when going through the
colonial universities. But unhappily we shall see that very often the
national middle class does not follow this heroic, positive, fruitful
and just path; rather, it disappears with its soul set at peace into
the shocking ways—shocking because anti-national—of a traditional bourgeoisie, of a bourgeoisie which is stupidly, contemptibly,
cynically bourgeois.

The objective of nationalist parties as from a certain given period
is, we have seen, strictly national. They mobilize the people with
slogans of independence, and for the rest leave it to future events.

When such parties are questioned on the economic program of the State that they are clamoring for, or on the nature of the regime which they propose to install, they are incapable of replying, because, precisely, they are completely ignorant of the economy of their own country.

The economy has always developed outside the limits of their knowledge. They have nothing more than an approximate, bookish acquaintance with the actual and potential resources of their country's soil and mineral deposits; and therefore they can only speak of these resources on a general and abstract plane. After independence this underdeveloped middle class, reduced in numbers and without capital, which refuses to follow the path of revolution, will fall into deplorable stagnation. It is unable to give free rein to its genius, which formerly it was wont to lament, though rather too glibly, was held in check by colonial domination. The precariousness of its resources and the paucity of its managerial class forces it back for years into an artisanal economy. From its point of view, which is inevitably a very limited one, a national economy is an economy based on what may be called local products. Long speeches will be made about the artisan class. Since the middle classes find it impossible to set up factories that would be more profit-earning both for themselves and for the country as a whole, they will surround the artisan class with a chauvinistic tenderness in keeping with the new awareness of national dignity, and which moreover will bring them in quite a lot of money. This cult of local products and this incapability to seek out new systems of management will be equally manifested by the bogging down of the national middle class in the methods of agricultural production which were characteristic of the colonial period.

The national economy of the period of independence is not set on a new footing. It is still concerned with the ground-nut harvest, with the cocoa crop and the olive yield. In the same way there is no change in the marketing of basic products, and not a single industry is set up in the country. We go on sending out raw materials; we go on being Europe's small farmers, who specialize in unfinished products.

Yet the national middle class constantly demands the nationalization of the economy and of the trading sectors. This is because, from their point of view, nationalization does not mean placing the whole economy at the service of the nation and deciding to satisfy the needs of the nation. For them, nationalization does not mean governing the State with regard to the new social relations whose growth it has been decided to encourage. To them, nationalization quite simply means the transfer into native hands of those unfair advantages which are a legacy of the colonial period.

Since the middle class has neither sufficient material nor intellectual resources (by intellectual resources we mean engineers and technicians) it limits its claims to the taking over of business offices and commercial houses formerly occupied by the settlers. The national bourgeoisie steps into the shoes of the former European settlement: doctors, barristers, traders, commercial travelers, general agents and transport agents. It considers that the dignity of the country and its own welfare require that it should occupy all these posts. From now on it will insist that all the big foreign companies should pass through its hands, whether these companies wish to keep on their connections with the country, or to open it up. The national middle class discovers its historic mission: that of intermediary.

Seen through its eyes, its mission has nothing to do with transforming the nation; it consists, prosaically, of being the transmission line between the nation and a capitalism, rampant though camouflaged, which today puts on the mask of neo-colonialism. The national bourgeoisie will be quite content with the role of the Western bourgeoisie's business agent, and it will play its part without any complexes in a most dignified manner. But this same lucrative role, this cheap-jack's function, this meanness of outlook and this absence of all ambition symbolize the incapability of the national middle class to fulfill its historic role of bourgeoisie. Here, the dynamic, pioneer aspect, the characteristics of the inventor and of the discoverer of new worlds which are found in all national bourgeoisies are lamentably absent. In the colonial countries, the spirit of indulgence is dominant at the core of the bourgeoisie; and this is because the national bourgeoisie identifies itself with the Western bourgeoisie, from whom it has learned its lessons. It follows the Western bourgeoisie along its path of negation and decadence without ever having emulated it in its first stages of exploration and invention, stages which are an acquisition of that Western bourgeoisie whatever the circumstances. In its beginnings, the national bourgeoisie of the colonial countries identifies itself with the decadence of the bourgeoisie of the West. We need not think that it is jumping ahead; it is in fact beginning at the end. It is already senile before it has come to know the petulance, the fearlessness or the will to succeed of youth. . . .

As regards internal affairs and in the sphere of institutions, the national bourgeoisie will give equal proof of its incapacity. In a certain number of underdeveloped countries the parliamentary game is faked from the beginning. Powerless economically, unable to bring about the existence of coherent social relations, and standing on the principle of its domination as a class, the bourgeoisie chooses the solution that seems to it the easiest, that of the single party. It does not yet have the quiet conscience and the calm that economic power and the control of the state machine alone can give. It does not create a State that reassures the ordinary citizen, but rather one that rouses his anxiety.

The State, which by its strength and discretion ought to inspire confidence and disarm and lull everybody to sleep, on the contrary seeks to impose itself in spectacular fashion. It makes a display, it jostles people and bullies them, thus intimating to the citizen that he is in continual danger. The single party is the modern form of the dictatorship of the bourgeoisie, unmasked, unpainted, unscrupulous, and cynical.

It is true that such a dictatorship does not go very far. It cannot halt the processes of its own contradictions. Since the bourgeoisie has not the economic means to ensure its domination and to throw a few crumbs to the rest of the country; since, moreover, it is preoccupied with filling its pockets as rapidly as possible but also as prosaically as possible, the country sinks all the more deeply into stagnation. And in order to hide this stagnation and to mask this regression, to reassure itself and to give itself something to boast about, the bourgeoisie can find nothing better to do than to erect grandiose buildings in the capital and to lay out money on what are called prestige expenses.

The national bourgeoisie turns its back more and more on the interior and on the real facts of its undeveloped country, and tends to look towards the former mother country and the foreign capitalists who count on its obliging compliance. As it does not share its profits with the people, and in no way allows them to enjoy any of the dues that are paid to it by the big foreign companies, it will discover the need for a popular leader to whom will fall the dual role of stabilizing the regime and of perpetuating the domination of the bourgeoisie. The bourgeois dictatorship of underdeveloped countries draws its strength from the existence of a leader. We know that in the well-developed countries the bourgeois dictatorship is the result of the economic power of the bourgeoisie. In the underdeveloped countries on the contrary the leader stands for moral power, in whose shelter the thin and poverty-stricken bourgeoisie of the young nation decides to get rich.

The people who for years on end have seen this leader and heard him speak, who from a distance in a kind of dream have followed his contests with the colonial power, spontaneously put their trust in this patriot. Before independence, the leader generally embodies the aspirations of the people for independence, political liberty and national dignity. But as soon as independence is declared, far from embodying in concrete form the needs of the people in what touches bread, land and the restoration of the country to the sacred hands of the people, the leader will reveal his inner purpose: to become the general president of that company of profiteers impatient for their returns which constitutes the national bourgeoisie.

P. T. Bauer
THE ECONOMICS OF RESENTMENT

Author of two books on Third World economic issues, Peter Bauer attacks here the notion that Western influence in less-developed countries is the cause of their poverty and stagnation as neo-colonial theorists generally maintain. Instead he argues the past benefits of Western rule and explains the present animosity of certain Third World elites and their supporters in the West to be the consequence of a psychological need for a scapegoat for the problems besetting these areas.

P. T. Bauer, "The Economics of Resentment: Colonialism and Underdevelopment," *Journal of Contemporary History* (London, January 1969), pp. 51–60; 62–67; 69. Reprinted by permission of Sage Publications Ltd. Footnotes omitted.

I intend to examine certain widely held and influential ideas on the relationship between colonial status and material progress, in particular on the supposed responsibility of colonialism for the material poverty of the underdeveloped world. (This idea itself is one aspect or instance of the more general notion of the alleged responsibility of the rich countries for the material backwardness of the poor countries. And this notion in turn is an example of economic or environmental determinism, the idea that external forces are largely responsible for the poverty of persons and groups.)

Over the last few decades, especially since the First World War, and to an even greater extent since the Second, statements and suggestions have abounded in publications, both in underdeveloped countries and in the West, asserting that the masses in underdeveloped countries are greatly concerned with their poverty, and alleging also that both in these countries and in the West it is widely recognized that the West has caused the poverty of the underdeveloped world.

It is in fact very doubtful how widespread these sentiments are in poor countries. Some familiarity with many of these countries suggests to me that the great majority of people know little about such matters, do not compare their lot with that of the population of distant countries, and do not ascribe any of their problems to present or past actions of Western countries. The great majority are concerned with their own daily lives; in Africa and Asia at any rate the vast majority normally know and care little about politics beyond the tribal or village level. But there are many vocal and politically influential people both in underdeveloped countries and in the West who have effectively canvassed the notion of Western responsibility for the poverty of the former. They have secured wide publicity and considerable political acceptance for this view, as well as for the related notion that the masses in underdeveloped countries both resent the international income differences and attribute them to exploitation by the West.

The readiness of the rulers in the West to accept the claims of these vocal groups to represent the general opinion of the peoples of the underdeveloped world, enhances the political effectiveness of these spokesmen, and lends a spurious plausibility to their claim to represent mass opinion. But their political success does not substantiate either the allegation of Western responsibility, or their pretension to represent mass opinion; political effectiveness has little to do with things as they are.

I shall argue first that it is untrue that the West has caused the poverty of the underdeveloped world. I shall then examine other, somewhat more speculative issues, and try to identify the groups and sections in both rich and poor countries who stand to gain from acceptance of the idea of Western responsibility for the poverty of underdeveloped countries, and to examine the reasons for their success in propagating this idea, especially in the West.

General Principle Fourteen of the first UNCTAD (United Nations Conference on Trade and Development) provides a convenient starting point for the discussion.

Complete decolonization, in compliance with United Nations Declaration on the Granting of Independence to Colonial Countries and peoples and the liquidation of the remnants of colonialism in all its forms, is a necessary condition for economic development and the exercise of sovereign rights over natural resources.

Leaving aside for the moment questions of meaning and interpretation of colonialism (especially "colonialism in all its forms"), it is untrue that colonial status is incompatible with material progress, so that its removal is a necessary condition for economic development. Some of the richest countries were colonies in their earlier history, notably the United States, Canada, Australia, and New Zealand; and these countries were already prosperous while they were still colonies.

Nor has colonial status precluded the material advance of the African and Asian territories which became colonies in the nineteenth century. Many of these territories made rapid economic progress between the second half of the nineteenth century, when they became colonies, and the middle of the twentieth century, when most of them became independent. The many obvious examples include Nigeria, Gold Coast—Ghana, Kenya, Malaya, and Hong Kong. Here are a few relevant statistics.

The rapid material progress of Gold Coast–Ghana is reflected in statistics which are somewhat more reliable and meaningful than they are elsewhere in Africa. The country became independent in 1957. By the mid-1950s the national income per head was about £70–£75. This is a low figure by Western standards but it was far higher than the corresponding figure in the independent African states; and it also reflected a substantial advance since the end of the nineteenth century, when the Gold Coast was very largely a subsistence economy. Real income per head approximately quadrupled between 1890 and 1960. The total population also approximately quadrupled.

Statistics of foreign trade are of particular interest for West Africa because well over 99.5 percent of the population is African: all agricultural exports (the bulk of all exports) are produced by them and practically all imports are destined for their use. In 1890 there were no exports (or production) of Gold Coast cocoa; by the mid-1930s these were about 300,000 tons annually, and by the early 1960s they were over 400,000 tons, all from farms established, owned, and operated by Africans; there are no foreign-owned cocoa farms. In 1890 combined imports and exports were less than £1 million annually; by the 1930s both imports and exports were in tens of millions; since the mid-1950s imports and exports have been about £100 million annually. Over this period there was a spectacular increase in imports of both consumer and capital goods. In 1890 there were no imports, or only negligible imports, of flour, sugar, cement, petroleum products, or iron and steel. In recent decades most of these have been on a massive scale. In the early 1890s there were about 3,000 children at school; by the mid-1950s there were over half a million. In the 1890s there were neither railways nor roads, but only a few jungle paths, and transport of goods was entirely by human porterage or by canoe. By the 1930s there was a substantial railway mileage and a good road system; by then journeys by road required fewer hours than they had required days in 1890.

Substantially the same applies to Nigeria between the end of the nineteenth century and 1960, when Nigeria became independent. Around 1900 exports and imports were each about £2 million annually; by the 1930s they were in tens of millions, and by the late 1950s they were about £150–200 million annually. Here again practically all exports are produced by Africans and practically all imports are destined for their use. In 1900 there were no exports (or production) of cocoa from Nigeria, and exports of oil palm products were one-tenth of their volume in the late 1950s. And here again there was a phenomenal increase in imports of mass consumer goods and capital goods over this period; in recent years there has also been a substantial increase in the local production of commodities previously imported.

The experience of Malaya has been somewhat analogous. In 1961, when the country became independent, the national income per head was about £100, far higher than elsewhere in Southeast Asia. In 1900 total domestic exports from Malaya were around £10 million a year; by the early 1960s they were several hundred million a year. In 1900 there were no exports of plantation rubber from Malaya; by the early 1960s they were around 700,000–800,000 tons annually, over half from Asian-owned properties.

Statistical information of the kind just presented can be easily multiplied, but by itself it cannot convey the profound and pervasive changes which have taken place in many parts of the underdeveloped world in recent decades, and which have changed the conditions of existence there. In many areas this progress has meant the suppression of slavery and tribal warfare and the disappearance of famine and of the worst epidemic and endemic diseases. It has meant the development of communications, the replacement of local self-sufficiency by the possibilities of exchange and the emergence and growth of cities. In West Africa slave-raiding and slavery were still widespread at the end of the nineteenth century; in 1900 the towns of Northern Nigeria, which are now centers of the groundnut trade, were important slave markets. In the 1890s there were still authenticated instances of cannibalism in Southern Nigeria. Again Malaya, which in the 1890s was a sparsely populated country of hamlets and fishing villages, has been completely transformed by the rise of the rubber industry, and has developed into a country with populous cities, thriving commerce, and an excellent system of roads.

The impact of these changes has often set up considerable strains because of personal, social, and political difficulties of adjustment to rapid change, especially the adjustment of attitudes and of social institutions. Many of the social and political problems of ex-colonial countries reflect difficulties of rapid and uneven advance, not those of stagnation and regression.

Thus the UNCTAD General Principle Fourteen that colonial status and economic progress are incompatible is patently untrue. Yet it has been formally and solemnly announced, published, and publicized by a United Nations conference made possible by the financial and moral support of the Western governments. But emphatic announcements do not turn into sense what is immediately demonstrable nonsense.

Although, as we have seen, it is untrue that colonial status is incompatible with material advance, the question whether colonial status has promoted material progress cannot be settled or demonstrated so conclusively, for the answer to that question depends in part on what political regimes would otherwise have prevailed in the colonial areas of Africa and Asia, and also on the assumed effects of their policies on economic development. However, it is highly probable that over the last century or so the establishment of colonial rule in Africa and Asia has promoted, and not retarded, material progress. With relatively little coercion, or even interference in the lives of the great majority of the people, the colonial governments established law and order, safeguarded private property and contractual relations, organized basic transport and health services, and introduced some modern financial and legal institutions. The resulting environment also promoted the establishment or extension of external contacts, which in turn encouraged the inflow of external resources, notably administrative, commercial, and technical skills, as well as capital. They also acquainted the population with new wants, crops, commodities, and methods of cultivation, and served to establish new markets for local produce and to open new sources of supply of a wide range of commodities. Thus a new outlook on material advance and on the means of securing it was engendered: for good or evil these contacts promoted the erosion of the traditional values, objectives, attitudes, and customs obstructing material advance.

It is unlikely (though this cannot be proved conclusively) that in the absence of colonial rule, the social, political, and economic environment in colonial Africa and Asia would have been more congenial to material progress. Indeed it was the presence of conditions unfavorable to material progress, especially the frequency of civil and tribal war and the prevalence of slavery, which led in most instances to the establishment of colonial rule. While it is not true that colonialism brought about poverty, there is some truth in the notion that poverty brought about colonialism.

The presumption that in Africa and Asia colonial rule has promoted rather than retarded economic development over the last hundred years, is supported by the material backwardness of the African and Asian countries in the tropics which have been independent longest. Most of these countries are materially extremely backward, usually much more so than the ex-colonies in the same region. Familiar examples include Liberia, Ethiopia, and to a lesser extent Thailand.

The notion that colonial rule has precluded, or at least retarded, economic advance, derives from several sources, or more precisely is compounded of several distinct but related ideas.

The first of these is the allegedly exploitative nature of political colonialism or imperialism. While the concepts of exploitation, colonialism, and imperialism are all ambiguous, their broad meaning is made fairly clear in the political and economic literature of the twentieth century. The notion of exploitation does not refer usually to plunder of the type which often accompanied military conquest before the nineteenth century, nor even to taxation of the colonies for the benefit of the metropolitan country. The alleged exploitation refers primarily to the conquest of markets for capital and commodities, supposedly necessitated by the otherwise inevitable decline (or even disappearance) of the rate of profit, and by the related need to find outlets for commodities unsaleable at home because of the insufficiency of purchasing power of the exploited masses. Well-known exponents of this view include J. A. Hobson, H. N. Brailsford, Leonard Woolf, and above all, Lenin. . . .

The suggestion that the poverty of Africa and Asia reflects external exploitation is clearly attractive to both actual and vicarious readers in underdeveloped countries. In developed countries the suggestion of exploitation evokes a guilt feeling, for which there seems to be a latent desire among many people. This may reflect dissatisfaction with the fruits of material progress; but more important in the context of underdeveloped countries is the role of a guilt feeling in promoting certain policies, particularly foreign aid, national and international development planning, and the expansion of the functions of the official international organizations. People who favor these policies are inclined to accept and promote the notion of colonial exploitation, and the guilt feeling which it arouses.

The obvious and familiar defects of the ideology of economic imperialism and colonial exploitation, especially in its Leninist version, include the following, among others: until the First World War (the period covered by this literature) the great bulk of capital exports from the advanced countries did not go to colonies, but to independent countries, mostly to other advanced countries; several of the richest countries were indeed not exporters but importers of capital; Great Britain, the leading colonial power, pursued an open-door, free-trade policy in its colonies. Most of this literature does not ask the obvious question: how could extremely poor people (or indeed materially primitive people as in Africa) pay for the capital and the commodities forced on them by capitalists in search of profits?

As already noted, the insubstantial nature of the thesis of imperialist exploitation has not diminished its political effectiveness. Numerous examples of this influence can be found in the writings of African and Asian politicians. For instance they abound in the writings of Dr. Nkrumah, who until his downfall was one of the most influential African leaders, and whose utterances were widely quoted and much respected not only in Africa but also in the West. Here is a typical nonsense passage:

> *Thus all the imperialists, without exception, evolved the means, their colonial policies, to satisfy the ends, the exploitation of the subject territories, for the aggrandizement of the metropolitan countries. They were all rapacious; they all subserved the needs of the subject lands to their own demands; they all circumscribed human rights and liberties; they all repressed and despoiled, degraded and oppressed. They took our lands, our lives, our resources and our dignity. Without exception, they left us nothing but our resentment. . . . It was when they had gone and we were faced with the stark realities, as in Ghana on the morrow of our independence, that the destitution of the land after long years of colonial rule was brought sharply home to us.*

A more recent, less familiar, but influential argument, rather different from the Leninist thesis, suggests that political colonialism has retarded the economic progress of the colonies by depriving them of the economic benefits of a sovereign national state. This view is clearly implied in some of the writings of Professor Gunnar Myrdal. He writes:

> *From one point of view, the most important effect of colonialism was related to the negative fact that the dependent nation was deprived of*

*effective nationhood and had no government of its own which could feel
the urge to take protective and fomenting measures in order to promote
the balanced growth of the national economy. Lack of political independence meant the absence of a unifying and integrating purpose for the
collectivity.... The political independence they have won for themselves,
or are now winning, is their most precious asset: the national state.*

Such suggestions overstate the potentialities of state power as an
instrument of economic progress. Inappropriate government policy
can retard material progress or even obstruct it altogether, especially when a government cannot maintain law and order, or when it
establishes extensive and close control over economic life. But
there is no reason to believe that the conduct of sovereign governments would have been more favorable to economic development
over the relevant period than that of the colonial regimes. The
contrary is strongly suggested by the experience of the independent
countries in the colonial regions of Africa and Asia in both the
nineteenth and the twentieth century.

Professor Myrdal and his followers frequently blame colonial
regimes for failure to pursue active economic development policies,
especially in undertaking comprehensive central planning in the
sense of state control of the composition and direction of economic
activity outside subsistence agriculture, which these writers regard
as a prerequisite of economic advance. Comprehensive central
planning, a policy which does not augment resources but only cen-
tralizes power, is neither a necessary nor a sufficient condition of
material advance. This is obvious both from the early history of
the developed countries, and from the recent history of the many
poor countries which have made substantial progress without this
policy. Indeed for a number of reasons, particularly pertinent in
Africa and Asia, such a policy is much more likely to obstruct than
to promote economic development, especially a rise in general living standards. But whatever the merits of central planning, it is
difficult to see how such a policy could have been undertaken by
the tribal chiefs or the sultans and rajahs whose authority was dis-
placed by the colonial powers....

Discussions on colonialism and underdevelopment often refer
to various types of colonialism. UNCTAD General Principle Fourteen quoted above is one of many examples.

Although political colonialism has many manifestations, the concept does have some definite meaning. A colonial government is not sovereign: it has to accept the instructions of the metropolitan government. In recent usage, colonialism has come to be applied to situations or relations without these political elements. The term has largely lost identifiable meaning, and has become a term of abuse of institutions, policies, governments, relationships, groups and individuals, disliked by the speaker or writer. It is often used to express disapproval of technically or materially successful countries, organizations, or groups. Two expressions or types of usage may be appropriately discussed here, namely economic colonialism and neo-colonialism.

The term economic colonialism is now widely used to refer to economic relationships between relatively more and relatively less prosperous countries, regions and groups, including economic relations within a country, as for instance between the North and the South in the United States or between West and East Pakistan. This usage, which is especially prominent in the recent literature of the economics of resentment, in effect identifies colonial status with relative poverty, and thereby deprives the former term of its usual and particular meaning. Moreover, it suggests that differences in income and economic attainment are reprehensible, and that the economic contacts in such situations are somehow damaging and degrading to the less prosperous partner. . . .

The suggestion that economic relations between rich and poor countries are biased against the latter often merges into the different and more influential notion that the prosperity of rich countries has been built up at the expense of the underdeveloped world.

The belief that the incomes of individuals and groups are somehow extracted from others rather than representing a return for the services rendered by themselves and their resources, has a long and disastrous history. In modern technical language it envisages economic activity as a zero-sum game, in which the gains of some reflect the losses of others. It has often been clearly noticeable in the economics and politics of envy and resentment, and has frequently been a major influence in the persecution and expulsion of ethnic minorities, particularly those which have achieved prosperity from poverty, Jews in Europe, Levantines and Indians in Africa, Chinese in Southeast Asia.

While this suggestion and the sentiments behind it long antedate

Marxist-Leninist writings, this literature, particularly in its Leninist version, has greatly promoted the spread and influence of the idea that the progress of the developed countries has been achieved at the expense of the underdeveloped world; that the wealth of the former has been extracted from the latter; and that the underdeveloped world is in fact an economic colony, or group of economic colonies, of industrial countries. In this literature private property incomes, notably return on private capital, imply exploitation; and service industries are generally unproductive. Thus the earnings of expatriate capital and of expatriate traders, administrators, and executives in underdeveloped countries are not regarded as incomes earned for resources and services provided to these countries, but rather as incomes and resources extracted from their populations who are thus in a state of economic subjection.

These ideas represent an extension of the concept of the exploitation of the proletariat from the domestic to the international sphere, with the population of the underdeveloped countries (most of whom are in fact agriculturalists) somehow identified with a domestic industrial proletariat. In fact, large parts of the underdeveloped world have little contact with advanced countries, and these parts are usually the poorest and most backward. Conversely, throughout the underdeveloped world the most prosperous areas are those with which the developed world has established wide-ranging contacts. It is plainly untrue that the rich countries have achieved their prosperity at the expense of the underdeveloped world.

The prosperity of rich countries such as, say, Canada, Australia, Japan, Switzerland, and Scandinavia, has quite obviously not been achieved at the expense of the underdeveloped world, with much or most of which, including the poorest parts, these countries have few economic contacts. Most of the rich countries which have contacts with the underdeveloped world were already materially far more advanced than the underdeveloped countries when they established contact with the latter. It is also relevant that on the eve of colonization material conditions were extremely primitive in the colonial regions, especially in sub-Saharan Africa and Southeast Asia.

Political independence is now often alleged to be unreal without economic independence; and the alleged lack of economic independence of many former colonies, as of other underdeveloped countries, is supposed to represent another category of colonialism, related to the other concepts and ideas examined in the preceding section. Unlike political independence or sovereignty, economic independence is an ambiguous term. The most plausible interpretation would be that of solvency, that is, the ability of a country to pay for the goods and services it uses without recourse to external grants and subsidized loans. Another possible, though less useful, interpretation would be the absence of external economic contacts. Yet another would be the ability to withstand adverse changes in external conditions without substantial dislocation. However, the literature of economic colonialism interprets economic independence quite differently.

In Marxist-Leninist literature any country in which there is substantial private foreign investment is regarded as economically dependent, since the return on such capital is seen as a form of exploitation which would not be tolerated by a truly independent country. As already noted, this argument, though politically effective, is invalid in logic and nonsensical in substance.

The presence of certain activities, especially manufacturing industry or the production of capital goods (heavy industry), is often canvassed as a criterion of economic independence. Large-scale development of domestic capital-goods industries, explicitly in order to achieve economic independence, has been a prominent objective and component of Indian economic planning since the mid-1950s. The pursuit of this policy, largely regardless of the cost and the methods of the process, or of the demand for the output, has been a major factor in India's dependence since about 1960 on large-scale external doles of food and foreign exchange. Somewhat similar results have accompanied the pursuit of so-called economic independence in a number of other underdeveloped countries, especially in Africa.

Neo-colonialism, which also figures prominently in current discussion, including the UNCTAD literature, is another exceedingly vague concept.

Dr. Nkrumah, a vocal opponent of neo-colonialism, writes as follows on this subject: ". . . our problems are made more vexed by the devices of neo-colonialists. . . . The greatest danger at present facing Africa is neo-colonialism, and its major instrument, balkanization. The latter term is particularly appropriate to describe the breaking up of Africa into small, weak states. . . .

The division of Africa into small states reflects the age-old presence and multiplicity of diverse ethnic groups and tribal societies and their demand for political independence, which has become more intense as the stakes in the fight for political power rise with the enlargement and enhancement of the powers of government. The economic effects of the division of an area into a number of independent states depend on the policies pursued by their governments. It is notable that even quite small countries have often progressed rapidly, as for instance Hong Kong and Israel, or are even among the most prosperous in the world, as Switzerland, New Zealand, and Holland. But in any case the process of political subdivision in Africa reflects local pressures and forces, as seen in the attempts of Biafra and Katanga to secure independence.

The failure of Dr. Nkrumah, as of other writers, to provide the term "neo-colonialism" with intelligible meaning is the more remarkable because of the importance assigned to the concept. His *Neo-Colonialism* (London, 1965), discusses the concept at great length, but interprets it largely as the operations of large foreign-owned corporations in underdeveloped countries, whose profits are said to reflect the exploitation of the local populations. This interpretation is in effect simply an application of the Marxist-Leninist idea of the exploitative nature of any return on private capital.

In recent years the term neo-colonialism has been introduced into discussions on foreign aid in three contexts. First, to protest against the imposition of conditions in the granting of intergovernmental aid; second, in support of the demand that aid should not be tied to purchases of specific commodities or from specific sources; third, in support of aid, especially of multilateral aid, on the ground that intergovernmental aid is necessary to avert the dangers of neo-colonialism. Whatever the merits of these arguments, the term neo-colonialism obscures the relevant issues instead of illuminating them.

These vague ideas and insubstantial arguments are designed to evoke definite emotions and promote specific policies. The principal consistent theme of the literature of colonialism, economic colonialism, and neo-colonialism, is the explicitly alleged or clearly implied responsibility of external, especially Western, forces and influences for the material backwardness and poverty of the former colonies, and more generally of all underdeveloped countries. Although, as already noted, this notion is untrue (indeed the reverse of the truth), it has a powerful political and emotional appeal. To use a felicitous phrase of Jacques Barzun's, the idea enables people to achieve "the desired status of victim." It is emotionally comforting to be told that external factors explain a failure to achieve specified goals, including material prosperity. . . .

We are familiar with the emotional dependence of psychoanalysts on their patients, of teachers on their pupils, and of priests on sinners. A similar relationship often exists between social reformers and those groups whose condition they ostensibly seek to ameliorate. The humanitarians and social reformers particularly need people who can be plausibly classified as helpless victims of causes and conditions beyond their control. And the classification of groups as helpless then actually promotes their helplessness, thus serving the psychological, political, and financial aims of the classifiers.

Many of these reformers, particularly the most vocal, seem much less interested in groups which cannot readily be classified as helpless even if they have to face formidable obstacles and difficulties and even if they are actually victims of political hostility. Indeed, self-reliant groups and individuals who are politically persecuted are often viewed with indifference or even disfavor by the most vocal and influential contemporary social reformers and humanitarians, as in the case of the Indian and Levantine minorities in Africa, or the Chinese immigrants in Southeast Asia, groups which started as very poor immigrants and many of whom, after attaining considerable prosperity, were subjected to partial or total expropriation or even expulsion. . . .

Much of the argument of this paper bears on an often ignored aspect of relations between the underdeveloped world and the West. I have referred to the presence of substantial groups in the West who support the notion that the West is to blame for the material backwardness of poor countries. Their attitudes and activities are related to a wider phenomenon; much of what is usually regarded as a confrontation or conflict between the developed and the underdeveloped countries is more nearly akin to an undeclared civil war in the West, where influential groups (especially among intellectuals) dislike or even detest aspects and institutions of their society, and consequently welcome and often promote influences which undermine them and weaken the society of which they are integral parts. There are various reasons for this attitude, including in many instances resentment of a society which does not give them the prominence and power they think they should have. These groups often regard the underdeveloped countries as allies in the civil war against Western society and its institutions, in the belief that they can promote their cause by supplying resources to the underdeveloped world in a confrontation with the West.

These considerations help to explain certain paradoxes in this general area of the relationship between developed and underdeveloped countries. The West provides most of the intellectual, political, administrative, and financial resources with which it is assailed from the underdeveloped countries; it is also the source of the arguments, sometimes genuine but usually spurious, directed against it by spokesmen who claim to represent the underdeveloped world, in particular the argument that the West has caused the poverty of the underdeveloped world. This argument, largely of Western origin, which has been so effective in undermining the self-assurance of the West, is not only false but the reverse of the truth. Whatever material progress has been achieved in the underdeveloped world was largely initiated and promoted by the West, which supplied the human and financial resources absent locally, and induced the necessary changes in attitudes, beliefs, motivations, and institutions. The West provides much of the money and personnel behind many policies and measures which weaken the West politically and financially, and which often harm Western personnel and capital in underdeveloped countries. The situation is most obvious in Africa, where the personnel required for the establishment and administration of economic controls, notably on external transactions and the deployment of foreign staff and capital, come largely from the West, and are usually financed from the West.

Peter Evans
NEO-COLONIALISM AND THE MULTINATIONALS

Many writers who warn against neo-colonialism argue that it leads to the stagnation of Third World economies. Peter Evans, on the faculty of the Sociology Department of Brown University, concedes instead that growth may occur (particularly when manufacturing as opposed to extractive investments are made), but questions the form of social structure that investments by multinational corporations will promote in less-developed countries.

Whether or not less-developed countries can better realize their economic aspirations by strengthening their ties with developed countries will remain in dispute as long as there are rich and poor countries. Dispute will be particularly sharp while the main instruments of such interconnection are identifiable institutions like the multinational corporation. It is easier to map the growth of the multinational corporation than to assess its consequences, but the need for an assessment cannot be ignored. As this essay's subtitle suggests, my main concern is consideration of arguments which are critical of the role of the multinational corporation.

The growth of the multinational corporation is undeniable. The value of the foreign subsidiaries and branches of United States-based corporations is more than $65 billion. Their sales have been rising faster than domestic sales of United States corporations, and their earnings are equivalent to about 20 percent of the net profits of American corporations. Statistics on investment by corporations based in other developed countries are more difficult to obtain, but it appears that in recent years foreign investment by West European firms is increasing even more rapidly than that of American firms. While locally owned firms will probably always retain some segment of their country's economy, it has been predicted that in another

Peter Evans, "National Autonomy and Economic Development: Critical Perspectives on Multinational Corporations in Poor Countries," reprinted by permission of the publishers from Robert O. Keohane and Joseph S. Nye, Jr., eds., *Transnational Relations and World Politics*, Cambridge, Mass.: Harvard University Press, Copyright 1970–1971, by the President and Fellows of Harvard College. Footnotes omitted.

twenty years 600 or 700 corporations will control most of the business of the non-Communist world. None of the 600 or 700 corporations is likely to be headquartered in poor countries, but almost all
will have subsidiaries in them. About one-third of United States foreign investment is located in less-developed countries, and almost
all the major multinational corporations have subsidiaries in these
countries. Such international economic interconnection presents a
poor country with a threat to its autonomy quite different from that
posed by other states.

With the growing predominance of the multinational corporation
increasing numbers of a poor country's economic actors become
responsible to superiors and stockholders who are citizens of other
countries. If a similar chain of command existed in public organizations, the poor country would be deemed a colony. Because multinational corporations are private economic organizations, chains of
command leading outside the state may multiply without ostensible
loss of political sovereignty. Yet, national autonomy, the ability of a
nation-state as a collectivity to make decisions which shape its political and economic future, has been diminished. But is this loss a
threat to general economic progress or only to the power of the
elite?

Evaluation of the role of national autonomy in fostering economic
progress depends on the evaluation of the effects of international
corporate investment. If one sees the economic and social effects
of the increased economic involvement of multinational corporations in less-developed areas as beneficial, then the nation-state
cannot help but appear as an anachronistic impediment to further
rationalization of the international economy. By creating irrational,
chauvinistic barriers in the path of multinational enterprise the
nation-state hampers the progress of its citizens. If, on the other
hand, one sees the multinational corporation as an instrument—
conscious or unwitting—for the preservation or exacerbation of the
economic disparities that currently separate rich and poor countries, then the nation-state becomes the focus of political organization, an instrument to be used to secure economic autonomy and
thereby to foster economic progress.

The multinational corporation, as an efficient technocratic solution to the problems of international economic organization, has numerous supporters in both rich and poor countries. They consider

international investment by private corporations an important, perhaps the most important, factor in stimulating progress in poor countries. Without these "mighty engines of enlightened Western capitalism" the prospects for the future prosperity of these countries would be dim indeed. The multinational corporation not only transfers capital to poor countries, it also provides them with the organizational and technological know-how necessary for the creation of a modern industrial society. The links between parent company and subsidiary are nurturing channels through which flow the resources needed by a less developed country for its economic growth.

Since this assessment of the role of the multinational corporation eliminates economic rationales, its proponents rely on political or psychological explanations for opposition to multinational enterprise. A recent text on multinational corporations has summarized this point of view nicely: "Two major sets of consequences emerge from the extension of corporate production across borders. The first set is economic consequences and is held almost universally to be beneficial. The second set is phrased in political or emotional terms; this includes the threat—often more apparent than real but nevertheless action provoking—which foreign investment poses to local autonomy, or sovereignty, or control." Raymond Vernon has taken a similar position, marveling "at the tenacity with which man seeks to retain a sense of differentiation and identity, a feeling of control, even when the apparent cost of the identity and the control seems out of all proportion to its value." For these observers the quest for national autonomy is a luxury, a psychologically desirable one perhaps, but one for which an economic price is paid.

Those who oppose the encroachments of multinational corporations in the third world spend little time analyzing psychological propensities for autonomy or self-differentiation. Since they are convinced that the effects of those "mighty engines of Western capitalism" are not to facilitate economic growth but to retard it, increased autonomy is an essential step toward hastening economic progress. While these opponents may agree that a sense of autonomy and control are psychologically gratifying, their main interest is explicating and documenting the retarding effects of asymmetric interconnectedness usually characterized as imperialism.

Spreading capital from rich to poor countries is one function classically attributed to international investment, but on examination the direction of the capital flow appears in doubt. Historical retrospects by critics have suggested that the Industrial Revolution in Great Britain was fueled by capital extracted from its colonies and that the development of the colonies suffered in consequence. Paul A. Baran, for example, has related India's failure to develop to the extraction of its surplus capital by British firms, an outflow which he claimed reached 10 percent of its national income in the beginning of the nineteenth century. Clifford Geertz has suggested a similarly negative role for the Dutch when comparing Indonesia's development with that of Japan.

Recent examinations of financial relations between the United States and Latin America also suggest that less-developed countries end up exporting more funds than they receive. From 1950 to 1965 remittances of income to United States parent companies exceeded net new private investment by $7.5 billion. An examination of United States Department of Commerce figures for the period 1965–1969 reveals an additional gap approaching $3 billion.

Some critics attribute the loss of capital by poor countries to exorbitant rates of return on foreign investment in these countries. Baran has noted that the profits of British, Dutch, and Belgian companies with investments in colonies were well in excess of the rate of return normal in their countries of origin. More recent data also substantiates this point. An analysis of British investment has confirmed the profitability of Asian and African ventures but suggests that high rates of profit were not possible without the organized political support of the home country. The lower rates of returns to British companies operating in Latin America can probably be explained by the fact that "there was greater stability within the Commonwealth and Empire and greater capacity to determine the investment climate."

A look at the current profitability of American foreign investment suggests that higher rates of return are still achieved on investments in poor countries. The rate of return on investments in less-developed countries in 1969 was more than double the rate of return on investments in developed countries. Separate examination of investment in extractive (mining and petroleum) industries and in manufacturing industries shows that high rates of return on extractive investment account for the difference. The following tabulation indicates earnings on United States direct investment in 1969 as a percentage of book value.

	All Investment	Manufacturing	Extractive
Developed countries	8.3%	10.8	3.0
Less developed countries	18.8%	8.9	27.6

While a combination of political dependency and concentration on extractive industry appears most conducive to exorbitant rates of return, the returns on investment in manufacturing industries may be underestimated by this analysis. In the first place, "fees and royalties" collected by United States firms from their direct investments are excluded. Were they added to earnings, rates of return would be increased by 15 to 20 percent. The overpricing of intermediate goods sold by parent companies to their subsidiaries may be an even more important source of extra returns from manufacturing investment in less-developed countries. A recent study of the pharmaceutical industry in Colombia suggests that return to parent companies from overpricing intermediate products is many times the return received from dividends and interest.

Even if profit rates on foreign investment were not excessive relative to domestic rates of return, foreign investment might still create a drain on the capital resources of a less-developed country in the long run. The lack of a termination date is an important feature of direct investment. With bonds and loans a borrower must eventually repay more than he borrows, but amortization at least diminishes his future obligation. With direct investment the recipient looks forward to interminable remittances and no guarantee that they will be matched by inflows of new capital. Initially a less-developed country may receive more in new investment than it must pay out in remitted income, but over the years the balance is likely to shift to its disadvantage. A comparison of Latin America, where United States investment has a long history, with Africa, where it is relatively recent, will serve as illustration. From 1965 to 1969 Africa received about as much new capital from the United States as it remitted in income. Remitted income from Latin America, on the other hand, was over three and one-half times the amount of new capital received.

Yet, multinational corporations could be making excessive profits and repatriating more capital than they invested and still contribute significantly to the economic growth of less-developed countries. If the organizational and technological know-how they contribute serves as the spark to the industrialization process, departure of capital is not an unreasonable price to pay. It must only be understood that the contribution of the multinational corporation lies primarily in the transfer of intangibles rather than in the transfer of capital.

Unfortunately, according to critics of the multinational corporation the past utilization of the organizational and technological resources of the corporation has diverted the productive energies of poor countries in directions unconducive to self-sustained economic growth. In 1950 H. W. Singer criticized investment in extractive industries in less-developed countries: "If we apply the principle of opportunity costs to the development of nations, the import of capital into underdeveloped countries for the purpose of making them into providers of food and raw materials for the industrialized countries may have been not only rather ineffective in giving them the normal benefits of investment and trade but may have been positively harmful." Singer based his criticism of extractive investment on the idea that it is designed to operate as an "enclave" relatively unconcerned with the growth of the local economy because the goods it produces are sold outside it. Baran has argued more strongly still that the effects of foreign investment in extractive industries are detrimental. He has concluded that "whichever aspect of economic development we may consider, it is manifestly detrimental to the prosperity of the raw materials producing corporations." Development would mean increased labor costs and probably higher taxes but would do nothing to increase the demand for the goods the extractive exporter is selling. When the attenuated interest of investors in extractive industries in local development is coupled with the high rate at which they remit their profits to the United States, it hardly seems necessary to invoke a psychological need for differentiation in order to explain hostility toward these foreign investors.

Defenders of extractive investment usually cite the resources made available to governments via taxation. This argument also leads us to the importance of political independence in effecting the redistribution of returns from the investor to the host country. If less-developed countries have been successful in retaining a larger portion of the income of extractive investment within their borders, it is because the state retained sufficient political autonomy to bargain with international firms. The existence of "aggressively nationalist groups" within a country has been a benefit to less-developed states in their bargaining.

Since mining and petroleum currently account for about 50 percent of the value of United States investment in less-developed countries, just as they did in 1950, arguments about the effects of extractive investment must continue to have an important place in any critique of the multinational corporation. In this same period, however, the value of American investments in manufacturing in less-developed countries has increased from $850 million to $4.7 billion. Investment in manufacturing industries may be a more stimulating outlet for the knowledge and skills of the multinational corporation, but it also raises a new set of problems.

The manufacturing firm, unlike the extractive exporter, has a direct stake in the growth of the local market. Because of this stake the manufacturing firm participates more actively in the life of the host country. The goods that it offers embody a way of life. In order to ensure their consumption the manufacturer must take on a role which bears a more than coincidental resemblance to that of the original international organization—the Roman Catholic church. For the church the transmission of values from Western Europe to less developed countries has been more an end than a means; the manufacturing firm becomes involved in the transnational transmission of ideals and values, although more as a means than an end. By introducing its wares and, even more important, by trying to convince people to consume them the manufacturing firm joins the church as an outsider helping to shape the culture of less developed countries.

The transfer of ideas may have no less economic impact than the transfer of capital, though it fits poorly into quantitative economic models. Supporters of the multinational corporation are likely to speak in terms of the transfer of neutral "skills" or "know-how" which will be useful to recipients in a less developed country in achieving whatever ends they may desire. Those who argue for greater autonomy are suspicious of the usefulness of the tools, but in addition they are afraid that the tools dictate the ends more nearly than the technocrats of developed countries would like to admit. Their arguments involve a range of issues from the ways in which people spend their paychecks to the kind of political philosophy they are likely to favor. These arguments are worth considering at some length.

As a transmitter of ideas and values, as well as a producer of goods, the multinational corporation becomes a means of encouraging consumptive emulation across societal boundaries. Thorstein Veblen's analysis of the ways the "leisure class" makes its own peculiar cultural standards normative for the social order as a whole now applies transnationally. Products and ideas developed in rich countries shape the values and ideas of citizens of poor countries. Or, to adapt Karl Marx's statement on the class nature of ideas, the nation which has the means of material production at its disposal controls the means of mental production and, in turn, the ideas of those who lack the means of mental production.

A short excursus on advertising expenditures should help make this argument more concrete. The United States Department of Commerce has estimated that sales of American manufacturing affiliates in less developed countries in 1968 were approximately $9 billion. Those corporations which own the bulk of United States overseas investment spend, on average, 4 percent of their sales receipts on advertising. We may estimate then that American manufacturing corporations are spending approximately $360 million each year in order to shape the consumptive habits of citizens of less developed countries. Rough as this estimate may be, it should stand as an indication of the magnitude of such expenditures. Expenditures by multinational corporations on the education of consumer preferences are less than the education budgets of national governments but not incomparably less. In Brazil, for example, use of the above percentages suggests that advertising expenditures by American manufacturing affiliates alone are over one-third of recurring public expenditures on all forms of education.

The contradiction between imported consumptive tastes and the productivity of local economies is disturbing. Ivan Illich, founder of the Center for Intercultural Documentation in Cuernavaca, has expressed his distress about this situation as follows: "The plows of the rich can do as much harm as their swords.... Once the Third World has become a mass market for the goods, products, and processes which are designed by the rich for themselves, the discrepancy between demand for these Western artifacts and the supply will increase indefinitely.... Each car which Brazil puts on the road denies fifty people good transportation by bus. Each merchandised refrigerator reduces the chance of building a community freezer." The example of the passenger car is a classic illustration of the diffusion of inappropriate patterns of consumption. A mode of transportation, developed in response to the historical, economic, and technological conditions of early twentieth-century America, was introduced by the multinational corporation and has become the mainstay of transportation systems in countries whose economic and social requirements make it altogether inappropriate. It has been estimated that automobile production facilities created by multinational corporations in Latin America are already ten times as great as they need be to meet the demands of the regional market. Yet, despite the resources devoted to their production, passenger cars are a form of transportation which can benefit only a minority of the population.

While ownership of a private automobile is beyond the reach of the average citizen of less-developed countries, production of passenger cars absorbs resources which might be used to produce trucks, buses, bicycles, and other forms of transportation more within the reach of all citizens. Automobile production may exert pressure on foreign exchange reserves by requiring increased importation of gasoline or of the raw materials and capital goods necessary to produce cars. Cars tend to be heavily concentrated in a few cities, and the resources necessary to build a road network to support such an individualistic mode of transportation are not available. Congestion in the cities of many less-developed countries is frequently worse than in most Western cities; pollution levels are also higher. The average city dweller in a less-developed country must sit in a bus each morning and evening stranded in a sea of passenger vehicles, breathing exhaust fumes and wishing he were able to add to the anarchy by purchasing his own automobile.

It is important to keep in mind that the disjunction between private consumptive longings and the welfare of the community does not have to be resolved in favor of the former. Barry Richman, an English management consultant, was struck by the extensive use of bicycles by the personnel of the factories he studied in the People's Republic of China (Communist China). Even managers and administrators, who in many poorer countries invariably move by car, rode bicycles to work. Consumer sovereignty is a concept of dubious empirical validity, and in less-developed countries "freedom to consume" is severely curtailed by poverty for all but the affluent elite. If collective decisionmaking at the national level could result in an allocation of productive resources more appropriate to the economic and social circumstances of the citizenry, it is hard to see how the freedom of the average individual can be said to have been diminished.

Without belaboring the issue further it seems plausible that multinational corporations help transmit standards of consumption which may well represent a misallocation of resources from the point of view of the welfare of the community as a whole. If this is true, then the distortion of consumer desires has a retarding effect on economic progress, and poor countries could achieve greater progress by exercising a greater degree of autonomy in shaping their consumptive norms. As Veblen has pointed out, the mark of a good borrower of technology is the ability to extricate the technology from the fetishes that grow up around its use in the culture of its origin. It is possible to reject the goods which rich countries have chosen as embodiments of their technology without rejecting the technology itself.

Consumer choices are not the only decisions affected by the internationalization of less-developed economies. Decisions about the allocation of productive resources are also directly affected. These decisions, however, are more likely to be made in corporate headquarters in New York or Tokyo than in capitals of less-developed countries. It might be argued that the geographical location at which an economic decision is made should have no effect on its outcome. If a rational man in Dar es Salaam will make the same decision as a rational man in New York, then the locus of decisionmaking is hardly vital. If, on the other hand, the outcome of a decision depends on the environment of the decisionmaker, the change becomes important. Increasingly, social scientists have adopted the latter view and look upon rationality as dependent on social position. No decision-maker can consider all the information that might be relevant—to say nothing of all the possible interconnections between the relevant facts. Time constraints and limited cognitive capacity ensure that rationality is always "bounded." The social position of the decisionmaker will determine the relative salience of different pieces of information and the ways the various pieces will be put together. Each decisionmaker brings to a problem not only a particular subsample of the relevant information but also a particular set of theories on how his information should fit together. . . .

Just as imported development strategies have proven irrational to their borrowers, strategies that looked irrational to developed countries have proven efficacious to late starters. David S. Landes has illustrated this nicely in his analysis of the differing rationales of British and German entrepreneurs in the latter half of the nineteenth century—when Germany was a "less-developed country": "The British manufacturer remained faithful to the classical calculus . . . making those investments which, given anticipated costs, risks, and sales, yielded the greatest margin over what existing equipment could provide. . . . The significance of this approach is best appreciated when contrasted with the technological rationality of the Germans. This was a different kind of arithmetic, which maximized, not returns, but technical efficiency."

The German kind of arithmetic, irrational as it may have appeared to established British entrepreneurs, proved efficacious. In broader terms Alexander Gerschenkron has shown that each of the European countries needed a distinctive system of banking, governmental involvement, and industrial organization suited to its own material circumstances in order to industrialize. Japan, with its direct governmental involvement in the creation of new industry and its cartelized, paternalistic method of industrial organization, also chose a path that looked irrational in terms of the cultural prescriptions of its predecessors but proved appropriate to its own circumstances.

Too great a reliance on development rationales evolved in other times and circumstances entails the same kind of disadvantages as absorption of alien standards of consumption. Greater reliance on indigenous ideas provides no guarantee of producing better strategies, but it increases the possibility of innovations shaped by the particular situation of a less-developed country. Poor countries are desperately in need of such innovations: Only by discovering rules that work for them do they have a chance to achieve parity. Following the rules that created the present system of international stratification can hardly be expected to eliminate this system.

Even if less-developed countries completely rejected the development theories proffered by developed countries, they would still be circumscribed in their choice of strategy by the predominance of foreign-owned firms in their economies. The presence of foreign-owned firms substantially limits the ability of a poor country to shape its own industrial structure. Gerschenkron's paradigm of European development and the experience of Japan suggest that the more backward a country, the more essential is initiative and direction by its government. Yet, governments of poor countries are often forced into roles more passive than those of governments in developed countries. European governments have been very active in engineering mergers to bring together locally owned firms and strengthen national industries. The government of a less-developed country, faced with an economy full of subsidiaries attached to foreign-based, private corporations, is much more limited in the kinds of organizational initiatives that it may take.

The automobile industry again provides a good example. As noted earlier production facilities for automobiles in Latin America exceed regional needs. At the national level the situation appears even more extreme. Argentina produces about 3 percent of the number of cars made in the United States, yet it was recently reported that Argentina had thirteen manufacturers competing in the local market. Since the assembly of automobiles is an industry with undeniable economies of scale, the cost of manufacture is grossly inflated by this fragmented industrial structure.

What action is open to a less-developed country faced with an industrial structure that is inefficient because it is a "miniature replica" of those of developed countries? The government of a small country is unlikely to be able to persuade Fiat, Volkswagenwerk, and General Motors Corporation to merge for its convenience. As long as it allows foreign-owned firms to compete freely for its internal market, it must either import automobiles and lose foreign exchange or produce them locally at production costs that may be as much as twice those at facilities utilizing efficiencies of scale. Since effective utilization of human resources is as important to a less-developed country as utilization of its land and minerals, it has been argued that a close bond between elites and masses is critical to a country's development. Yet, a populist orientation is rare in traditional societies, and the experience of colonialism is likely to increase the separation between elites and masses. The multinational corporation may also help to maintain an external orientation among elites.

Nationals working at the local level strive to absorb the cultural perspective of the organizations that provide their livelihood and their work environment. The ability to identify with the corporation as an organization and to acquire the cognitive and stylistic norms that prevail within it is an important prerequisite of executive success. The socialization of local elite personnel is reinforced by the employment of foreign personnel in key high-level positions. If corporations are successful in inculcating a sense of organizational identity, the probability that the local economic elite will act on the basis of national identification diminishes.

The relation between foreign economic linkages and attitudes toward domestic politics has been nicely illustrated in a recent paper on Brazilian entrepreneurs. It was found that entrepreneurs in firms dependent on foreign corporate support felt that the proper functioning of society required only an alliance of upper-class groups. Entrepreneurs in firms independent of foreign economic interests were much more likely to feel that salaried employees and wage workers should share in political power.

This analysis implies that policies favoring foreign investors should rarely be found in conjunction with policies that stress a higher level of participation and effort from the populace. An impressionistic glance at less-developed countries appears to confirm this hypothesis. Tanzania's choice of the policy of *kujitegemea* ("self-reliance") in 1967, for example, was spelled out in a two-pronged manner. One prong was the nationalization of foreign-owned investment; the other was an attempt to increase the economic and political participation of the people of the country by diminishing the distance between the people and their leaders and convincing them that it was only through their own cooperative efforts that the country would grow. A contrasting example is that of the military government which ascended to power in Brazil in 1964. It was successful in improving the climate for foreign investors but was suspicious to the point of paranoia of widespread political participation.

If regimes can hope to mobilize either foreign investors or their own constituents but not both, then the alienation of the populace from its government must be counted as one of the "opportunity costs" of policies favoring foreign investors. This cost may be especially large in very poor countries in which agriculture is primitive and dominant and the low productivity of agricultural labor is a major concern.

A related argument revolves around the role of the state as a bargaining agent. It has already been noted that governments with little political independence, for example, colonies, were most likely to provide foreign investors with exorbitant returns. It was also observed that the prevalence of nationalist sentiments within a populace might be a useful resource to governments in bargaining with foreign investors. If economic dependency reduces political autonomy, then the very countries which have the largest amounts of foreign investment will be least likely to secure their fair share of the fruits of this investment. China in the nineteenth and early twentieth centuries might be considered a case in point.

A determinate relation between economic dominance by foreign-owned firms and a particular combination of political strategies cannot be proven by a few examples. Nonetheless, the examples suggest that the predominance of foreign-owned firms has political consequences which, in turn, have implications for the future economic progress of a poor country. If a state's ability to mobilize the energies of its populace and to bargain effectively are considered economic assets, then penetration by multinational corporations must be considered an economic threat to the degree that it undermines political autonomy or increases the distance between the citizenry and its leaders.

A range of arguments leads to the conclusion that the increased economic interconnectedness between rich and poor countries fostered by large corporations is not without negative consequences. Some of these arguments, for example, that multinational corporations inculcate an inappropriate set of consumer desires and promulgate unsuitable development theories, are not amenable to quantitative estimation. Other arguments—that less-developed countries lose capital as a result of direct investment or that profit rates are excessive—are potentially subject to rigorous analysis, though a great deal of work is yet to be done. Despite the need for more information and analysis it does not seem wise to assume that increased international interconnectedness via the multinational corporation automatically increases benefits to both rich and poor countries. Less-developed countries cannot count on having their welfare maximized by relying on the unseen hand of economic interchange mediated through the organizational framework of the multinational corporation.

Rejection of reliance on foreign-owned firms almost inevitably leads to diminished reliance on private enterprise in general. Leaving industrialization in less-developed countries to private enterprise is tantamount to leaving it in the hands of foreign enterprise. Individual entrepreneurs in less-developed countries are rarely a match for their gigantic competitors. More often they find that their self-interest demands playing a cooperative, subordinate role. Managing the subsidiary of a multinational corporation is usually a more attractive possibility than competing against it.

Weakness of the local entrepreneurial class forces countries in search of greater autonomy toward more socialist forms of economic organization. Emphasis on collective rather than individual decisionmaking increases. Much more initiative will be required of the state. Throughout the discussion the importance of the state as the only organization with sufficient leverage to bargain with the multinational corporation has been stressed. Far from being an anachronistic impediment, the state appears to be the only organization that citizens of a poor country might utilize to defend their interests.

Having decided to move in the direction of a more autonomous society in which the state is a major entrepreneur, the poor country is then faced with the knotty problem of creating a state whose actions and decisions reflect the interests and desires of the populace.

In most poor countries the state is primarily the instrument of the elite. If increased national autonomy results only in the creation of more cumbersome, ineffective bureaucracies or in the more effective domination of the local populace by a local elite, it is hardly a step forward. Presently constituted public bureaucracies are poor models. The building of efficient, responsive public organizations must become a primary goal for a poor country in quest of greater autonomy.

A poor country which rejects interconnectedness based on the multinational corporation must also find new means of relating itself to other countries. Autonomy does not mean autarky any more than "self-reliance" means "self-sufficiency." The possibility of autarky would make the achievement of autonomy much easier, but autarky is not possible for any but the largest of the less-developed countries. For most poor countries greater autonomy must mean increased control over external economic relations, not their absence. Arguments against the further strengthening of the ties that currently bind poor countries to developed countries should not be construed to imply the wisdom of isolation. One way for less-developed countries to achieve increased control would be cooperating in areas in which they face similar problems, for example, coordination between poor countries exporting the same product. Replacing a private, asymmetric type of integration with a more public, symmetric interconnectedness may offer the best hope of greater autonomy.

Moving toward greater autonomy is essentially choosing to orient economic decisions around the political constituency of the nation-state rather than to allow the locus of decisionmaking to gravitate toward private, profitmaking corporations based in rich countries. There is good reason to believe this policy is an economically rational choice, but it provides no ready-made solutions to the problems of poor countries. It is rather the selection of a new paradigm, a new framework in which to seek solutions.

Tom Soper

THE EUROPEAN ECONOMIC COMMUNITY AND AFRICA

Since its creation in 1958, the character of the Common Market's relation to Africa has been attacked by some as a manifestation of neo-colonialism, while defended by others as a mutually advantageous association. Mr. Soper, Director of Studies at London's Overseas Development Institute, published this defense of the relationship in 1965. Since then the Second Yaoundé Convention was signed (1969), with funds for Africa increased to $1 billion for a five-year period. In February 1975, these arrangements were once again renewed with the conclusion of still another convention at Lomé, Togo. The entry of Great Britain into the European Economic Community has meant that these latest accords have brought about the association of most of Commonwealth Africa with the Common Market. This ends the virtual French monopoly over EEC loans and grants since the African states of French expression must now share the advantages of association with the countries of the former British Empire.

Since the coming into force of the Treaty of Rome on January 1, 1958, the European Common Market has always been a matter of immense significance and concern to Africa. This is so, primarily, because from the outset a substantial part of Africa has been formally associated with the EEC. In 1958 the African associate members consisted of the then French West and Equatorial Africa, Madagascar, French Somaliland, the French Cameroons and Togoland, the Belgian Congo, Ruanda-Urundi and Italian Somaliland; that is to say, all the African dependencies of the Six. Morocco and Tunisia in North Africa also had special relations with the EEC, although this relationship was not regularized as a special part of the Treaty of Rome, as was that which bound the Tropical African dependencies to Europe. Algeria was at the time a part of France and thus was included in the provisions of the Treaty of Rome. A section of the Convention of Association annexed to the Treaty was also applicable to her. Excluding the Mahgreb countries—which are not being considered in this article—a total of some 50 million persons

Extracts from "The EEC and Aid to Africa" by Tom Soper, *International Affairs*, London, July 1965, pp. 463–477. Reprinted by permission of the Royal Institute of International Affairs. Footnotes omitted.

in Africa, or between a fifth and a quarter of the total population of
the continent, were linked to the EEC. Since 1958 African associate
membership has changed only slightly. Guinea, under President
Seku Touré, has opted out, and two ex-British dependencies have
come in: British Somaliland, consequent upon its joining Italian
Somaliland to become the new state of Somalia; and the Southern Cameroons, consequent upon its joining the French-speaking
Cameroons to become the new Republic of Cameroun.

Although not associated with it, Commonwealth African countries
have also shown great interest in the EEC. Pan-Africanism has been
a theme of overwhelming importance among some of their leaders,
and if a quarter of the continent has a special relationship with
Europe there is bound to be concern among the rest; secondly, two
Commonwealth African countries have been sucked into the EEC
already; and thirdly, some of the others already have close economic relations with the Six through trade and send a not insubstantial proportion of their exports to them—in the case of Ghana
and Nigeria as much as a third. As the Treaty of Association ex-
tends preferential treatment to the exports of those countries associated, this discriminates against those which are not. At the
present time Anglophone African interest has reached the point
where Nigeria has been negotiating with the EEC for many months
in order to obtain a form of association, and Kenya, Tanzania and
Uganda have just opened formal negotiations.

To understand the nature of the association it is important to
look back to the situation in 1956, just before the Treaty of Rome
was signed. France at this time was an imperial power and her
overseas dependencies experienced the closest possible economic
relationship with her. Broadly speaking, something like two-thirds
of the exports and imports of the French Empire in Africa went to,
and came from, France. In France itself the market for French-
African products was protected and guaranteed, and special prices
in excess of the world market price were paid to primary producers.
French companies had a preferential right of establishment in the
dependencies, French exports to them and special advantages and
there was a substantial program of French public investment in
them. Thus it was that France, when the point came of having to
decide whether or not to sign the articles of the Treaty of Rome,

was faced with an extremely awkward predicament. She was, in effect, being asked to join a community of European states which, among other things, was forming a customs union, the provisions of which naturally applied to the member states alone and not to third countries. The effect of this was that France, in the absence of special provisions, would have had to apply a common community tariff against countries who were not members of the union; and these included the French Empire overseas. She was therefore faced with the two extreme choices of having to sever her historic connections with her dependencies, or to ask that they should be included as members of the EEC.

Severance was something that France herself could not contemplate. Yet inclusion was simply not practicable, for this would have meant that the dependencies would have had to be treated on complete economic equality with the Six. This would have prevented any of them from protecting its industries against the Six; it would have required acceptance of a common external tariff against the rest of the world; and the mockery of trying to thrash out a common agricultural policy, a common transport policy, a harmonization of social policies, and so on, for countries as diverse as Western Germany and Senegal.

In the event a compromise was reached; a compromise which was extended not only to the dependencies of France but, in principle, to those of the other five member states of the EEC as well. In practice this had relevance, in addition to France, to Italy, Belgium and Holland. This was a logical extension, as a basic philosophy of the Treaty of Rome is that the members treat each other in exactly the same way. Thus it was that special terms of association were worked out, terms which were applicable to the following:

French West Africa, including: Senegal, the Sudan, Guinea, the Ivory Coast, Dahomey, Mauretania, the Niger and the Upper Volta; French Equatorial Africa including: the Middle Congo, Ubangi-Shari, Chad and Gaboon; St. Pierre and Miquelon, the Comoro Archipelago, Madagascar and dependencies, the French Somali Coast, New Caledonia and dependencies, the French Settlements in Oceania, the Southern and Antarctic Territories; the Republic of Togoland; the French Trusteeship Territory in the Cameroons; the Belgian Congo and Ruanda-Urundi; the Italian Trusteeship Territory in Somaliland; and Netherlands New Guinea.

The terms of association were embodied in Part IV of the Treaty of Rome, which continues *sine die,* and in an implementing convention annexed to the Treaty, which was to operate for five years. It was provided that the exports of associate countries should be able to enter the market of the Six duty free; that associates could protect their own industries if they wished to, even against the Six, although they could not give less-advantageous terms to the Six than they gave to other countries; that they should suppress any discrimination towards individual member states of the Six; that they should benefit from a Development Fund which could provide grants to a total of $581 million over the five-year period. Of this, $511 million was earmarked for French possessions overseas. This Fund was built up from contributions by the European member states, with over a third provided by Western Germany and over a third by France. Seventy percent of the expenditure of the Fund was to be devoted to economic projects—mainly infrastructure—and 30 percent to social projects, mainly schools and hospitals.

There is no doubt that these provisions gave considerable benefits to the associates. They would have duty-free access to a dynamic European market of 170 million people; they were not prevented from protecting their own economies, and they were the beneficiaries of a Development Fund of some size, and one which was over and above any bilateral aid they were already receiving. The advantages to France were that she had managed to join the EEC with all that that entailed, and yet had been able to retain her historic ties—economic, cultural and social—with her overseas Empire. The French mission, far from being undermined, had in effect been reinforced, notably by German contributions into areas that had become so permeated with the French culture and with commercial and industrial links that they were unlikely to be susceptible to Teutonic influences—if indeed any such influences were contemplated.

Western Germany itself, and to a lesser extent Holland, were not entirely satisfied with the association arrangements. For Germany it meant a concentration of a part of their aid program into a section of the developing world—primarily Francophone Africa—with which they had no special economic interest. Germany's concern with the poorer countries of the world was far wider than that of France. Latin America, Asia and Anglophone Africa, in terms of trade, and public and private investment, all meant more to her. But by agreeing to the terms of the association she was required to place $200 million over a five-year period at the disposal of a Fund which would invest most of it in Francophone Africa; special trading privileges were to be given to overseas countries with which Germany did little business, and, in many instances, tariffs had to be imposed against the imports of certain commodities from other countries with which Germany did considerable business. The Dutch shared these views, and were reluctant to back a system that appeared to them as being too exclusive.

In the interests of European unity, however, and to ensure that France came into the Common Market, the dissidents among the Six gave way. The only significant encroachment on French interests overseas was that the Right of Establishment was, in accordance with the principle of equality among the Six, extended to all the members and not restricted to France. This meant that any rights that French industry had in establishing itself in French dependencies could no longer be exclusively applicable to France alone but had to be shared with the other five European member states.

The Convention of Association embodying these terms expired on December 31, 1962. By this time, a number of important political developments had taken place: the French Empire in Tropical Africa had achieved independence as fourteen separate states; independence had also been gained by Madagascar, and by the Belgian and Italian territories in Africa. On achieving independence these countries had the option of continuing with the association or opting out; and all, except French Guinea, elected to continue. Thus when the time came to consider the terms under which a new convention of association should be worked out, the underlying political situation was very different from what it had been in 1956–1957. The new association that was ultimately agreed on is, in fact, a negotiated treaty between twenty-four states: the six of Europe and the eighteen associates. The association indeed—known as the Yaoundé Convention and signed at Yaoundé in July 1963—is an Afro-Malagasy association and in this it differs from the first convention of association, which, as we have seen, although primarily African, was not exclusively so.

A second important different between the two conventions is that the Development Fund has been considerably enlarged both in size and, more significantly, in scope. Over a second five-year period, a total of $730 million has been made available for public investment in the associated countries. Of this, $620 million is in the form of grants but, unlike the previous Fund which was entirely grants, the remaining $110 million is in the form of loans. Of this, $46 million is available at very low interest rates, repayable over a maximum of 40 years and with up to a 10-year grace period. The remaining $64 million is also for loans but on harder terms, carrying the rate of interest employed by the European Investment Bank at the time the loan agreement is reached and repayable over 25 years. These hard loans come not directly from the Development Fund, but from the European Investment Bank—set up by the EEC to assist in the advancement of the less-developed parts of Europe. The Fund, however, in order to soften the terms, may assist in the provision of a rebate of up to 3 percent.

There is also a considerable diversification of purposes to which financial assistance from the Fund can be put. The first Fund could finance only basic economic infrastructure and social investments. The new Fund has powers not only to do this, but also to support production schemes providing normal financial returns, industries for processing agricultural products, and surveys. In the field of technical cooperation it can support staff and vocational training programs. In order to assist in the stabilization of commodity prices it has powers to place credits at the disposal of local funds or bodies concerned with this problem. It can provide aid to assist certain associated countries in the transition from protected markets and artificially high prices to a competitive market. . . .

A third major development from the first convention is the creation of institutions for the association. The first had none, but at the request of the eighteen Afro-Malagasy countries there was now been set up an Association Council consisting of the EEC Council of Ministers, the EEC Commission and one member of the government of each associated state. There are also an Association Committee, a Parliamentary Conference, and a Court of Arbitration consisting of five members acting by majority vote.

A fourth major development is that the Yaoundé Convention is open-ended. That is to say, other countries with economies comparable in character and stage of development to those already associated can apply for full association by adherence to the

Yaoundé Convention as it now stands; *or* for an association of a special type based on reciprocal obligations in trade; *or* for a simple trade agreement. Under the first convention there was no possibility of extending the membership through the articles of association themselves. Any third country wishing for a form of association with the EEC could negotiate through Article 238 of the Treaty of Rome, a means of linkage that was valid for any country in the world.

In the case of the British application in 1961, as full membership was asked for and not association, the application was made through Article 237. Towards the end of these negotiations, it was announced that the Six had agreed that should Britain become a member of the Common Market, the option of association as at that time operating—that is, that which was based on the first convention of association—should be open to Commonwealth Africa and certain other Commonwealth countries with broadly similar economies. This agreement represented a major concession on the part of France. By agreeing to allow the benefits of association to be shared, the differential advantages accruing to Francophone Africa were of course diluted. The wider a preference is shared, the less advantageous it is. So far as Africa was concerned, Commonwealth adhesion to the EEC would have meant an additional 100 million Anglophone Africans on an existing base of 50 million Francophone Africans. And the Anglophone increment was in general economically more advanced than the Francophone.

At the time it looked as if France had agreed to the intended widening of the association in part because British membership would have meant that exports from Francophone Africa would have free access to the British market as well as to that of the Six, and that this would help to some extent to compensate for any losses suffered by the existing associates through the adhesion of Commonwealth African countries. Further, there would have been an additional British contribution to the Development Fund, which would have added to its potence but probably not have changed its essentially French character. But, as was seen from subsequent events, all this was window-dressing. The British application for membership was vetoed, and there was therefore no question of Commonwealth African countries becoming associated with the EEC on this basis. But even before the veto those Commonwealth

African countries which had expressed their views were virtually unanimous in condemning the association. The one real exception was Sierra Leone, which nonetheless failed to follow up its expressions of interest.

Negotiations between Britain and the Six were broken off in 1963. By then the new terms of association between the EEC and the eighteen associates were nearly settled. Ratification was delayed as a result of Dutch and German irritation over the French action blocking British membership, but in the course of time tempers cooled and the Yaoundé Convention came into force on June 1, 1964, nearly a year after its signing. There is no doubt that this delay in ratification as a result of a purely internal European disagreement over British membership of the Common Market had adverse effects on Anglophone African opinion. Commentators were quick to point out that if association were so beneficial to Africans then it was a pity that their interests were brusquely pushed aside as soon as European matters were involved.

From the point of view of practitioners of aid the most fascinating thing about the association agreements is that an extremely tidy and logical bundle has emerged from most unlikely origins. The starting point in 1956–1957 was a compromise agreement, in the interests of European solidarity, to accommodate on the one hand France's special position as an imperial Power, and on the other hand the disinclination of the five other members of the EEC to link themselves too formally to that situation. A further stage was reached in 1960 when the associated countries themselves achieved political independence and all, with the exception of French Guinea, elected to continue with the association until the end of the first-year period. Then came the long and hard-fought negotiations between the Six and the eighteen Afro-Malagasy states, resulting in the Yaoundé Convention, which was clearly based on the 1958–1962 Convention but equally clearly developed far beyond it. It has emerged as a closely integrated program of trade and aid with the donor-recipient relationship formally institutionalized.

Taking the financial provisions of both conventions of association, some $1.25 billion has, so far as Africa is concerned, been earmarked for development assistance over 10 years. This is equivalent to approximately £450 million or £45 million a year. This is just under a quarter of the yearly total British aid program, and about a half of the British aid that is currently directed towards Africa each year. Capital assistance from the Fund has also now reached a rate of disbursement that is roughly equal to capital assistance supplied bilaterally from France, although French technical assistance makes the total French bilateral contribution much higher. Even so, EEC assistance from the Fund cannot be thought of as a small additional investment: it is a substantial proportion of the total aid.

But it is the characteristics of EEC assistance to its Afro-Malagasy associates that are so illuminating, rather than the actual quantity of aid provided. In the first place, the associates know precisely how much financial assistance *in toto* will be available over a five-year period. They may regard it as generous or mean as they like, but they have the great advantage of a degree of certainty. Not only are they certain as to the total amount, they know how much is available in grants, how much in loans and what the terms of the loans will be. Further, they know that so much will be devoted to one category of investment, and so much to another. . . .

So far, apart from ex-British Somaliland and the ex-British Southern Cameroons which became associates of the EEC almost as an after-thought following their political unification with other African states, no Commonwealth African country has joined. Their attitude, indeed, has in general been one of considerable suspicion, and there has been a tendency to echo the views of the President of Ghana who has been hostile from the outset. Charges of neocolonialism have been made; that the Six are striving to recover their political "losses" in Africa through economic ties; that the association is intended to keep African countries as primary producers in perpetuity, and that it is an obstacle to the growth of manufacturing industry; that it is dividing Africa between those which are associated and those which are not and is inhibiting the development of African Common Markets.

In fact, these charges can be countered. On *neo-colonialism—* the association has come about through hard-fought negotiations between eighteen independent Afro-Malagasy countries and six independent European ones. If the outcome is considered to be neo-colonial in character, then the Ghanaian charge is a gratuitous indictment of the motives and ability of the Afro-Malagasy governments who have entered into the agreements. On *primary products and industrialization*—the association has provided help in the stabilization of prices of commodities, which all African countries are asking for; it is opening its markets free of duty to all products from associates, including manufactured goods; it has overtly declared that one of the objects of the association is to "further the industrialization of the associated states and the diversification of their economies in order that they may achieve stability and economic independence," and part of the available financial assistance is specifically earmarked for industrial development. On *African Common Markets and intra-African cooperation*—the commercial relationship between the Six and the eighteen is based on the concept of a free-trade area. This means that any individual associate can establish what tariffs it likes against third countries.

There has, indeed, been an instance of an associated country applying tariff duties against another associated country. As an example of intra-African economic cooperation—which is so essential for economic development—this is deplorable, but it is significant as an indication of the freedom of action that is in practice experienced by associates. There is nothing that prevents African countries from forming their own customs unions; indeed, the EEC is anxious to encourage as much intra-African economic cooperation as possible. It is specifically stipulated in the association agreement that the Yaoundé Convention "shall not preclude the maintenance or establishment of customs unions or free-trade areas among associated states," and, further, that it "shall not preclude the maintenance or establishment of customs unions or free-trade areas between one or more associated states and one or more third countries insofar as they neither are nor prove to be incompatible with the principles and provisions of the said convention."

Why then is it that Commonwealth African countries have been so suspicious of the association agreements? One possible explanation is that they were not as fully informed as they might have been in the early stages about the exact nature of the association. For this Britain must shoulder some of the responsibility, although in fairness it must be acknowledged that when the British negotiators were seeking for membership of the EEC the terms of the Yaoundé Convention were not themselves settled, and thus it was difficult to be precise as to what a Commonwealth African country would ultimately be undertaking if it opted for association. It is clear too that, rightly or wrongly, it appeared to the political leaders of Commonwealth Africa that Britain was negotiating on their behalf. With independence either achieved or just about to be, this alone was sufficient to create suspicion. "It is all very well for Mr. Macmillan," commented Mr. Ali Mazrui of Kenya, "to tell British television viewers that he obtained 'excellent terms' for British subjects in Africa. What was wrong was that the Rome Treaty left it to Mr. Macmillan to negotiate the terms."

There was also the fact that the nature of the machinery of association was alien to Anglophone African ways of thought and traditions. To the Francophone African a treaty which spelled out declarations of intent, articles of agreement, rights and obligations was the obvious way of establishing a trade and aid relationship. To Anglophone Africans this seemed unnecessary and dangerous. They seemed to have less faith than their Francophone neighbors in the usefulness of negotiating with Europeans. Once you have signed on the dotted line you are committed and caught! In fact six-months' notice can be given if an associate wishes to leave, but the fear of perpetual involvement in Europe seems to have remained among many Anglophone Africans who are always stressing the importance of purely African activities as opposed to European ones. Further, the exact nature of the Treaty can only be precisely clarified in its actual operations. And Commonwealth African countries were worried about qualifying clauses such as that which encouraged the establishment of customs unions among associates and third countries provided they did not conflict with the principles of the Convention. What exactly were these principles and who was to judge as to whether a particular course of action was incompatible or not?

But, as the operations of the association have been seen in practice, a softening of Anglophone African attitudes seems to have emerged. An East African delegation representing Kenya, Tanzania and Uganda has just started formal talks with the EEC. Nigeria has already been involved in negotiations for many months, and the talks have now neared a crucial and decisive stage. The basis of the Nigerian application is not full adherence to the Yaoundé Convention but a trade agreement with reciprocal obligations. This would involve preferential access to the Common Market for many of Nigeria's products. Nigeria in return would have to give a cer-

tain preference to various imports into her economy from the Six—
a somewhat difficult proviso for her as she has traditionally been an
"open-door" trading country.

Some progress was made on this point, and Nigeria indicated
that she was prepared to dispense with the customs element in import duties on twenty-six items from the Six, amounting to about 4
percent of their exports to her in 1963. In return, Nigeria had asked
for a gradual reduction of tariffs by the Six on Nigerian exports of
cocoa, palm oil, groundnuts and plywood. But it now seems that
France has demanded a considerable enlargement of the tariff
preferences that Nigeria is proposing, in spite of the fact that the
other five member states were satisfied with the original offer. It
may be that the French see in Nigeria a powerful nation, comparable in numbers to the combined populations of all the existing associates, and one whose present economic standards and
future potential constitute a threat to them. The French have always
felt themselves to be in a special way responsible for protecting the
interests of Francophone Africa, and if the privileges of association
are shared with another African country they are naturally diluted.
Whether these considerations will be strong enough to prevent
Nigerian association remains to be seen.

Suggestions for Additional Reading

Two shortcomings limit most books on European decolonization: their focus is too narrow and they are chronological rather than analytic or interpretive in presentation. All too often the result is a kind of date-by-date account of the relation between the imperial power and a single (or regional) colonial possession. The different forces leading to decolonization—nationalist determination on the part of the colonial subjects; economic interest; past precedent; national psychology; international strategic calculations on the part of the Western states—are haphazardly introduced if mentioned at all. As a consequence, there are few good works on the decolonization processes of the different European powers, much less adequate comparative studies that conceptualize the entire period. The one substantial work in English that attempts to be comparative Rudolf von Albertini's *Decolonization: The Administration and Future of the Colonies, 1919–1960,* is unfortunately not exempt from these criticisms (which are even more true of H. Grimal's *La décolonisation, 1919–1963*). It is ironic, moreover, that after all the criticism of studies of imperialism as too centered on the European actors (a charge that connotes ethnocentrism), many studies of decolonization are biased in the other direction, being far more detailed about the colonial nationalists than about the European policymakers. Hopefully these observations will be taken more as a challenge than as a discouragement by students of these problems.

There are several bibliographies of works on the British Empire and the decolonization process, one of the most recent being an appendix to Nicholas Mansergh's *The Commonwealth Experience* (1969). One might also consult Robin Winks, *The Historiography of British-Empire—Commonwealth Relations* (1966), and Philip Curtin, "The British Empire and Commonwealth in Recent Historiography," *American Historical Review* (October 1959). Mansergh has also edited a series entitled *Speeches and Documents in British Commonwealth Affairs, 1931–1952* (1953; two volumes), and *1952–1962* (1963, one volume). In addition, Max Beloff's *Imperial Sunset* (1967), Correlli Barnett's *The Collapse of British Power* (1972), and Ian Drummond's *British Economic Policy and the Empire, 1919–1939*

(1972) deal with the period before 1945, and so offer a good introduction to postwar decolonization. Although a great deal is known about the details of the transfer of power in India, much still remains to be done interpretatively. Unfortunately one of the more interesting works has not yet been translated from the French: Georges Fischer's *Le Parti travailliste et la décolonisation de l'Inde* (a review of this book by V. G. Kiernan appears in the *New Left Review*, March-April, 1967). Other works include M. A. Fitzsimons, *The Foreign Policy of the British Labour Government, 1945–1951* (1953); Barbara Ward, *India and the West* (1961); and a collection of documents edited by Nicholas Mansergh, *The Transfer of Power, 1942–1947* (1970). There is a good deal of factual material as well in H. Grimal's *De l'Empire britannique au Commonwealth* (1971), and in H. V. Hodson's *The Great Divide* (1969).

In relation to the decline of British power in the Middle East, the best work is probably Elizabeth Monroe's *Britain's Moment in the Middle East, 1914–1956* (1963). More popular accounts can be found in Peter Mansfield, *The Ottoman Empire and Its Successors* (1973), and Ann Williams, *Britain and France in the Middle East and North Africa* (1968). Books dealing with local nationalism but devoting attention to British policy in the area include most notably Maxime Rodinson, *Israel, A Colonial-Settler State?* (1967), G. Antonius, *The Arab Awakening: The Story of the Arab National Movement* (1965), and, from a Zionist perspective, Christopher Sykes, *Crossroad to Israel, 1917–1948* (1965).

While the work excerpted from John Hatch earlier in this volume is specifically on the British in Africa, his *Africa: The Rebirth of Self-Rule* and *History of Postwar Africa* (1965) also deal with this theme. Contemporary works on Africa are, of course, quite numerous, but surprisingly few of them deal at any length with the politics of decolonization from the European angle. One might, however, consult Dennis Austin, *Politics in Ghana, 1946–1960* (1964), and *West Africa and the Commonwealth* (1957), for a discussion of West Africa. East Africa is the subject of Dan Horowitz's "Attitudes of British Conservatives towards Decolonization in Africa," *African Affairs* (January 1970), and the comment on this article in the July 1970 edition of the same journal by David Goldsworthy.

Interesting overviews of the process of British decolonization may be found in the memoirs of the principal actors, Prime Ministers Attlee, Churchill, Eden and Macmillan, and men of lesser rank such as Hugh Dalton and L. S. Amery. Many of the overviews are disappointing, however, either being superficial—the books of John Strachey and Colin Cross come to mind—or missing the forest for the trees as in the case of David Goldsworthy's *Colonial Issues in British Politics, 1945–1961* (1971). An interesting account of the economic issues involved is Michael Barratt-Brown's *After Imperialism* (1963). A fruitful approach that awaits fuller development would be to place the imperial question within the context of relations between Great Britain and the United States as Gabriel Kolko, for one, has done in *The Politics of War: The World and United States Foreign Policy, 1943–1945* (1968), Chapter 12 especially.

Competent overviews of the decolonization process are as lacking in the case of France as in that of Great Britain. Nevertheless, a number of good monographs exist. A. W. De Porte's *De Gaulle's Foreign Policy, 1944–1946* (1968) is particularly useful in regard to the Levant. D. Bruce Marshall's *The French Colonial Myth and Constitution-Making in the Fourth Republic* (1973) similarly provides a good starting point for the study of postwar French colonial affairs. Several books supply excellent accounts of the French involvement in Indochina after 1945, although they generally give more insight into the situation in Indochina than that in France: Joseph Buttinger, *Vietnam: A Dragon Embattled* (1967; two volumes); Donald Lancaster, *The Emancipation of French Indochina* (1961); Ellen Hammer, *The Struggle for Indochina, 1940–1955* (1967); and Philippe Deviller, *Histoire du Viet Nam de 1940 à 1952* (1952). Georgette Elgey's *La République des illusions, 1945–1951* (1965), and *La République des contradictions, 1951–1954* (1967) contain detailed descriptions of the French political scene during this period.

In regard to Algeria, two books with insight into the French mind are by Raymond Aron: *La Tragédie algérienne* (1957) and *l'Algérie et la République* (1958). Dorothy Pickles' *Algeria and France* (1963) and Thomas Oppermann's *Le Problème algérien* (1961), provide a good deal of information on French-Algerian relations but are weak on interpretation.

These two great colonial wars are seen with some unity by Alfred Grosser in *La IVè République et sa politique extérieure* (1967) and by Raoul Girardet in *L'Idée coloniale en France* (1972). But in my opinion the best overall study of the nightmare of Fourth Republic decolonization comes in a book not surprisingly on the military: John Ambler's *Soldiers against the State* (1968). Nevertheless, few books on the Fourth Republic give the colonial imbroglio the central position it deserves. De Gaulle's colonial policy similarly awaits its historian. W. W. Kulski's *De Gaulle and the World* and Philip Williams and Martin Harrison's *Politics and Society in de Gaulle's Republic* handle the topic in rather mediocre fashion. One might, however, consult Edward Kolodziej's *French International Policy under de Gaulle and Pompidou: The Politics of Grandeur* (1974), and certain parts of Stanley Hoffmann's *Decline or Renewal? France Since the 1930s* (1974).

Very little has yet been done on Dutch and Belgian decolonization, which merits close attention. In addition to the three works excerpted earlier in this text, however, one might consult *Political Awakening in the Belgian Congo* (1964), by René Lemarchand; *Indonesia and the Dutch* (1962), by Leslie Palmier; *Nationalism and Revolution in Indonesia* (1952), by George Kahin; and "The Netherlands after the Loss of Empire," by Henri Baudet, *Journal of Contemporary History* (January 1969).

The most spirited debate over decolonization is whether any such thing actually occurred. Theorists of "neo-colonialism" and "dependency" argue that the economic ties of most Third World nations constitute such checks on sovereignty that it is misleading to speak of decolonization (see the Introduction). They are opposed by political economists who maintain that the peoples of the less-developed countries possess considerably more effective autonomy than before and, more importantly, that their insertion into the international economic system is in most cases clearly to their advantage. There are two main arenas of dispute: the relations between Europe and Africa and those between the United States and Latin America. In both cases the principal focus is on the character of an international order dominated militarily by the United States and economically by the multinational corporations. The tone of the debate is acrimonious. Dependency theorists are usually radical and often Marxist—although Gunnar Myrdal, Raul Prebisch, and François Perroux, three more conventional economists, may also be leagued in this camp. Typically the works of the more radical read like calls for revolution against the international capitalist system, responsible in their view for virtually all the hardships of the Third World (this is not true of Myrdal, Prebisch or Perroux). To the contrary, the proponents of the established order usually concede minor shortcomings in the system, but insist that the presented arrangement internationally is beneficial to most of its members, to the less-developed peoples as well as to those of the industrial nations. Furthermore, they usually deplore what they call the stridency and "partisanship" of their radical counterparts and appeal instead for more "objective" scholarship.

The literature on this subject is voluminous and rapidly growing. For the point of view of the dependency theorists one might begin with James Cockroft et al., *Dependence and Underdevelopment: Latin America's Political Economy* (1972); Arghiri Emmanuel, *Unequal Exchange* (1972); Jagdish Bhagwati, editor, *Economics and the World Order* (1973); and Samir Amin, *Neo-colonialism in West Africa* (1974). Rebuttals may be found in Charles Kindleberger, *American Business Abroad* (1969), Lecture 5; and especially in Benjamin Cohen, *The Question of Imperialism* (1973). A solid historical account arguing the benefits of the European presence in Africa may be found in Lewis Gann and Peter Duignan's *Burden of Empire* (1967). Writings on the relations between the European Economic Community and Africa frequently make the case for mutual advantage as well. See, for example, "Commonwealth Africa and the Enlarged European Community," *African Affairs* (October 1972), by the Staff of the Economic Department of Standard Bank Limited; and "The Common Market and Its Colonial Heritage," by Carol Ann Cosgrove, *Journal of Contemporary History* (January 1969). To date the best work in the field is by I. W. Zartman, *The Politics of Trade Negotiations between Africa and the EEC: The Weak Confront the Strong* (1971). Two issues of *Foreign Policy,* Spring and Summer 1974, also carry a series of articles on the multinationals and their role in the world economy, as does the Fall 1974 edition of *Foreign Affairs.* Of particular interest is an exchange between Ronald Müller and Richard Barnet—co-authors of *Global Reach: The Power of Multinational Corporations* (1974)—and Raymond Vernon, long a major apologist for the new world order based on the multinationals.

With such a vast topic as decolonization, the reading list is virtually endless. But the subjects falling under this heading are so interesting, varied and complex, the major issues still so open for debate, and the conclusions so important for policy formulation that the field promises to be stimulating for years to come.

1 2 3 4 5 6 7 8 9